EQ6

USER
MANUAL

Lessons and Reference

The Electric Quilt Company
419 Gould Street, Suite 2
Bowling Green, Ohio 43402

EQ6 User Manual

Copyright © 1991-2006

The Electric Quilt Company
419 Gould Street, Suite 2
Bowling Green, OH 43402 USA

419/352-1134 (general)
800/356-4219 (sales only)
419/352-4332 (fax)
Find us online at: www.electricquilt.com

CREDITS:
Software Programmer: Dean A. Neumann
Book Editor: Andrea Poulimenos Bishop
EQ6 programming and book team: Heidi Gernheuser, Penny McMorris, Jenny Novinsky, Ann Rutter, Sara Seuberling, Sara Woodward

Quilt design shown on front cover designed by Michelle Linnell of Corpus Christi, Texas, USA.

Any corrections and/or clarifications to sections of this book after it has been printed can be found online at:
www.electricquilt.com > Support > Frequently Asked Questions > EQ6

Table of Contents

More Copyright Information

Copyright of Designs

Blocks: Any blocks you design (without copying a design from existing copyrighted quilt blocks) are yours to copyright. Blocks from the EQ Libraries are copyright-free when used in your designs, except for the blocks designed by Debbie Sichel, Judy Vigiletti, and Rita Denenberg. These blocks are clearly marked by the Block Name. You may not distribute or sell collections of block designs from EQ6.

Quilts: Any quilts you design (without copying an existing copyrighted quilt design) are yours to copyright.

When making or publishing a pattern, you do not need to mention that the pattern was made in EQ6 (we love it if you do, of course). If you have a question about copyright, contact us.

Block Name on the notecard

A Special Note to Teachers

We love the fact you are teaching our software and are happy to help you in any way we can. Please contact us for special teacher EQ6 CDs. You may install the software on computers in a classroom or computer lab to teach your class PROVIDED that no copies of the software are given to students and all copies of the software are uninstalled from all computers at the conclusion of the class. If the computer lab technician will not install the software without a written letter of permission, please applaud their actions and give them our thanks. Then, contact us at customer service and we can send you a written letter of permission once we have all the necessary information (your name, class name, dates, times, computer lab name, etc.). Also, you may want to write our webmaster and let them know that same information, so they can advertise your class on the Classes and Tutorials page.

A Special Note to Quilt Shops

You may install a copy of the software on your store computer PROVIDED it remains the store copy and is not distributed or resold. You should register that copy through The Electric Quilt Company, because it would be eligible for an upgrade if a newer version is ever released. You are allowed to leave it running for you, your employees, and your customers to use, demo and print.

A Special Note to Libraries and Guilds

It is a serious violation of the license agreement to lend software. Software remains on the computer even after the CD has been returned. Each time the software is lent, it is an instance of software piracy.

ELECTRIC QUILT 6
Complete Quilt Design Software

EQ6

Introduction

Thank You for Buying Electric Quilt 6

Welcome to the world of computer quilting! We can't wait to show you all the great features of Electric Quilt 6. This user-friendly software will help you to design quilts and blocks, color with real fabrics, and print patterns to follow. Let's get started.

How do I start?

Install – Please refer to page 7 of this book.

First Run – The computer that EQ6 is installed on will need to be connected to the Internet the first time you run the program for activation and registration. Please see pages 7-8 of this book.

Learn to Use – Go through the lessons at the front of this book. These six lessons will teach you how to use the program. Later, repeat any of the lessons for more practice and try using different blocks and fabrics than used in the lesson.

Get Answers – Keep this book next to you at the computer and use it as a reference to look something up. Watch the help videos which come with EQ6 by clicking on the Watch a Video tool. Look up answers in the EQ6 Help File by clicking HELP > Contents.

What do I do if I need help?

Please don't become frustrated, especially if you are new to computers. It isn't easy to "drag the scrollbar" or "double-click" if you're using a computer for the first time. Just keep practicing. You'll get it. And the more you do it, the easier it will become.

If you have read through the lessons in this book, looked up your question in the index of this book or the EQ6 Help File, and you still need help, there are many resources available.

E-mail – Send us your questions: **techsupport@electricquilt.com**
If you are having difficulties with a specific project or design, feel free to attach EQ6 projects or pictures to help us "see" how to help you.

Call – Talk to a real person on our technical support line: 419-352-1134
(Monday-Friday, 9-5pm Eastern)

Fax – Fax your questions to us: 419-352-4332

Mail – Although this isn't an instant answer like e-mail, here is our mailing address:
The Electric Quilt Company
419 Gould Street, Suite 2
Bowling Green, OH 43402-3047
USA

Web site – Read message forums, frequently asked questions, and much more: **www.electricquilt.com**

Companion Books – Purchase any of these books for more practice and creative ideas using EQ6.

Classes – Check our Web site for listings in your area or visit www.quiltuniversity.com.

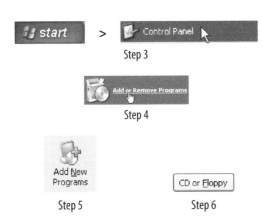

Step 3

Step 4

Step 5   Step 6

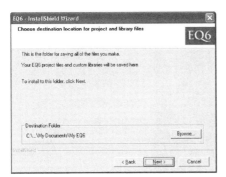

The second installation location is where your project files and custom libraries will be saved by default. Please make a note of this location.

Please note:
EQ6 uses the My Documents folder of the computer user who installed EQ6 to store your EQ6 projects and Custom Libraries. If you are installing EQ6 for another person, please install EQ6 from the computer user account that will be using this software.

Desktop Icon

What if I have an earlier version of EQ?

If you have EQ2, EQ3, EQ4, or EQ5 installed, you do not need to uninstall those programs before installing EQ6. The full version of EQ6 is a complete, stand-alone program. If you purchased EQ6 as an upgrade from EQ5, EQ6 requires that EQ5 be loaded on the computer before installing EQ6. Please do not give away or sell your previous versions of EQ if you got this new software as an upgrade – it is a violation of software licensing.

Installing EQ6

Before you begin the installation, turn off any programs that may be running on your computer.

1   Insert the EQ6 CD into your CD-ROM drive.

2   The installation should start automatically.

3   If the installation does not start automatically, click **START > Control Panel**.

4   Double-click **Add or Remove Programs**.

5   Click **Add New Programs** in the left column.

6   Click the **CD or Floppy** button and then follow the instructions on the screen.

You should be able to click **Next** through the entire installation to get the normal installation. If you browse and change either of the installation paths be sure to create a new folder each time for the files. In other words, click Browse, change the drive letter and type EQ6 in the path typing box. This will create the folder for you. Click **OK** and **Yes** to continue with the installation.

Running EQ6

The installation creates an icon on the Windows Desktop and under Electric Quilt in the program groups. To run EQ6, double-click the desktop icon or use the menu and click **START > All Programs > Electric Quilt > EQ6 > EQ6**.

The first time you open EQ6 you will see an "activation" screen that will unlock EQ6, then ask you to register your program. See the following page for activation and registration instructions.

Activating EQ6

The computer needs to be connected to the Internet for activation. Activation is a process that unlocks EQ6, using your License ID and Password as the keys. You will only need to activate the first time EQ6 is started on a computer.

The activation process will start automatically the first time you run EQ6. You will need to have your License ID and Password available. They are located on the inside back cover of this book. Follow the instructions on the screen to complete the activation.

Please note: EQ6 software provides a total of 4 activations. Each time you replace your current computer with a new one, activating EQ6 on the new computer will use one of your activations. For example, if Betty spends part of the year at her second home, installing EQ6 on computers in both homes would use two activations. If Betty's computer hard drive needs to be replaced, installing EQ6 on the new hard drive would also use an activation.

For more information on EQ6 activation, please see our website: www.electricquilt.com > Support > Frequently Asked Questions > Electric Quilt 6 > Activation.

Registering EQ6

After the activation has been successfully completed, you will be asked to register EQ6. The fields with an asterisk (*) are required. If your address does not include a State or Province, please enter AA.

Choosing Inches or Centimeters

You can use inch or centimeter measurements in EQ6.

1   **Click FILE > Preferences > Measurement** (under Workspace).

2   Click on the measurement you'd like to use.

3   Click **OK**.

Notes
- Once you change the measurement units the program will continue to use those units until you change them again.

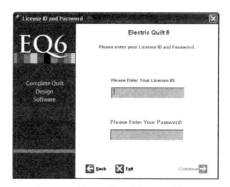

Enter your License ID and Password from the inside back cover of this book

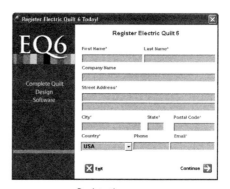

Registration screen

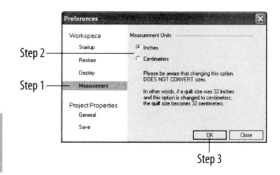

Step 2

Step 1

Step 3

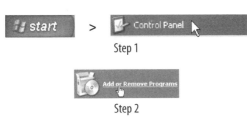

Step 1

Step 2

Step 4

Uninstalling EQ6

1   Click **START > Control Panel**.

2   Double-click **Add or Remove Programs**.

3   Find EQ6 in the list below and click on it.

4   Click the **Change/Remove** button next to the name.

5   Choose **Remove** and follow the instructions on the screen.

Notes for Laptop/Touchpad Users

In the directions, we will refer to click+drag, SHIFT+drag or other combinations involving dragging an object. When using a computer with a mouse, these directions are quite simple. If you are using your touchpad, you will want to be sure you understand the following steps so the lessons and documentation referring to dragging work for you.

Click+Drag

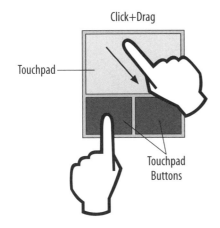

Touchpad

Touchpad Buttons

Click+Drag (Example: Scrollbars)
Click and hold the left touchpad button.
Run the index finger of your other hand repeatedly across the touchpad diagonally.
Release the left touchpad button when you are finished.

Shift+Click+Drag

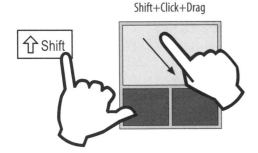

⇧ Shift

SHIFT+Click+Drag (Example: Setting items on Layers 2 and 3)
Hold down the SHIFT key.
With the same hand, click and hold the left touchpad button.
Run the index finger of your other hand repeatedly across the touchpad diagonally.
Release the left touchpad button and SHIFT key when you are finished.

Ctrl+Click+Drag

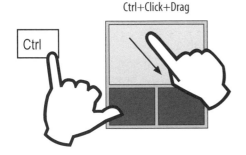

Ctrl

CTRL+Click+Drag (Example: Drawing perfect shapes)
Hold down the CTRL key.
With the same hand, click and hold the left touchpad button.
Run the index finger of your other hand repeatedly across the touchpad diagonally.
Release the left touchpad button and CTRL key when you are finished.

What's New in EQ6

General

- Projects and My Libraries are in the My Documents folder linked to your user name (C:\Documents and Settings\...)
- Quick quilt projects
- Scaling of fabric
- Display Dynamic Help
- Use of JPEGs, GIFs, TIFFs and more
- High resolution image exporting
- New blocks, fabrics, layouts, photos, embroidery, thread
- Restore default for entire program
- Worktable tools for quickly changing worktables
- Large video screen with more videos

Quilt Worktable

- Show/Hide Layers
- Keep width and height equal on the Layout tab
- Adjustable origin rulers for Quilt worktable
- Center a block in the quilt on the graph pad
- Create a quilt layout from a block drawing
- Aligned border styles
- Fussy cut position of fabric is saved with the quilt

Toolbars

- Save in Sketchbook is now Add to Sketchbook
- Plain Block tool replaced by Erase Block tool
- Set Embroidery and Set Photo have their own tools and are separate from the Set Block tool
- New Paintbrush tools
- Random Recolor tool
- Rotate Fabric tool
- New Thread tools
- Set Applique Text tool
- Set Auto Borders tool
- Freehand, Brush Stroke, Polydraw, Rectangle, and Ellipse tools in PatchDraw
- Most recently used fabrics and colors
- Customizable toolbars
- Restore default tools

Libraries

- New Thread and Photo libraries
- Save your own quilt layouts, photographs, embroidery or thread color to library
- Copy is now Add to Sketchbook
- Cut, copy and paste features added
- Fabric and Thread Library search by color
- Import your own embroidery (EXP format only)
- Import sketchbook items from closed projects
- Multiple select (CTRL+A) to add items to the Sketchbook with one click
- Link to other EQ product libraries from within the Library
- Search for blocks by category

Sketchbook

- Divided into more sections (Quilts, Blocks, Fabrics, Colors, Embroidery, Photos, Thread)
- Sorting
- View more than one quilt at a time
- Double-click on an item to edit it
- Expanded notecards that can be moved and pinned
- Select coloring on Blocks palette
- Add Plain Block

Printing and Exporting

- Rotate templates in 90 degree increments
- Resizable Foundation Pattern box
- Foundation units labeled inside patches
- Large key block option for templates and rotary cutting
- Borders & setting triangles clip automatically
- Mirror option when printing block
- Export high resolution images in BMP, GIF, JPG, PNG, and TIFF formats

Block Worktable

- PatchDraw completely reworked
- Special grids for circles, eight pointed stars, and more
- Serendipity options – Frame Block, Tilt Block, & Merge Blocks
- Format options when importing an image to trace

ELECTRIC QUILT 6
Complete Quilt Design Software

Lessons

Lesson One

In this lesson we will take a tour of the software, making several quilts as we go. You'll see some of the blocks and fabrics which come with EQ6 and you'll learn how to:

- Create a New Project

- Tour the Workspace

- Start New Quilts

- Adjust the Layout

- Learn about the Speed Keys

- Learn about the Sketchbook

- See All the Blocks in the Library

- See Block Names

- Search for Blocks

- Add Blocks to the Sketchbook

- Set Blocks in a Quilt

- Recolor Blocks in a Quilt

- Fill One Last Quilt with Blocks and Fabrics

- Watch Help Videos

Ready? Set? Go at your own pace as you work these lessons. Now that you have EQ6, we want you to use and love it. So if you get stuck or have questions, e-mail or call us. (Our contact information is on page 6.) We'll do our best to help.

Remember as you are working that these are just computer files. You are not committing these decisions to fabric unless you want to. It is ok to make mistakes and mess up these files; just create a new project whenever you want to start fresh.

If you're using a laptop or touchpad, please see page 9 before starting this lesson.

Create a New Project

1 Double-click the EQ6 icon on your Windows Desktop. You'll see the EQ6 splash screen play.

2 When the Tip of the Day displays, click **Close**.

3 Next a Project Helper appears giving you three options: Create a new project, Open an existing project, or Start with a quick-quilt project. Let's leave it on **Create a new project**.

4 The typing cursor is already in the box for the project name. So, type: **Lesson One**

Notes

• Some people like to repeat the lessons in this book. If you repeat this lesson, you can either delete the old Lesson One (see page 111) or name this one differently (Lesson One – second time).

5 Click **OK**.

6 On the top toolbar click the **Work on Quilt** button. It's the very last button which looks like a quilt with four blocks.

Tour the Workspace

Look at the top of your screen. Just under the title "Lesson One" you will see FILE, EDIT, VIEW, etc. This is called the menu bar. We will always CAPITALIZE these words in our instructions, so you know that we are referring to the menu bar.

You have a toolbar below the menu bar and another toolbar down the right side of your screen. At the bottom of your screen are tabs. You don't need to know what all these menus, tools, and tabs do yet, but just know they are here and these are the places we will instruct you to click.

Right now we are on the Quilt worktable. We know this because after the word LIBRARIES in the menu bar we see the word QUILT, and the last button on the top toolbar is pressed in. If you point the mouse at this last button on the top toolbar without clicking, you will see its tooltip says "Work on Quilt." Buttons and tabs have tooltips which can be seen by hovering over each one individually.

Step 2

Step 3

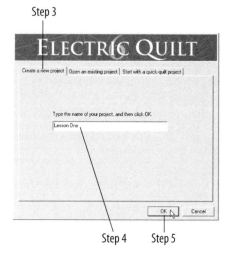

Step 4   Step 5

Step 6
Work on Quilt

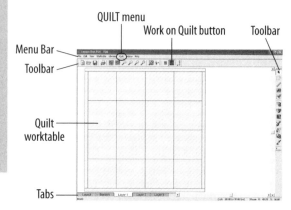

Work on Block

BLOCK menu

Work on Block button

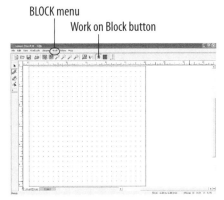

Block worktable

Work on Quilt

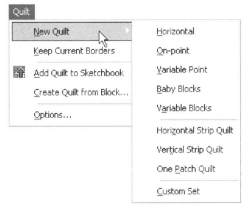

Start a new quilt from the Quilt menu

We can switch to the Block worktable easily. **Click the Work on Block button** on the top toolbar (it is second to last button on that toolbar and looks like a single block). Do you see how it now says BLOCK in the menu? The Block worktable has its own tools, menus, and tabs as well. We'll learn about those later in the block lessons.

These are the two places you can be – the Quilt worktable or the Block worktable. Now that you know where you are, let's switch back to work on a quilt and start designing!

Click the Work on Quilt button, so you see the quilt on your screen again.

Start New Quilts
Let's see what kinds of quilts we can make.

7   On the menu bar, click **QUILT > New Quilt > Horizontal**. This is a horizontal layout.

8   On the menu bar, click **QUILT > New Quilt > On-point**. This layout is on-point. There is also a Variable Point option where you can stretch your diamonds.

9   Click **QUILT > New Quilt > Baby Blocks**. This is a baby blocks or tumbling blocks layout. There is also a Variable Blocks option where you can stretch your tumbling blocks.

10   Click **QUILT > New Quilt > Horizontal Strip Quilt**. This layout consists of horizontal rows, each of which can be changed independently. It is great for Row quilts and Bargello quilts. There is also a Vertical Strip Quilt option where you have columns instead of rows.

11   Click **QUILT > New Quilt > One Patch Quilt**. The hexagon or *Grandmother's Flower Garden* layout you see is one of the many patches you can have repeated all over the quilt.

12   Click **QUILT > New Quilt > Custom Set**. This is a blank quilt layout waiting for you to set in blocks of all different sizes.

Notes
• Each layout can be edited to fit your needs. The possibilities are endless. Let's start simple, however, and just do a new horizontal quilt.

13   Click **QUILT > New Quilt > Horizontal**.
Look at the quilt on your screen and count the number of blocks horizontally and vertically.

Adjust the Layout

14   At the bottom-left corner of your screen, click the **Layout** tab.

15   On the right you will see a big gray box (or palette) with *Horizontal Layout* at the top. Under the Number of blocks section, it reads horizontal: 4 and vertical: 4. Let's change the number of blocks horizontal to be 1. **Click the left arrow button next to Horizontal three times to get to 1.** This new quilt would make a great table runner.

16   On the top toolbar, click **Add to Sketchbook**. We'll see what this does later.

17   **Click the right arrow buttons next to Horizontal and Vertical to add more blocks until both say 5.**

18   On the top toolbar, click **Add to Sketchbook**.

19   If there is a check in *Keep width and height equal*, under **Finished size of blocks**, click in the checkbox to uncheck it.

Step 13

Step 14

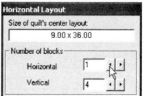

Step 15

Step 16
Add to Sketchbook

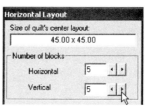

Step 17

Step 18
Add to Sketchbook

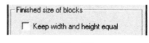

Step 19

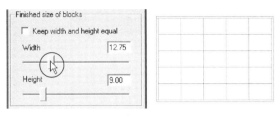

Step 20

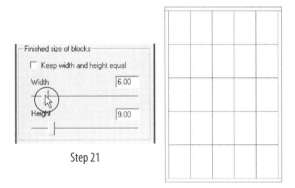

Step 21

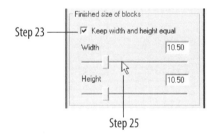

Step 23

Step 25

Using the slider bars

Drag the rectangle

Click to the sides

Type

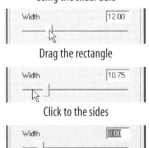

20 Click on the rectangle for **Width** and drag it slowly *to the right* on the line. The blocks (and the quilt) become wider. If you're using a laptop touchpad, and you're having problems, see page 9.

21 Drag the rectangle slowly *to the left* on the line. The blocks and quilt become thinner.

22 Let's try **Height**. Click on the rectangle for Height and drag it slowly back and forth to the left or right. Everything becomes taller or shorter depending on the direction you are sliding.

23 What does the checkbox do? Click in the checkbox for *Keep width and height equal* to place a checkmark there.

24 Click on the rectangle for **Width** and drag it back and forth to the left or right. Do you see how Height moves together with Width now?

25 Try clicking on the line to the left or right of the rectangle for Width. Watch how Width and Height move together in increments.

26 Try sliding the rectangle for **Height** and clicking to the left or right of the rectangle for Height. The same thing happens. The checkbox locks the sizes together keeping width and height equal.

Notes
You can change the size in three different ways:
- *Drag the rectangle* – Position your cursor over the rectangle. Click, hold and drag it to the left or right.

- *Click to the sides* – Position your cursor over the line to the left or right of the rectangle. Click once on the line and watch how the size changes in increments.

- *Type* – Double-click on the current size so it turns shaded. Type a new number.

Lesson One

27 There is a faster way to make changes to this box. Press your keyboard **TAB key** over and over. Watch how sometimes the numbers have the focus (turn shaded blue, gray, or green) and sometimes the lines or checkboxes have the focus (dotted box around the line or checkbox). Whenever the text is shaded, you can type over the number.

28 Press the **TAB key** until the number for Number of blocks, Horizontal is shaded.

29 Type: **3**

30 Press the **TAB key** so the Vertical number turns shaded.

31 Type: **3**

32 Press **TAB, TAB** so the Width number turns shaded.

33 Type: **12**

34 Press **TAB, TAB** so the Height number turns shaded.

35 Type: **12**

36 Press **TAB, TAB, TAB, TAB** (a total of four times) so the Sashing Width number turns shaded.

37 Type: **4**

38 Press **TAB, TAB** so the Sashing Height number turns shaded.

39 Type: **4**. You now have a 3x3 horizontal quilt with 12" (finished) blocks and 4" (finished) sashing. Great job!

Notes
- When you look at a finished quilt you don't see seam allowances. Even though a fabric block starts at 12½" square, once it is sewn in it will be 12". In EQ6 we are designing what the finished quilt will look like, so we need to use finished sizes as well. Seam allowance is added to the finished block sizes when we print, which we will see later in Lesson Three.

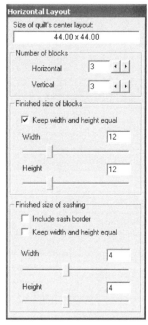

Layout settings made in steps 29-30

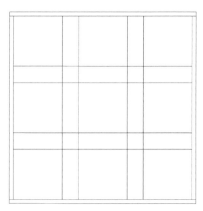

3x3 horizontal quilt with 12" (finished) blocks and 4" (finished) sashing

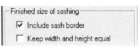

Step 40

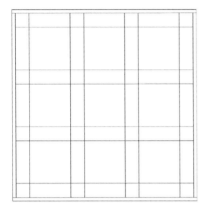

Quilt with sash border

Step 41

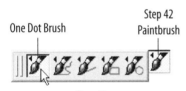

One Dot Brush

Step 42
Paintbrush

Step 43
Click and hold to see the flyout

Sketchbook Fabrics and Colors palette

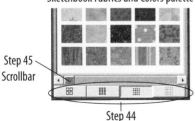

Step 45
Scrollbar

Step 44
Use the display buttons to change
the number and size of fabrics shown

40 Before we set blocks and color, let's see what the sash border checkbox does. Click **Include sash border** to place a check next to it. The sashing was only between the blocks earlier. Now it is around the outside as well. In case you missed it, click to uncheck, and then click to recheck the checkbox for *Include sash border*.

41 As you can see, the **Layout** tab lets you adjust the quilt layout. Let's skip the Borders tab for now and go to the next one. Click the **Layer 1** tab at the bottom of your screen.

Notes
- The quilt is covered in gray "hatching" lines. Whenever you see these lines, know that they mean nothing is set there.

Learn about the Speed Keys

42 On the right-hand toolbar, click the **Paintbrush** tool. The Sketchbook Fabrics and Colors palette will appear.

43 EQ6's Paintbrush has five brush styles and we want the first style. Click and *hold* on the **Paintbrush** tool until the flyout menu appears. Be sure to click the first style which is called the **One Dot Brush**.

44 At the bottom of the Fabrics and Colors palette, you will see buttons with squares on them. These display buttons control how many swatches you see at a time. Feel free to click back and forth on them. Let's leave ours set to the third display button so we can still see detail in the fabrics, but also see a lot of fabrics at one time.

45 Above that you have a scrollbar. Slide the scrollbar left or right to see all the swatches in this project.

46 Let's color! **Click any fabric swatch in the palette to select it.**

47 Click in the large center square of your quilt. Don't worry if the fabric looks different in the quilt than it does in the palette. Fabrics placed in the quilt scale appropriately according to the block size.

48 Click once in each of the other large squares with this same fabric.

Notes
• When using any of the Quilt tools, it is never a "drag and drop" from the palette, it's a "click, click." Click in the palette to select the item. Click directly on the quilt to place it.

• If you ever make a mistake coloring, click EDIT > Undo or press CTRL+Z on your keyboard.

49 Click a different fabric swatch in the palette.

50 Click in the quilt on all the sashing strips. Do you see how slow this is going to color these blocks and strips the same color? This is what our speed keys are for.

51 Click a new fabric swatch in the palette.

52 **Hold down your keyboard CTRL (Control) key**.

53 Click in a large center square. All 9 squares will color together.

54 Click to choose a new swatch in the palette.

55 Still holding down the CTRL key, **CTRL+click** in the vertical sashing. All the vertical sash strips will color together.

56 **CTRL+click** in the quilt on the horizontal sashing. All the horizontal strips will color together.

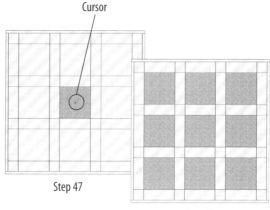

Cursor

Step 47

Step 48

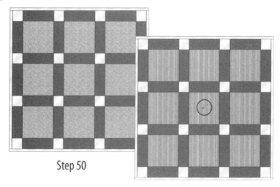

Step 50

Steps 52-53

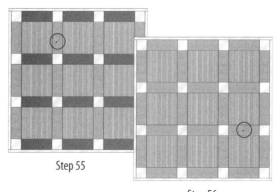

Step 55

Step 56

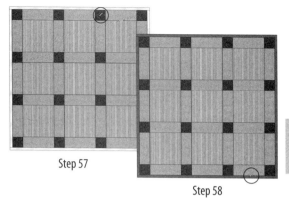

Step 57

Step 58

Step 61

57 Click in the palette to choose a new fabric swatch. **CTRL+click** in the quilt in the cornerstones (small squares between the sashing).

58 Click in the palette to choose a new fabric swatch. **CTRL+click** in the border.

Notes
- **Your first speed key is the CTRL key. CTRL = everything (no pun intended).**

59 Release the CTRL key. Click in the palette to choose a new fabric swatch.

60 Hold down your keyboard **ALT (Alternate) key**.

61 Click in the large, top-left square in your quilt and watch what happens.

62 If you missed it, click in the palette to choose a new fabric swatch and **ALT+click** in the large, top-middle square in your quilt. Release the ALT key.

Notes
- **Your second speed key is the ALT key. ALT = alternates.**

Lesson One

Learn about the Sketchbook

On the top toolbar are two important red buttons.

• **Add to Sketchbook** – puts the item in your Sketchbook *(The arrow shows you are adding it to the Sketchbook.)*

• **View Sketchbook** – lets you see what is in your Sketchbook. *(The glasses show you are viewing the Sketchbook.)*

Why do you want to add items to your Sketchbook? Your Sketchbook is tied to the current project name (Lesson One). If you add something to the Lesson One Sketchbook, it will be there the next time you return to this project. If you don't add it, it won't be there.

63 On the top toolbar, click the **View Sketchbook** button to see the Sketchbook. Along the left side are buttons for the Sketchbook sections.

64 Click the **Quilts** section to see the quilts in this project.

65 Below the quilt picture, you will see a scrollbar, the word Unnamed, and either *Quilt 1 of 2* or *Quilt 2 of 2* depending on the quilt you are viewing. **Click in the middle of the scrollbar to see the other quilt.** These are the quilts we saved in steps 16 and 18.

66 Where is the quilt we just colored? It isn't in the Sketchbook. That is because we haven't added it yet. Click **Close** in the bottom-right corner (or the X in the title bar) of the Sketchbook.

67 Click **Add to Sketchbook** on the top toolbar.

68 Click **View Sketchbook** on the top toolbar. The Quilts section now says it has 3 quilts (_ of 3).

69 Click the right arrow on the scrollbar beneath the quilt until you reach quilt 3 of 3. The colored quilt is in here, so we are OK now.

70 Click **Close** or the X in the title bar to put the Sketchbook away. You will be back to the Quilt worktable with your quilt in front of you.

Step 63
View Sketchbook

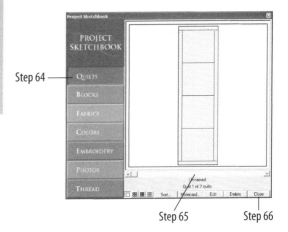

Step 64 —

Step 65   Step 66

Step 67
Add to Sketchbook

Step 68
View Sketchbook

Title Bar

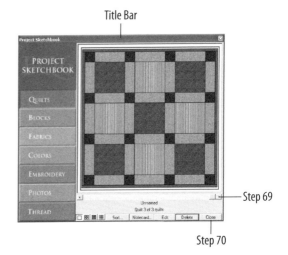

Step 69

Step 70

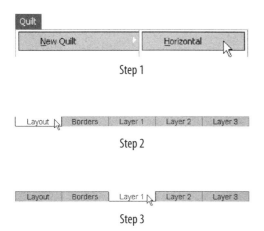

Step 1

Step 2

Step 3

Paintbrush tool

Step 6
Add to Sketchbook

Step 7
View Sketchbook

☕ Coffee Break

A Coffee Break is free time. Look for the Coffee Break symbols in each lesson. The coffee symbols mean you can stop reading and work at your own pace for as long as you'd like. When you're ready to return to the lesson, find the end of the Coffee Break and begin reading and working again.

If you ever take a Coffee Break, decide to close and save the project, and then turn off your computer for the night, you will need to re-open the same project to the same screen to start where you left off. In this case, it would be project *Lesson One*, on the Quilt Worktable, on Layer 1, with the Paintbrush tool.

Practice what you've learned:
1 QUILT > New Quilt > Horizontal.
2 Change the way the quilt is laid out on the Layout tab.
3 Click the Layer 1 tab and color with the Paintbrush tool.
4 CTRL+click to color every spot.
5 ALT+click to color alternate spots.
6 Add to Sketchbook.
7 View Sketchbook.

Please remember, this is only practice. Don't get frustrated (or we'll switch you to decaf coffee during the Coffee Breaks). Try to start at least 2 different horizontal quilts, color them, and add them to the Sketchbook.

You'll get a chance to delete any or all of the practice projects you make in these lessons. We just want to be sure you understand the basics of how to set up a horizontal quilt, color it, and add it to the Sketchbook so you will be able to find it again later.

So add quilts to the Sketchbook like crazy. Remember, no one will make you sew these!

Lesson One

See All the Blocks in the Library

71   On the top menu bar, click **LIBRARIES >
Block Library**. The Block Library will appear.
It is divided into four basic parts:

- *Sections* – In the top-left are buttons for the
five sections (Library, My Library, etc.).

- *List* – Below the sections is a list of block styles
you can browse. The list has a scrollbar beside it.

- *Blocks* – To the right you will see a large group
of blocks in the selected style with a scrollbar
below them.

- *Buttons* – Along the bottom you will see many
buttons.

72   Click the **Library** section and click the up arrow
on the scrollbar next to the list until you reach
the top.

73   **Click the minus sign (-) next to the name
1 Classic Pieced.** You will now see all 9 libraries
that come with EQ6, where all the thousands
of blocks are located. The first three are full
of pieced blocks, then there are three full of
appliqué, followed by quilting stencils, and
more block styles. Don't go wandering just yet;
there will be another Coffee Break for you to
play with blocks later.

74   Click the plus sign (+) next to **1 Classic Pieced**.

Step 71

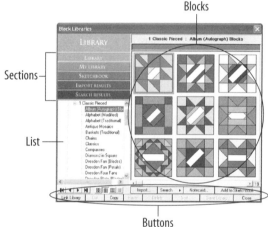

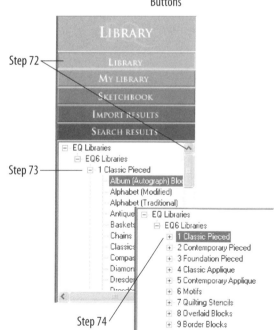

Lesson One

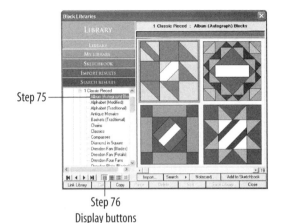

Step 75

Step 76
Display buttons

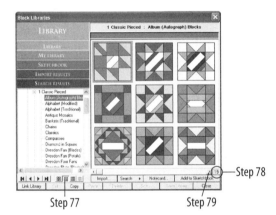

Step 78

Step 77   Step 79

Step 84
Tooltip

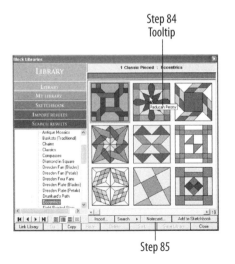

Step 85

75 Click the first name below it: **Album (Autograph) Blocks**.

76 Remember the squares below the Fabrics and Colors palette which controlled how many fabrics we saw at a time? The library has these display buttons too. Click the first button with 4 squares on it. You will see 4 blocks at a time.

77 Click the next button with 9 squares on it. Now you'll see 9 at a time. These buttons are great for seeing more of a block's detail.

78 If you look above the Add to Sketchbook button, you'll see a number. This is the number of blocks in this style.

79 Although we only see 9 blocks right now, we can use the scrollbar below the blocks to see all 19. Click repeatedly on the right arrow of the scrollbar beside 19.

80 Stop when you don't see any new blocks appear.

81 So, we've seen all the blocks in Album (Autograph) Blocks, but what about the rest of 1 Classic Pieced? Click in the list on **Alphabet (Modified)**.

82 Press your keyboard down arrow repeatedly to go down through the list.

83 Stop when you see some blocks you like or when you reach Wheels. Remember that you may see 9 blocks now, but you can just scroll horizontally to see the rest. The real number of blocks in each style appears to the right of the scrollbar above the Add to Sketchbook button.

See Block Names

84 Position your cursor over a block without clicking, to see the tooltip. This is the block name.

85 Click the block to select it and then click the **Notecard** button. This is another way to see the block name.

Notes

Every block has a notecard. In the notecard there are four fields:

- *Name* – This is name of the block as designated in EQ6.

- *Reference* – This is usually blank, unless you or someone else has typed some reference information in there.

- *Library* – This shows you which library and which style the block is from.

- *Notes* – This is usually blank, unless you or someone else has typed some notes in there.

86   Click the **X** in the top-right corner of the notecard to close it.

Search for Blocks

87   When you are looking for blocks in the library you can search in one of three ways:

- *by sight* – click through the library until you see what you want.

- *Search by Notecard* – search the block notecards for a specific word.

- *Search by Category* – search according to predetermined categories we have marked the blocks by.

Let's search by notecard. Click the **Search** button, then click **By Notecard**.

88   Be sure there is a check next to every search field. If one is missing, click in the box to put a check there.

89   Let's search for some blocks. In the top, long box, type: **Nine**

90   Click the **Search** button at the bottom, then click **OK** when the message appears telling you how many blocks were found.

91   Position your cursor over each block for a moment without clicking, to see the block names. Each block contains the word "Nine," whether it is *Nine Patch, Double Nine Patch,* or *Four Times Nine.*

Step 86

Name
Reference
Library
Notes

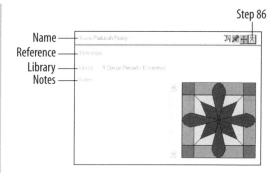

Step 87

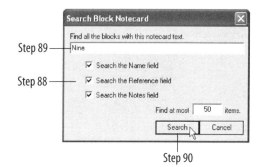

Step 89

Step 88

Step 90

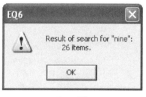

Step 90

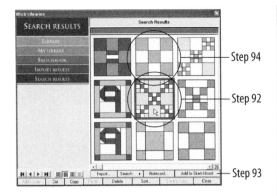

Step 94

Step 92

Step 93

Step 95

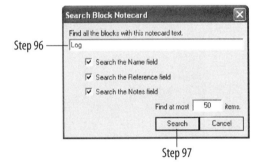

Step 96

Step 97

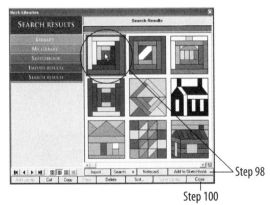

Step 98

Step 100

Birds in the Air

Snowball Variation

Notes

- Blocks go by many different names. You may call a block *Variable Star* and we may call it *Sawtooth Star*. When you search by Notecard, you are searching the Name field of the Notecard as it has been named in the EQ6 library.

- You will get more search results if you type less of the name (*Star* versus *Connecticut Star Variation*).

- Whenever you search, there is a box labeled "Find at most ____ items." If you leave it set to 50, but it can find 300, it will still only return 50 results. Change this number as you need to. It can go as high as 999.

Add Blocks to the Sketchbook

92 Find and click on the *Double Nine Patch* block to select it (see picture above for step 92).

93 Click the **Add to Sketchbook** button in the bottom-right corner of the Library. The block will "disappear" to show it was added. Don't worry, you can't "use up" a block. It is not gone forever and will be back the next time you view that style.

94 Find and click on the *Nine Patch* block (see picture) to select it. Click **Add to Sketchbook** again.

95 Let's search for other blocks. Click **Search > By Notecard**.

96 This time let's find a *Log Cabin*, so type: **Log**

97 Click the **Search** button, then click **OK** when the number of results are reported.

98 Select the first block in the top-left corner and click **Add to Sketchbook**.

99 Repeat steps 95-98 for:

Birds (*Birds in the Air* block)

Snowball (*Snowball Variation* block)

100 Click **Close** to put the library away.

Lesson One

Set Blocks in a Quilt

101 Start a new horizontal quilt by clicking **QUILT > New Quilt > Horizontal**. (If you get a beep and a message, it means you didn't add your last quilt from the Coffee Break to your Sketchbook. Click *Yes* to add it.) A new horizontal quilt will appear.

102 Click the **Layout** tab to change the way your quilt is laid out.

103 Be sure the numbers match the image to the right and read 4, 4, 9.00, 9.00, 0.00, 0.00.

If they do not, type: 4 (TAB) 4 (TAB, TAB) 9 (TAB, TAB) 9 (TAB, TAB, TAB, TAB) 0 (TAB, TAB) 0.

104 Click the **Layer 1** tab so we can set blocks.

105 On the right-hand toolbar, click the **Set Block** tool. The Sketchbook Blocks palette will appear with the blocks you added from the library.

106 Click the *Double Nine Patch* block in the palette to select it and click in any empty space in your quilt.

Step 101

Step 102

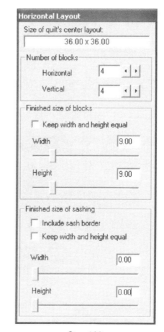

Step 103

Step 104

Step 105
Set Block

Step 106

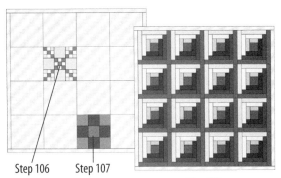

Step 106   Step 107

Step 109
CTRL+click to set the *Log Cabin*
in every block space

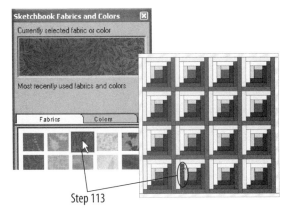

Step 111
Add to Sketchbook

Step 112
Paintbrush

Step 113

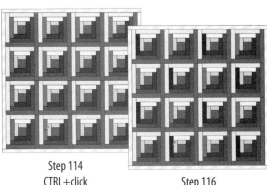

Step 114
CTRL+click

Step 116
ALT+click

107 Click the *Nine Patch* block in the palette and click in the quilt. You'll notice that setting blocks works the same way as coloring. Select it in the palette and click in the quilt.

108 Well if clicking is the same, what about CTRL+click? Click the *Log Cabin* block in the palette to select it.

109 Hold down your keyboard **CTRL** key and click in the quilt. The Log Cabin will fill every block space.

110 Release the CTRL key.

111 Click **Add to Sketchbook** on the top toolbar to add this quilt to your project.

Recolor Blocks in a Quilt

112 Click the **Paintbrush** tool on the right-hand toolbar.

113 Click a fabric in the palette and click a patch in a quilt block. Just that patch will color.

114 Click a different fabric in the palette and **CTRL+click** *that same patch* in the quilt. Do you see how CTRL+click colors the patch in all the blocks?

115 Release the CTRL key.

116 Click a different fabric in the palette and **ALT+click** *that same patch* in the quilt. Do you see how ALT+click colors the patch in alternate blocks?

117 Release the ALT key.

118 Finish coloring this quilt (and the border), using the Paintbrush tool, CTRL+click, and ALT+click.

119 Click **Add to Sketchbook** to put this quilt in your project.

Fill One Last Quilt with Blocks and Fabrics

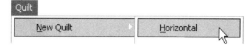

Step 120

120 Start a new horizontal quilt by clicking **QUILT > New Quilt > Horizontal**.

121 Click the **Layout** tab and make the settings match the picture to the right: 5, 5, 9.00, 9.00, 0.00, 0.00.

122 Click the **Layer 1** tab.

123 Click the **Set Block** tool on the right-hand toolbar.

124 CTRL+click the *Snowball Variation* block in the quilt.

125 ALT+click the *Double Nine Patch* block in the quilt.

126 Click **Add to Sketchbook** to put this quilt in your project.

127 Click the **Paintbrush** tool on the right-hand toolbar.

128 Click different fabrics in the palette and use **CTRL+click** to color the blocks in the quilt and the border.

129 Click **Add to Sketchbook** to put this quilt in your project.

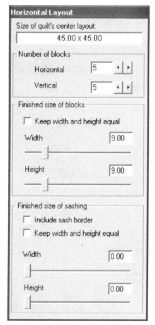

Step 121

Step 123
Set Block

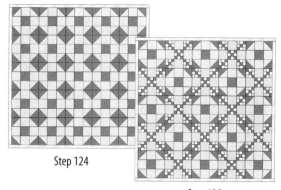

Step 124

Step 125

Step 126
Add to Sketchbook

Step 130

Watch Help Videos

130 Be sure your computer's speakers are turned on, then click **VIDEOS > Designing Quilts > Starting a New Quilt** on the top menu bar. Watch the entire video. This is everything that we just covered in this lesson.

131 At the bottom of the video screen, click **Select a Video > Using the Quilt Tools > Set & Erase Tools**. Watch the video.

132 At the bottom of the video screen, click **Select a Video > Using the Quilt Tools > Paintbrush Tool**. Watch the video.

Notes

- The EQ6 videos are a great way to learn about the different tools, tabs and buttons to see how they work. They are also a great way to review the steps to do a specific task if you haven't used the program in a while.

Great job! Do you realize how far you've progressed? You now know how to start new quilts, get blocks from the library, set them in quilts, color, and add the quilts to the project so you can find them again!

Now turn the page for another Coffee Break!

Lesson One

☕ Coffee Break

Now is your free time to play with blocks from the library. Go explore the Block Library and add blocks to your Sketchbook so you can set them in quilts. Use any blocks from Libraries 1 Classic Pieced through 5 Contemporary Applique.

Practice what you've learned:
1 QUILT > New Quilt > Horizontal.
2 Change the way the quilt is laid out on the Layout tab.
3 Click the Layer 1 tab.
4 LIBRARIES > Block Library > pick a style in the list > click a block > click Add to Sketchbook. Add 5-10 of your favorites. Close the library when you're done.
5 Set blocks with the Set Block tool.
6 CTRL+click to set blocks in every spot.
7 ALT+click to set blocks in alternate spots.
8 Click the Paintbrush tool to color.
9 CTRL+click to color in every spot.
10 ALT+click to color in alternate spots.
11 Add to Sketchbook.
12 View Sketchbook.

Try at least 2 quilts then come back for the next lesson.

Homework

Since the EQ6 videos are such a great way to learn how the tools work, watch the video called "Rotate & Flip Tools." You will find it in: VIDEOS > Using the Quilt Tools > Rotate & Flip Tools.

Once you watch it, practice using the Rotate and Flip tools on single blocks (click), alternate blocks (ALT+click), and all the blocks in the quilt (CTRL+click).

Blocks will only appear to rotate or flip if they are not the same on all sides. The *Log Cabin* and *Birds in the Air* blocks are ideal for rotating and flipping. Blocks like the *Nine Patch* or *Double Nine Patch* will not show any change.

133 Click the large **X** in the top-right corner to close EQ6 when you are finished.

Lesson One

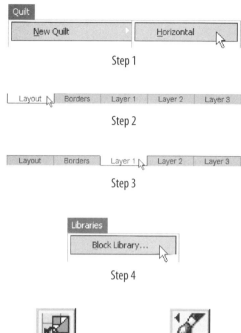

Step 1

Step 2

Step 3

Step 4

Step 5
Set Block tool

Step 8
Paintbrush tool

Step 11
Add to Sketchbook

Step 12
View Sketchbook

Step 133

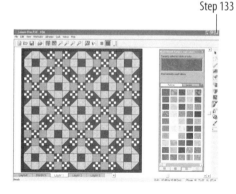

Lesson Two

In this lesson we will continue our software tour, making several on-point quilts as we go. You'll play with borders and fabrics that come with EQ6 and learn how to:

- Open an Existing Project

- Edit a Quilt from the Sketchbook

- Play with the Symmetry Tool

- View the Display Dynamic Help

- Create a New Project

- Start an On-Point Quilt and Adjust the Layout

- Use the Tape Measure Tool

- Get a Block from the Library

- Get Fabrics from the Library

- Learn about the Fabric Library

- Recolor with the Random Recolor Tool

- Review the Sketchbook

- Make a Medallion Quilt

- Add Borders to Your Medallion

- Line up Borders

- Clone Borders

- Play with Auto Borders

Remember to go at your own pace as you work though these lessons and e-mail us, or give us a call if you have a question. (Our contact information is on page 6.)

If you are using a laptop or touchpad, please see page 9 before starting this lesson.

Open an Existing Project

1 Double-click the **EQ6** icon on your Windows Desktop. You'll see the EQ6 splash screen play again. When the Tip of the Day displays, click Close.

2 Click the **Open an existing project** tab of the EQ6 Project Helper. Here you will see two lists of projects (most recently used and existing).

3 In either list, find and click on your **Lesson One.PJ6** project. To the side, you will see one of the quilts in this project.

4 If you like, you can click the third arrow (below the quilt) several times to review the quilts from Lesson One.PJ6.

5 Click **OK** to open the project. The Sketchbook will appear.

Edit a Quilt from the Sketchbook

6 In the Sketchbook's left column, click the **Quilts** section.

7 Click the right arrow at the end of the scrollbar below the quilts until you see the quilt you added with all the Log Cabin blocks. (It should be the third or fourth quilt in the Sketchbook.)

8 Choose either of these two ways to edit this quilt from the Sketchbook:

• double-click in the center of the quilt

• click the quilt to select it and click the **Edit** button at the bottom of the Sketchbook

Play with the Symmetry Tool

9 On the right-hand toolbar, click the **Symmetry** tool. Rotating and flipping is great as we learned in the Lesson One Homework, but the Symmetry tool is much more fun.

10 **CTRL+click** on your quilt with the Symmetry tool.

Step 2

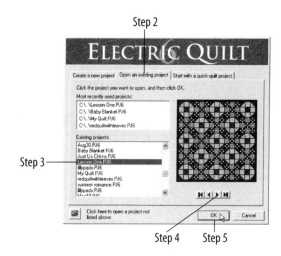

Step 3

Step 4   Step 5

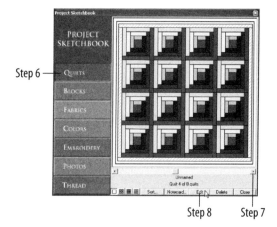

Step 6

Step 8   Step 7

Step 9
Symmetry

Just a few examples of the rotations created by the Symmetry tool

Step 11
Add to Sketchbook

Step 12
Display Dynamic Help

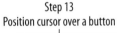

Step 13
Position cursor over a button

Description of the
button appears here

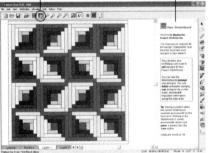

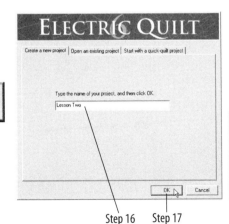

ELECTRIC QUILT

Create a new project | Open an existing project | Start with a quick-quilt project |

Type the name of your project, and then click OK.

Lesson Two

Step 15
New

OK   Cancel

Step 16   Step 17

Notes

- The Symmetry tool automates rotating and flipping. It works on every block in the quilt (which is why you need to hold down the CTRL key when using it). There are 16 different versions before you return to the first version.

- The Symmetry tool works with groups of four, so you may find that quilts with 4, 8, or 12 blocks across and down work best for the effect. Odd numbered blocks may make the quilt feel unfinished.

11   Click the **Add to Sketchbook** button on the top toolbar for any versions of the quilt you like.

View the Display Dynamic Help

12   Click the **Display Dynamic Help** button on the top toolbar. A new window pane will appear at the side of your screen. Display Dynamic Help is great if you forget what a tool does and need a quick reminder.

13   Position your cursor (without clicking) over any button in the top or right-hand toolbars. Watch how the description changes when you hover over each toolbar button. You don't need to read them all now; just know the descriptions are there if you need help.

14   Click the **Display Dynamic Help** button on the top toolbar to turn it off again.

Create a New Project

15   On the top toolbar, click the **New** button. (If the last quilt you made is not in the Sketchbook, you will get a message about adding it. Click Yes.) You will automatically be taken to the *Create a new project* tab of the Project Helper.

16   Type: **Lesson Two**

Notes

- Some people like to repeat the lessons in this book. If you repeat this lesson, you can either delete the old Lesson Two (see page 111) or give this one a slightly different name (Lesson Two – second time).

17   Click **OK**.

Start an On-Point Quilt and Adjust the Layout

18 On the menu bar at the top, click **QUILT > New Quilt > On-point**. A blank on-point layout appears.

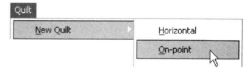

Step 18

19 In the bottom-left corner of your screen, click the **Layout** tab. Let's play with the settings to see how this type of layout works.

Step 19

20 Under **Select a style**, click the dot next to the first choice, then the second, and back again to see how the two styles differ. One has a quarter-square triangle in the corner; the other has a seam in the corner. Leave it set to the *first choice*, so the quilt on your screen matches the images for this lesson.

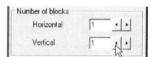

Step 20

21 Under **Number of Blocks**, click the left arrows next to **Horizontal** and **Vertical** until both read **1**. This is one on-point block and could be fun if you were designing a medallion.

Step 21

22 Let's save this for later. Click the **Add to Sketchbook** button on the top toolbar.

23 Click the right arrow next to **Vertical** until it reads **5**. Let's make a table runner.

Step 22
Add to Sketchbook

24 Under **Finished size of blocks**, click, hold, and drag the slider rectangle on the line. Watch the blocks in the quilt as you slide the rectangle back and forth. Notice how the blocks always remain on-point squares.

25 Double-click the number for **Finished size of blocks** and type: 9

26 Under **Finished size of sashing**, click, hold, and drag the **Width** slider rectangle back and forth to see what it does. Notice when the sashing size is too close to the block size, it is difficult to distinguish between the two on the quilt. Also notice when sashing is set to 0.00, there is no sashing.

27 Drag the slider rectangle for **Width** to the left, until it reads 0.00, so there is no sashing.

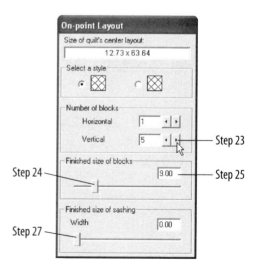

Step 23

Step 24

Step 25

Step 27

Step 28
Tape Measure

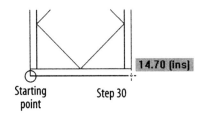

14.70 (ins)

Starting point   Step 30

Quilt: 14.73 by 65.64 (ins)   Mouse H: 14.73   V: 65.64

Starting point   Step 31

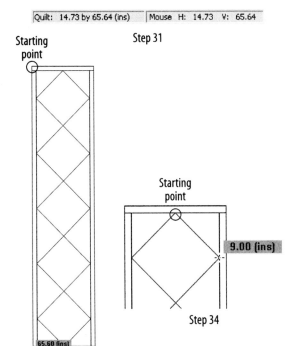

Starting point

9.00 (ins)

Step 34

65.60 (ins)

Step 32   Starting point

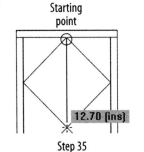

12.70 (ins)

Step 35

Use the Tape Measure Tool

28 On the right-hand toolbar, click the **Tape Measure** tool. It lets you drag a line across the quilt to measure approximately how long it is.

29 Position your cursor over the *lower-left corner* of the quilt border.

30 Click, hold, and drag your cursor straight across to the *lower-right corner* of the quilt border. You will see a size (close to 14.70) in a blue box that changes as you move your cursor.

31 Look at the bottom of your screen for the word *Ready*. You'll see *Quilt: 14.73 x 65.64 (ins)* in the same line. This is the finished size of your quilt.

32 Position your cursor over the *upper-left corner* of the quilt border and click, hold, and drag straight down to the *lower-left corner.* You will see a number very close to 65.64.

Notes
- The Tape Measure is especially useful if you ever question a size when printing. Remember, the Tape Measure is an approximation and is more accurate the closer you click and stop near the points of the actual object you are measuring.

- You can also verify what each number in the Layout box does by measuring with the Tape Measure tool.

33 In the top-middle of your quilt, is the corner of the first on-point block. Still using the **Tape Measure** tool, position your cursor here.

34 Click and hold as you drag diagonally down and right to an adjacent corner (following the edge of the on-point block). This number should be close to 9, which we set on the Layout box.

35 Starting from the same point, but dragging to the opposite corner (through the center of the block) you'll see that this size is close to 12.73.

Get a Block from the Library

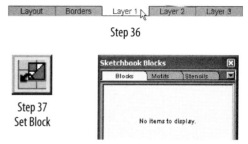

Step 36

36 At the bottom of your screen, click the **Layer 1** tab.

37 On the right-hand toolbar, click the **Set Block** tool. Oops, it says "No items to display" in the Blocks palette, because we haven't gotten any from the library yet.

Step 37
Set Block

Sketchbook Blocks palette is empty

38 On the top menu bar, click **LIBRARIES > Block Library.**

39 In the buttons at the bottom, click **Search > By Notecard.**

Step 38   Step 39

40 Type: **Ohio**

41 Click the **Search** button, then **OK** when the results are reported.

Step 40

42 Click to select the first block, *Ohio Star*, then click **Add to Sketchbook**.

43 Click **Close** to put the library away. The Blocks palette is still showing.

Step 41

44 Click the *Ohio Star* block in the palette to select it.

Step 42

45 Hold down the **CTRL key** and click in one of the five large on-point squares of the quilt.

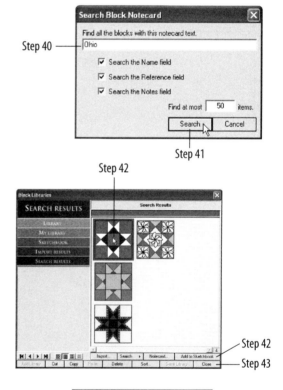

Step 42
Step 43

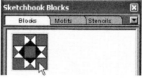

Step 44

Step 46

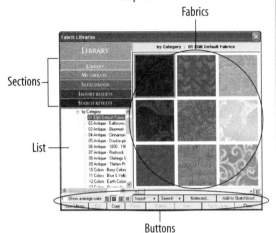

Sections

List

Fabrics

Buttons

Get Fabrics from the Library

46 On the top menu bar, click **LIBRARIES >
Fabric Library.**

Learn About the Fabric Library

The Fabric Library looks and functions similarly to the Block
Library we studied in Lesson One. It is also divided into four
basic parts:

- **Sections** – In the top-left are buttons for the five sections
  (Library, My Library, Sketchbook, etc.).

- **List** – Below the sections is a list of fabric styles you can
  browse. The list has a scrollbar beside it.

- **Fabrics** – To the right you will see a large group of fabrics
  in the selected style with a scrollbar below them.

- **Buttons** – Along the bottom you will see many buttons.

In the list, you will see the three main fabric libraries that
come with EQ6 if you scroll. Fabrics are organized by Category,
by Color, and by Manufacturer.

47 Drag the vertical scrollbar next to the list up or
down until you see *by Color.*

48 If there is a plus sign next to the name, click the
name **by Color** to open it. If there is a minus
sign, it is already open.

49 Click the first style, **01 Yellow**, under *by Color.*

50 Press your keyboard down arrow until you reach
06 Rust. In the Block Library it was important
to see a block's detail, but here in the Fabric
Library we may want to see more fabrics at a
time.

51 Below the list are the display buttons with
squares on them that control how many fabrics
you see at a time. Click the fourth button.

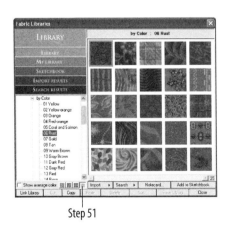

Step 48

Step 49

Step 47

Step 51

52 Click in the list on **07 Gold**.

53 *(Optional)* Click the **Close** button in the bottom-right corner of the library and click **LIBRARIES > Fabric Library** again from the top menu bar. Notice how the library opens in the last place you visited.

54 **Click a gold fabric swatch to select it.**

55 Click the **Add to Sketchbook** button in the bottom-right corner of the library. The fabric will disappear to show it was added to your Sketchbook. We just added one fabric, but there are many ways to add items to your Sketchbook.

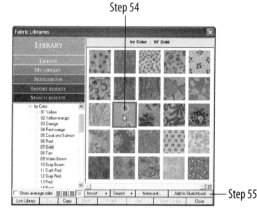

Step 54

Step 55

56 Click a gold fabric.

57 Hold down your keyboard **SHIFT key.**

58 Click a different gold fabric. Notice how the SHIFT key lets you select the two fabrics you clicked and all the fabrics in between.

59 Click the **Add to Sketchbook** button to add the entire group.

60 Drag the vertical scrollbar next to the list down until you see *22 Bright Blue*.

61 Click **22 Bright Blue** in the list.

62 Click a bright blue fabric.

63 Hold down your keyboard **CTRL key.**

64 Click four fabrics that are not side by side. Notice how the CTRL key lets you select scattered fabrics.

65 Click the **Add to Sketchbook** button in the library to add the entire group.

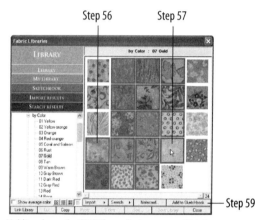

Step 56   Step 57

Step 59

Holding down the SHIFT key selects a range of fabrics

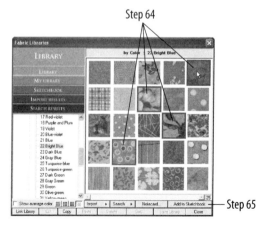

Step 64

Step 65

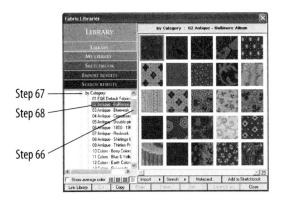

Step 67
Step 68
Step 66

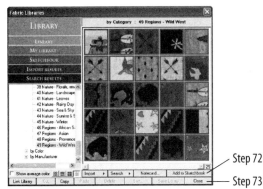

Step 72
Step 73

Step 71 - Hold down the CTRL key and the letter A on your keyboard to Select All

66 Drag the vertical scrollbar next to the list up until you see *by Category*.

67 If there is a plus sign next to the name, click the name **by Category** to open it. If there is a minus sign, it is already open.

68 Click the second style, **02 Antique - Baltimore Album**, under *by Category*. (This library is organized further by the style names. There are groups called Antique, Colors, Geometric, Holidays, etc.)

69 Press your keyboard down arrow to go through the list. Stop when you reach some fabrics you really like or when you reach **49 Regions - Wild West.**

70 Click on a fabric swatch.

71 Press **CTRL+A** on your keyboard to select all the fabrics in this style.

72 Click the **Add to Sketchbook** button in the library to add all the fabrics in this style.

Notes
- To summarize, here are the four ways to select items in the library:
  Select One – click one item
  Select a Range – click one, hold down SHIFT, and click the last item in the range
  Select Scattered Items – click one, hold down CTRL, and click others
  Select All – click one, press CTRL+A

- Now that you've learned this, don't get so eager that you go into every category, press CTRL+A to select all the fabrics, and Add to Sketchbook. Every fabric you add increases your project's file size. If your file size is gigantic, your project may "move slower" depending on your computer's ability to process such large files. Add only the fabrics you need.

73 Click the **Close** button to put the library away.

74 Click the **Paintbrush** tool on the right-hand toolbar.

75 Drag the scrollbar beneath the fabrics to the right until you see your new fabrics. They will be at the very end.

Step 74
Paintbrush

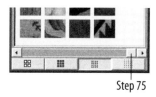

Step 75

76 Click a fabric in the palette and **CTRL+click** on the border of the quilt. (Remember, the fabric rescales on the quilt.)

77 Click a different fabric in the palette and **CTRL+click** one of the "setting triangles" just inside the border. This quilt does not need to be pretty because what we are going to do next is completely random and will change it anyway.

78 Click the **Add to Sketchbook** button on the top toolbar.

Recolor with the Random Recolor Tool

79 The Random Recolor tool is not on your right-hand toolbar by default, so let's add it. **Right-click on the Paintbrush tool and click Add/Remove Buttons.**

80 Find **Random Recolor** in the list and click on it. Now we just need to turn the list off.

81 Click in the white space outside of your quilt to deselect the list and turn it off.

82 Click the **Random Recolor** tool on the right-hand toolbar to use it.

83 In the Random Recolor box under *Modify color*, click the word **Randomize** to place the dot there.

84 **Click on your quilt to see what happens.** The first thing you'll notice is your entire quilt changes to solid colors.

85 If you click on your quilt again, you'll see those colors change randomly.

86 Continue to click on your quilt at least five times or until you find a fun combination.

Steps 76 & 77
Color the quilt using
CTRL+click

Step 78
Add to Sketchbook

Button Size ▶
Button Style ▶
Add/Remove Buttons
Restore Default Tools

Step 79

✓ Swap All Colors
Random Recolor
Set Thread
✓ Eyedropper

Step 80

Step 82
Random Recolor

Random Recolor ✕
Modify color
○ Shift Hue   20 ◂ ▸
○ Saturation 10 ◂ ▸
○ Brightness 10 ◂ ▸
● Randomize

Step 83

Step 84

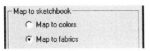

Step 87

Step 89
Add to Sketchbook

Step 88

87 In the Random Recolor box under *Map to sketchbook*, click **Map to fabrics**.

88 Click on the quilt. Your quilt will change from the modified solid colors to the closest matching fabrics out of your Sketchbook.

89 Click the **Add to Sketchbook** button on the top toolbar.

90 Repeat steps 83-89 twice to recolor and add two new quilts to the Sketchbook.

Notes
- The Random Recolor tool is one that is not on the toolbar by default. We left off some tools to keep the toolbar simple as you learn. Also, depending on your screen area and size of the EQ6 window, not all the tools will fit. It's a good idea to know how to add and remove buttons in such cases. You may want to watch the video on Adding New Tools (VIDEOS > Using the Quilt Tools > Adding New Tools) for more information.

☕ Coffee Break
Now is your time to play with on-point quilts and the Random Recolor tool at your own pace. Feel free to play with any blocks from Libraries 1-5 and any fabrics from the Fabric Library.

Practice what you've learned:
1 QUILT > New Quilt > On-point.
2 Change the way the quilt is laid out on the Layout tab.
3 Click the Layer 1 tab.
4 LIBRARIES > Block Library > pick a style in the list > click a block > click Add to Sketchbook. Add as many blocks as you need. Close the Library when you're done.
5 LIBRARIES > Fabric Library > pick a style in the list > click a fabric > click Add to Sketchbook. Add as many fabrics as you need. Close the Library when you're done.
6 Set blocks with the Set Block tool.
7 Color with the Paintbrush tool.
8 Randomize color with the Random Recolor tool.
9 Map to fabrics from the Sketchbook with the Random Recolor tool.
10 Add to Sketchbook.

Try at least 2 quilts then come back to learn about borders.

Step 1

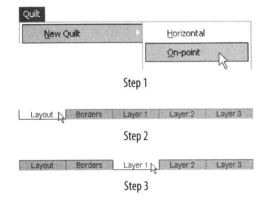

Step 2

Step 3

Step 4

Step 5

Step 6
Set Block

Step 7
Paintbrush

Step 8
Random Recolor

Step 10
Add to Sketchbook

Lesson Two

Review the Sketchbook

91 Click the **View Sketchbook** button on the top toolbar.

92 Click the **Quilts** section.

93 Below the quilts are the display buttons with the squares on them that control how many quilts you see at a time. Click the second button.

94 Drag the scrollbar beneath the quilts back and forth to see the quilts in this project.

95 Scroll all the way to the left to the first quilt. This is the empty 1x1 on-point quilt we made in step 22.

96 Double-click the quilt to edit it to the worktable.

Make a Medallion

97 Click the **Borders** tab at the bottom of your screen. Every quilt starts with a plain, 1.00 inch, Long Horizontal border. It is highlighted on the quilt in gray right now. We can see this in the Borders box because Select a border style is set to Long Horizontal and Left, Top, Right, and Bottom are set to 1.00.

98 On the Borders box under **Select a border style**, click the arrow at the end of the word Long Horizontal to drop down the list and drag the vertical scrollbar down to the bottom.

99 Click **Tile Squares** and your border style will change on the quilt. Tile Squares is a great border because it does the math and figuring for you. This is why the numbers for Left, Top, Right, and Bottom are grayed out and set to 4.25. The only part you can change is the number of square blocks horizontally in the border.

Step 91
View Sketchbook

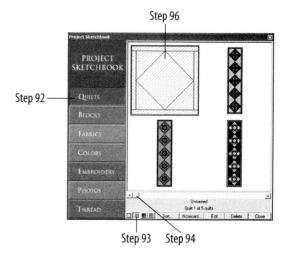

Step 96

Step 92

Step 93   Step 94

Step 97

Quilt with 1.00" Long
Horizontal border

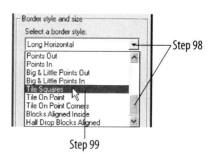

Step 98

Step 99

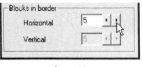

Step 100

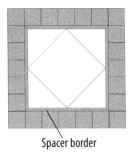

Spacer border

Step 101

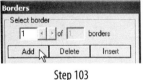

Step 103

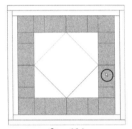

Step 104

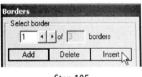

Step 105

Inserted border

Step 107   Step 106

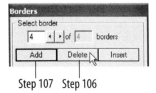

100 Under Blocks in border, click the right arrow for **Horizontal** twice to change it from 3 to **5**. Tile Squares always keeps perfectly square blocks around the outside of your quilt. If the center of your quilt cannot be evenly divided to make square blocks, it adds a spacer border of the perfect width to be able to do so.

101 Let's look at the other border styles available. **Click the drop down arrow at the end of the word Tile Squares > drag the vertical scrollbar on the list up to the top > click on the word Mitered.**

102 Press your keyboard down arrow to go through the list to see all the styles. See if you can figure out the difference between a style and its *Half Drop* version. Stop when you reach Half Drop Blocks Aligned.

Add Borders to Your Medallion

103 Click the **Add** button twice on the Borders box. You will see two plain (1.00 inch Long Horizontal) borders added around the outside of the quilt.

104 If you ever want to select a border, you can click on it in the quilt. Position your cursor over the inner **Half Drop Blocks Aligned** border in the quilt and click on it.

105 Click the **Insert** button once on the Borders box. Insert adds a plain border in front of the selected border.

106 Let's clean up our borders and start over. Click the **Delete** button on the Borders box until there are no more borders and the Delete button grays out.

107 Click the **Add** button once.

Notes

There are three buttons at the top of the Borders box:
- *Add* – adds a border around the outside of the quilt
- *Delete* – deletes the selected border
- *Insert* – inserts a border in front of the selected border

Line up Borders

108 You can line up borders with the inside of your quilt or each other. **Under Select a border style > click the drop down arrow > find and click the style Points In.**

Step 108

109 Under Lock size adjustments > click to put a check next to All. This will lock all the border slider bars together, so they move as one.

110 Click and hold any slider rectangle (Left, Top, Right, or Bottom) and drag it slowly to the right until it reads 3.00. Remember, these sliders work the same as those on the Layout tab. You can drag the rectangle or click to the sides of the rectangle. So, if you miss 3.00, you can click to the side of the rectangle on the line to make it jump in increments toward your goal.

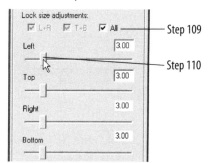

Step 109

Step 110

111 Click the **Add** button to add a border. The new outer border is automatically selected.

112 Click the drop down arrow next to Long Horizontal and click to change it to **Blocks**.

113 Under **Blocks in border**, click the right arrows next to **Horizontal** and **Vertical** until both read **6**.

114 Change the size of the border to 2.00, by clicking on a line (Left, Top, Right, or Bottom) to the right of the slider rectangle.

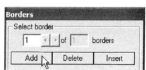

Step 111

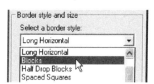

Step 112

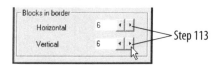

Step 113

Notes

- We're on our way to making our medallion now that we've covered some border basics. Look at the two borders on your quilt. The inner Points In border lines up well with the on-point center square of our quilt. The Blocks border, however, does not line up well with the Points In border. This is when you need "aligned" borders.

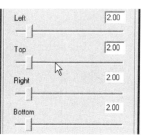

Step 114

Medallion quilt with Points In and Blocks borders

Step 115

Step 116 ——

Step 117 ——

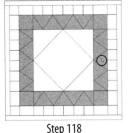

Step 118

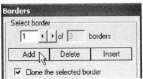

Step 118

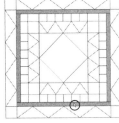

Step 119

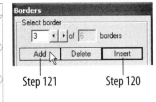

Step 121   Step 120

Step 124 ——

Step 123 ——

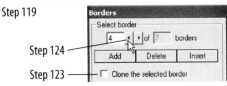

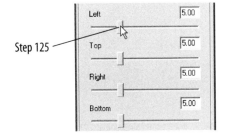

Step 125 ——

115 Under Select a border style > click the drop down arrow > click on Blocks Aligned Inside near the end of the list. The Aligned border now matches at the corners and fits the 6 blocks in the border to line up with Points In.

116 Click the **Add** button to add a plain 1.00 inch Long Horizontal border.

Clone Borders

117 Just below the Add, Delete and Insert buttons, click to put a check next to **Clone the selected border.**

118 Click in the quilt on the Points In border to select it > click the Add button. You just cloned and added a border with the same settings to the outside of your quilt.

119 Click the Long Horizontal border on the quilt (just inside the Points In border you added) **to select it.**

120 Click the **Insert** button twice.

121 Click the **Add** button once.

123 Click to uncheck **Clone the selected border.**

124 You can also select borders using the arrows above the Add, Delete, and Insert buttons. **Click the left facing arrow three times so you have border 4 of 7 selected.**

125 Change the size of this border to **5.00** by dragging any rectangle or clicking to the side of it. All the sides will move together because they are still locked together by All (under *Lock size adjustments*). Remember this wide plain border, because we are going to add fun things to it in a few steps.

126 Click the **Layer 1** tab at the bottom of your screen.

Lesson Two

Play with Auto Borders

127 Let's add another tool to the toolbar. **Right-click the Paintbrush tool on the right-hand toolbar > click Add/Remove buttons.**

128 Find the **Set Auto Borders** tool in the list and click on it. Click away from the list in the white space around your quilt to close it.

129 Click the **Set Auto Borders** tool.

130 On the Auto Borders palette, click the drop down arrow for Select a style > find and click on Curved in the list.

131 Click a curved border in the palette.

132 Click on your quilt in the wide plain border.

133 Click a different border in the palette and click on that wide border again.

134 Click the **Add to Sketchbook** button to save this quilt.

Step 127

Step 128

Step 129
Set Auto Borders

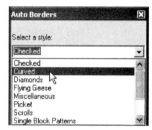

Step 130

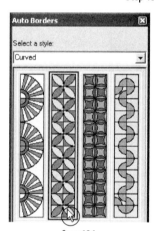

Step 131

> ☕ **Coffee Break**
> Now to play with borders and the Set Auto Borders tool!
>
> Practice what you've learned:
> 1 QUILT > New Quilt > Horizontal or QUILT > New Quilt > On-Point.
> 2 Change the way the quilt is laid out on the Layout tab.
> 3 Click the Borders tab. Change the border style and size.
> 4 Add, Insert, and Delete borders.
> 5 Clone borders.
> 6 Align borders to make interesting patterns.
> 7 Click the Layer 1 tab.
> 8 Get blocks from the Block Library.
> 9 Get fabrics from the Fabric Library.
> 10 Set blocks with the Set Block tool.
> 11 Color with the Paintbrush tool.
> 12 Add to Sketchbook.
>
> Try at least 2 quilts then come back to learn about printing in the next lesson.

135 Click the large **X** in the top-right corner to close EQ6 when you are finished.

Step 134
Add to
Sketchbook

Step 132 - Click on the wide Long Horizontal border

Lesson Three

Now we're going to focus on printing. Our goal is to understand what can be printed and how to do it:

- Start a New Project and Add Library Blocks

- Learn More about the Block Worktable

- Preview Different Printout Styles

- Print a Foundation Pattern

- Use a Quilt from the Layout Library

- Learn about Basics by Style Library Layouts

- Understanding the Layout Library

- Set Blocks into a Basics by Style Layout

- Play More with Auto Borders

- Color with the Spraycan

- Name the Quilt on its Notecard

- Print Templates

- Print Large Foundations

- Print Fabric Yardage Estimate

- Print Borders

Remember to go at your own pace as you work these lessons and e-mail us, or give us a call if you have a question. (Our contact information is on page 6.)

Printing requires that you have a printer installed (or just a printer driver) on the computer you are using. Click START > Printers and Faxes to see if you have one installed. If there is nothing in the list, then please install a printer or printer driver before proceeding.

If you are using a laptop or touchpad, please see page 9 before starting this lesson.

Lessons

Start a New Project and Add Library Blocks

1   Double-click the **EQ6** icon on your Windows Desktop. You'll see the EQ6 splash screen play again.

2   When the Tip of the Day displays, click the **Next** button a few times and read some tips. You may not understand them now. But you'll know the Tips are here for help and inspiration.

3   Click **Close** to close the Tip of the Day.

4   On the **Create a new project** tab of the EQ6 Project Helper, type: **Lesson Three**

Notes
• Some people like to repeat the lessons in this book. If you repeat this lesson, you can either delete the old Lesson Three (see page 111) or name this one differently (Lesson Three – second time).

5   Click **OK**.

6   On the top menu bar, click **LIBRARIES > Block Library**.

7   Click **Search > By Notecard**.

8   Be sure all three search fields are checked. Click any that are unchecked.

9   Under *Find all the blocks with this notecard text*, type: **Broken Dishes**

10   Click the **Search** button, then click **OK** when the number of results are reported.

11   **Click on a *Broken Dishes* block to select it > click the Add to Sketchbook button.**

12   Repeat steps 7-11 to find and add these blocks:

   • *Compact Car*

   • *Twenty-Five Patch*

13   Click **Close** to put the library away.

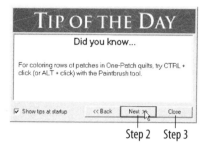

Step 2   Step 3

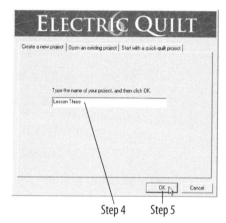

Step 4   Step 5

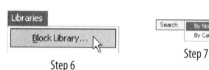

Step 6

Step 7

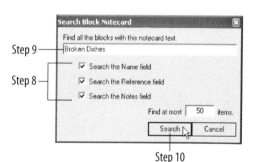

Step 9

Step 8

Step 10

Broken Dishes   *Compact Car*   *Twenty-Five Patch*

Lesson Three

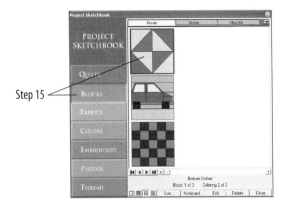

Step 15

Learn More about the Block Worktable

14 On the top toolbar, click the **View Sketchbook** button.

15 **Click the Blocks section > double-click the Broken Dishes block.** This puts the *Broken Dishes* block onto the Block worktable. (Notice the top menu bar now says Block, not Quilt, and you have drawing tools on the left.) The Block worktable is used mostly for drawing. We'll draw in a later lesson. But, for now we will only use one button and one tab.

Step 16

Step 18

16 At the bottom of the screen, click the **Color** tab. You'll see the block in color now. We're going to preview and print from the Block worktable to show you it's possible. If you only need a pattern and not an entire quilt, it's quick to just grab a block from the Library and print it.

Preview Different Printout Styles

17 On the top toolbar, click the **Print** button. You'll see eight printout types – but only four are available right now. Let's see each one.

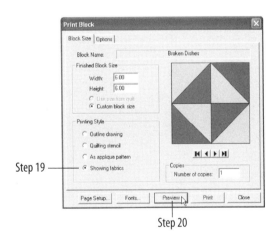

Step 19

Step 20

18 Click **Block**. Notice there are four *Printing Styles:* Outline drawing, Quilting stencil, As appliqué pattern, and Showing fabrics.

19 Click **Showing fabrics**.

20 Click the **Preview** button. This is what the printout would look like. As you can see, Print > Block > Showing Fabrics gives you a picture (not a pattern) of the block in color. You can try out the other Print Block styles later on your own.

Step 21

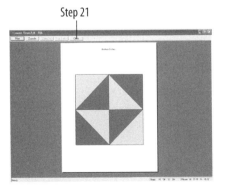

21 Click **Close**.

22 Click **Print** *(optional)*. Or, click **Close** to return to the Block worktable.

23 On the top toolbar, **click the Print button > Foundation Pattern.**

24 Click the **Preview** button. This is what a foundation pattern for *Broken Dishes* would look like. It is numbered, so you can sew A1 to A2 to A3 to A4 and B1 to B2 to B3 to B4 and then sew sections A and B together. Even if you don't plan to foundation-piece a block, previewing a block's foundation pattern may show you how to sew the block together if you're a new quilter.

25 Click **Close**.

26 Click **Print** *(optional)*. Or, click **Close** to return to the Block worktable.

27 On the top toolbar, **click Print > Templates.**

28 Click the **Preview** button. This previews a template printout for *Broken Dishes*. Notice that since the block design repeats one triangle eight times, you need only one template. (These templates work great when you cut them out, tape them beneath your clear ruler, and rotary cut around them.)

29 Click **Close**.

30 Click **Print** *(optional)*. Or, click **Close** to return to the Block worktable.

Step 23

Step 24

Step 25

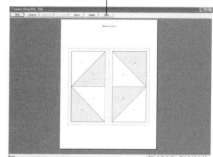

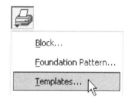

Step 27

Step 28

Step 29

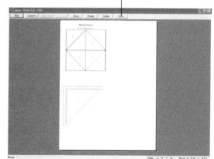

Step 31

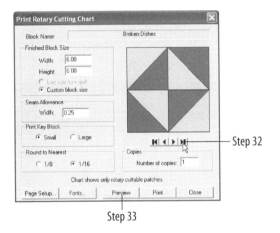

Step 32

Step 33

Step 34

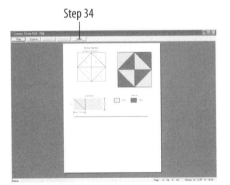

31 On the top toolbar, **click Print > Rotary Cutting.**

32 Here's something to notice: For this printout, you need to do one more step and select the coloring you want. On the right side of the Print Rotary Cutting Chart box, **click the fourth coloring arrow below the picture of the block** to choose the block coloring.

33 Click the **Preview** button. Here is a rotary cutting chart for *Broken Dishes* in the coloring we just specified. There is still only one patch marked "A," but the colors to the side say how many patches you need of each.

34 To zoom in for a closer look, **click the Zoom In button > point to the area you want enlarged > click and hold as you drag the cursor diagonally to make a box > release the mouse**. What you enclosed in the box will zoom. Click **Close**.

35 Click **Print** *(optional)*. Or, click **Close** to return to the Block worktable.

Notes
- Size? Always think *finished size*. Seam allowance, if needed, will be added automatically.

- Previewing printouts helps you ensure your final printout will be perfect, with the pattern names, finished sizes, line thickness, mirroring and other options, as you want.

- Missing a patch on the rotary cutting printout? Those patches are missing for a reason: they are not normally considered rotary-cuttable. Print the same block again, as templates, deleting all but the "missing" patches. Then use these templates beneath your clear rotary cutting ruler.

- Need a quick pattern? Just "print and run": Click the block in the Library > click Add to Sketchbook > Close > click View Sketchbook > double-click the block to send it to the Block worktable. Then print. No need to design a quilt!

Lesson Three

Print a Foundation Pattern

36 On the top toolbar, **click the View Sketchbook button > click the Blocks section > double-click the Compact Car block** to put it on the worktable. Let's try out some of the many foundation printing options. (Be sure to see the detailed information in the Printing section of this manual about all the options.) It doesn't matter which tab you are on.

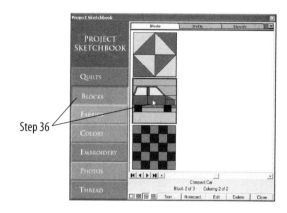

Step 36

37 On the top toolbar, **click Print > Foundation Pattern.**

38 At the top, click the **Options** tab. (Normally you'll always go to "Options" to set your pattern size.)

Step 38

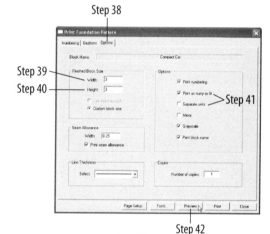

Step 39

Step 40

Step 41

Step 42

39 Imagine you want a small pattern repeated on one page. Under *Finished Block Size*, notice the Width box is highlighted. **Type: 3**

40 **Press your keyboard TAB key** to highlight the Height box. **Type: 3** again. This means you want a 3" x 3" pattern. Just below, notice "Use size from quilt" is not enabled (it's gray). Since you are printing from the Block worktable, your only choice is Custom Size – the Width and Height you set.

41 Under Options, **click to *check* Print as many as fit** if it is not checked. **Click to *uncheck* Separate units** if it is checked.

42 Click the **Preview** button. You now have four small car patterns, headed east.

43 Click **Close**. Let's mirror them.

Step 43

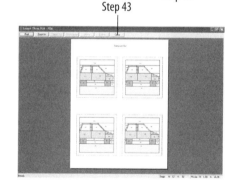

44 Click the **Options** tab again. Under Options, **click to *check* Mirror** if it is not checked.

45 Click the **Preview** button. Your four cars now head west. *Tip:* Normally you should mirror any directional foundation pattern. (To make sewn cars face right, car patterns would need to face left.)

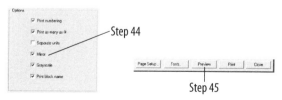

Step 44

Step 45

Step 46

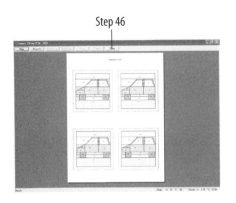

Step 48

Step 49

Step 50

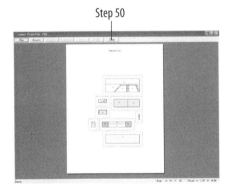

46 Click **Close**.

47 Click the **Options** tab again.

48 This particular block must really be sewn in separate units. So let's separate those units. Under Options, **click to *check* Separate units**.

49 Click the **Preview** button. Now your pattern is properly separated into units. But notice you have units *for only one full pattern,* not four, even though *Print as many as fit* is still checked. (Just know that if you "separate units" you can only have one pattern on the page. So don't "separate units" if you want many small patterns.)

50 Click **Print** *(optional)*. Or, click **Close**, and **Close** again to return to the Block worktable.

Use a Quilt from the Layout Library

51 Now let's print patterns from blocks set in a quilt. Rather than make our own layout, we'll use one from the Library. On the top menu bar, click **LIBRARIES > Layout Library**.

52 Drag the vertical scrollbar down (if necessary) > click Basics by Style > click Stars.

53 These look like blocks, but are actually quilt layouts. The first layout is selected. Click **Add to Sketchbook**. Click **Close**.

Step 52

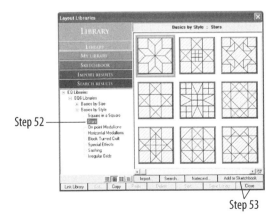

Step 53

Lesson Three

Learn about Basics by Style Library Layouts

Step 54
View Sketchbook

54 On the top toolbar, click the **View Sketchbook** button.

Step 54
View Sketchbook

55 **Click the Quilts section > click the Star quilt layout > click the Edit button.** Notice you are now back on the Quilt worktable because you edited a quilt. *Reminder:* The Work on Quilt button on the top toolbar also takes you to the Quilt worktable.

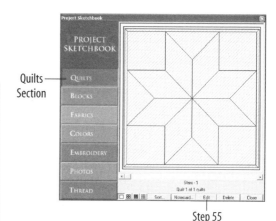

Step 55

Understanding the Layout Library
The Layout Library has two categories:

- **Basics by Size (mattress size).**
  These handy layouts are sized for beds (and more). They are identical to regular layouts you would make by clicking QUILT > New Quilt > and choosing any style *other than Custom Set.* So (and this is the important part) **it is easy to adjust block size and number for these quilts on the Layout tab.**

- **Basics by Style (on-point medallions, star layouts, etc.)**
  These are Custom Set quilts. Custom Set is the *only layout style without pre-set block spaces.* So we've pre-set some blocks into the large, empty, layout space for you. But this means **adjusting the blocks of these quilts is not so simple. So, these layouts are easiest to use in the size they come.**

Step 56

56 We're on the Layer 1 tab. Click the **Layout** tab. Where did the star go? This is why many *Basics by Style* layouts are difficult to adjust. You see only one empty space, without the pre-set blocks of the star. We'll work more with Custom Set in the next lesson. For now, let's see why these *Basics by Style* layouts are fun to use.

Layout | Borders | Layer 1 | Layer 2 | Layer 3

Step 57

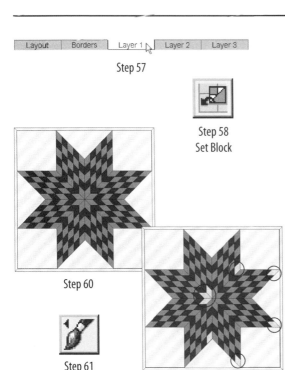

Step 60

Step 61
Paintbrush

Step 58
Set Block

Step 62

Step 63
Rotate Block

Step 64

Step 65
Paintbrush

Step 65 - Color the background

Set Blocks into a Basics by Style Layout

57 Click the **Layer 1** tab.

58 On the right-hand toolbar, click the **Set Block** tool.

59 Click to select the *Twenty-Five Patch* block in the palette.

60 **Click on each of the 8 star points to set the block into each point.** Notice that the square blocks skew to fit the diamond shape. You should now have a *Lone Star*.

61 Click the **Paintbrush** tool. Click any fabric in the palette.

62 **CTRL+click one star point in the center of the star.** You'll notice not all 8 points of the center color – don't worry if some points color on the outside. We want to do this so we can fix the way the blocks are rotated. Layouts from the library are blank (filled with "hatching lines") and blank quilts cannot keep rotations. For any layouts like this, you will need to rotate the blocks to be able to CTRL+click and color efficiently.

63 On the right-hand toolbar, click the **Rotate Block** tool.

64 **Click any of the 8 Twenty-Five Patch blocks in the quilt that do not have the fabric-colored point in the center.** Click the blocks until all 8 points colored with fabric meet. Now that your blocks are perfectly rotated, you can color easily.

65 Let's color the background where you see the gray "hatching lines." **Click the Paintbrush tool > click a fabric or color in the palette > click each large square and triangle around the star**, coloring the plain background behind the star.

Play More with Auto Borders

Step 66

66 Let's change the border, then print patterns. Click the **Borders** tab.

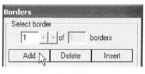

Step 67

67 Click **Add** to add a border.

68 Under *Lock size adjustments*, make sure **All** is checked.

69 **Change the size of this border to 5.00 by clicking repeatedly on the line** (Left, Top, Right, or Bottom) to the right of the slider rectangle. We could choose a different border style here, but instead we'll use an auto border.

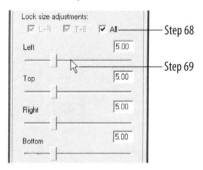

Step 68

Step 69

70 Click the **Layer 1** tab.

71 On the right-hand toolbar, click the **Set Auto Borders** tool. (See 302 if the tool is not on your toolbar.)

72 On the Auto Borders palette, **click the down arrow next to Select a style > scroll down, find and click on Single Block Patterns** in the list. ("Single Block" denotes the whole border was drawn as one very long block to fit a whole border side. Only these "Single Block" borders can be printed as one pattern. All other borders must be printed one shape (block) at a time.)

Step 71
Set Auto Borders

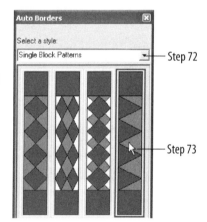

Step 72

Step 73

73 Drag the horizontal scrollbar below the border images to see them all. **Click to select any Single Block border.**

74 **Click in the wide border of your quilt.** You should now have a pieced outer border and plain inner border.

75 **Click to select a different border from the palette and click your wide border again.** Try out as many other Single Block borders on your quilt as you want.

Step 74 - Your border may not look like the one pictured above if you used a different Single Block Patterns border

Step 76
Set Block

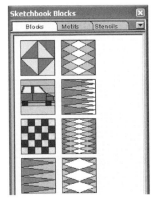

Auto Border blocks always appear as squares
in the palette and in the Sketchbook

Step 77
Spraycan

All borders have been colored.

76 On the right-hand toolbar, click the **Set Block** tool. Each time you use an Auto Border, EQ6 automatically adds the blocks of that Auto Border to your Sketchbook. If you look at the last blocks in the palette, they look odd. This is because they are displayed squeezed into a square. On your quilt they are stretched out long. But they are the same blocks.

Notes
- You can set a block into any space- block, sash or border (except for Mitered borders). If the space is not square, then the block stretches to fit the space. (Just like the *Twenty-Five Patch* block stretched to fit the diamond of our star.) But, no matter what, blocks will always display as squares in your Sketchbook and in the palette.

Color with the Spraycan

77 Your auto border is colored in grays and your mitered border has yet to be colored. Let's recolor quickly. On the right-hand toolbar, click the **Spraycan** tool.

78 **Click to select any fabric or color in the palette.**

79 **Click any patch in your auto border.** Any patches of the same color on that border strip will also recolor.

80 **Click to select a different fabric or color in the palette > hold down your keyboard CTRL key > click the mitered border.**

☕ Coffee Break

Take a break and play with the Spraycan tool. Recolor the quilt and borders as you'd like.

The Spraycan sprays all similarly colored patches in one block with the selected fabric or color. CTRL+click sprays all similarly-colored patches in all blocks on that layer.

Practice what you've learned:

1 Click on a patch in a *Twenty-Five Patch* block in the quilt with the Spraycan.

2 CTRL+click on a patch in a *Twenty-Five Patch* block in the quilt with the Spraycan.

3 Click on a patch in a Single Block Patterns border in the quilt with the Spraycan.

4 CTRL+click on a patch in a Single Block Patterns border in the quilt with the Spraycan.

If you make mistakes, do not get frustrated. The point is to learn, not create a perfect quilt coloring. Remember, you can go back a step by immediately choosing EDIT > Undo from the menu bar at the top of your screen.

If too many patches begin coloring together with the Spraycan tool, click or CTRL+click with the Paintbrush tool to separate them. Then switch back to using the Spraycan to audition colors.

Spraycan tool

Step 1 - Click on a
Twenty-Five Patch block

Step 2 - CTRL+click on a
Twenty-Five Patch block

Step 3 - Click on the
Single Block border

Step 4 - CTRL+click on the
Single Block border

Name the Quilt on its Notecard

81 Now that your quilt is colored, let's add it to the Sketchbook. On the top toolbar, click the **Add to Sketchbook** button to keep this quilt.

82 Click the View Sketchbook button > click the Quilts section.

83 Your new quilt will be the last one in the Sketchbook. Use the right arrow at the end of the scrollbar to find your quilt. **Click on your quilt to select it.** If you are viewing more than one quilt at a time, be sure the last quilt has a blue outline around it.

84 It now says *Unnamed* beneath the quilt. Let's name it. Click the **Notecard** button. A notecard appears, with a typing cursor blinking, ready for you to type.

Step 81
Add to Sketchbook

Step 82
View Sketchbook

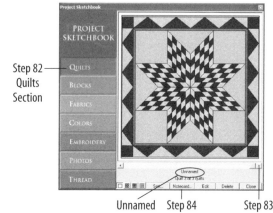

Step 82
Quilts
Section

Unnamed   Step 84   Step 83

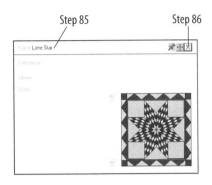

Step 85   Step 86

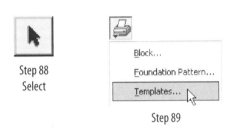

Step 88
Select

Step 89

Step 91

Step 91

Step 92

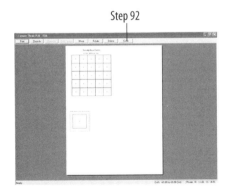

Step 93

85 Type: **Lone Star**.

86 Click the **X** in the top-right to close the notecard. Below the quilt it now says *Lone Star*.

Notes

- When you print a design, its Name in the Sketchbook will appear at the top of the printout. (It will say *Unnamed* until you type a name for it in the Sketchbook on its notecard.)

- To add a copyright notice to your EQ6 printout for an original block or quilt, type all of the following on the notecard's Name line: block or quilt name, copyright symbol, year, your name. For example: Peace Dove ©2006 Erin Grey. To type a © symbol, hold down your keyboard ALT key and type 0169.

- Don't confuse names: *Notecard* names appear at the top of printouts. *Project* names appear on your hard drive, to identify the entire project file and help you remember what's inside. Your project may contain many quilts, each with a different name.

87 Click the **Close** button to close the Sketchbook.

Print Templates

88 When you print from the quilt, EQ6 can use the size at which you set the block on the quilt. On the right-hand toolbar, **click the Select tool > click the top-right Star point to select it for printing.**

89 On the top toolbar, **click Print > Templates**.

90 Notice under Finished Block Size, *Use size from quilt* is selected. Let's see what happens when we don't use the size from the quilt. **Click to put the dot next to** *Custom block size* (any size will do).

91 Click **Preview**. *Eeeek.* This pattern is for a square.

92 Click **Close**.

93 **Click to put the dot next to** *Use size from quilt.* This tells EQ6 to figure the size perfectly from the quilt on the screen.

94 Click **Preview**. This pattern is for a diamond. On the left-hand page, you see a little block picture (key block). On the right-hand page is your template. (Only one template is needed since all diamonds are the same size.)

95 The left-hand page has room for the template, so let's move it there. At the top, **click the Move button > click, hold and drag the template to the left page**. Don't worry-empty pages don't print.

96 Click **Print** at the top of this Preview screen.

Print Large Foundations

97 Perhaps you'd prefer foundation-piecing these diamonds in rows. The star point should still be selected. If not, click it with the **Select** tool.

98 On the top toolbar, **click Print > Foundation Pattern > click the Options tab**. *Use size from quilt* is already selected.

99 Make sure **Print numbering** and **Separate units** are *checked* under Options. (Separate units *must* be checked; Print as many as fit *must not* be checked, if you plan to move or delete sections.)

100 Click **Preview**. You see a multi-page printout with rows of diamonds.

Notes

• Don't worry when printouts span multiple pages. When printing large patterns it's unavoidable. Notice that guidelines print to indicate how to fit multi-page patterns together. Match guidelines by moving one sheet to match the adjoining sheet's guideline (the dots and dashes of the guidelines should be perfectly on top of one another). Use small strips of transparent tape to fasten them together, and sew right over the tape.

• How the selected block is oriented on the quilt determines how the pattern is oriented on your printout. For example, each star point in this quilt faces a different direction. If you choose one pointing up and to the right, that's how it will be oriented on your printout. (Preview several star points to see how each fits on the paper.) To maximize paper saving, it's important to select the best orientation.

Step 94

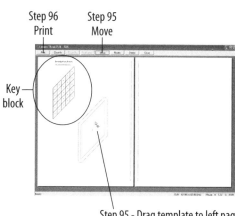

Step 96 Print | Step 95 Move

Key block

Step 95 - Drag template to left page

Step 98

Step 98 Options tab

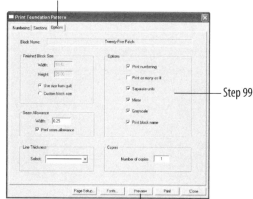

Step 99

Step 100

Lesson Three

Step 101
Zoom In

Drag a box around
the area to zoom

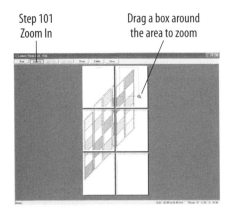

Step 102

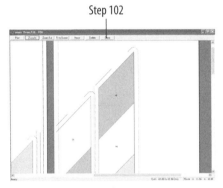

Zoomed in area

Step 104

101 To zoom in for a closer look, **click the Zoom In button > point to the area you want enlarged > click and hold as you drag the cursor diagonally to make a box > release the mouse**. What you enclosed in the box will zoom. Now you can see the sewing order numbers. You don't need to print.

102 Click Close > click Close. You are now back on the worktable without printing.

Print Fabric Yardage Estimate

103 EQ6 will estimate fabric yardage for your quilt. Remember, these are estimates and are often generous. On the top toolbar, **click Print > Fabric Yardage**.

104 On the Print Fabric Yardage box, let's leave the fabric width set for 40 inches. Click **Preview** to see the yardage chart. You can zoom in if you want.

Notes
Here is how EQ6 figures yardage:
- It adds the seam allowance you select to each patch.

- It places an imaginary rectangle around each patch at the seam allowance.

- It places these rectangles on fabric of the selected Fabric Width.

- Each time a "row" is filled, it begins a new row, counting the entire strip as required yardage.

- The result is usually an over estimate. Shapes like on-point sashes tend to give exceptionally large yardage figures.

- The estimate for the border generally requires a length of fabric as long as the longest border strip. If you want a border pieced in strips, use the Blocks border style.

- Backing and binding are not estimated.

105 When you are done previewing, **click Close > click Cancel** to return to the worktable.

Print Borders

106 On the right-hand toolbar, **click the Select tool > click an outer border strip to select it for printing**. The whole border strip will be selected (except the corner, which would need to be printed separately). Since we used a Single Block Patterns Auto Borders style, you can print the whole border side as one long strip. Had we used a style from the Borders tab, only one block or triangle would select and print.

107 On the top toolbar, **click Print > Foundation Pattern**. You see the border block as a square, rather than a long rectangle as in your border.

108 Click the Options tab > make sure *Use size from quilt* is selected.

109 Click **Preview**. You'll see the whole border, stretched over several sheets of paper. We won't print.

110 Click **Close**.

Homework

You've done a lot. So here's some homework to relax with. Watch two videos under Simple Tasks:

- Print Paper Piecing Templates – see how to print a whole sheet of English paper piecing templates – the kind you might use to hand-piece a Grandmother's Flower Garden quilt. See VIDEOS > Simple Tasks > Printing Repeated Shapes.

- Make a Quilt Label – see how to design and print a quilt label, or even a gift card. See VIDEOS > Simple Tasks > Making a Quilt Label.

---

111 Click the large **X** in the top-right corner to close EQ6 when you are finished. Click "Yes" for any pop up boxes if you want to keep the unsaved quilts in your Sketchbook.

Step 106
Select

Step 106
Click on a border strip to select it

Step 107

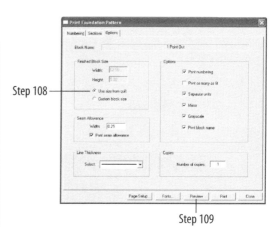

Step 108

Step 109

Step 110

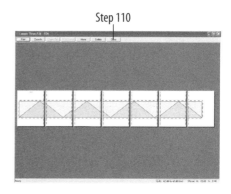

Lesson Four

You've learned to start new quilts, add borders, set blocks, color, and print while using the Layout, Borders, and Layer 1 tabs. This is as much as many easy quilts need. Now it's time to see what the other layers do, as well as learn about Custom Set quilts. This lesson is more advanced than the others, but we'll walk you through it:

- Create a New Project

- Add Blocks and Motifs to the Sketchbook

- Add Stencils to the Sketchbook

- Understand the Sketchbook Blocks Palette

- Set Blocks on Layer 1 of a Custom Set Quilt

- Move and Resize blocks with the Adjust Tool

- Rotate Blocks with the Adjust Tool

- Turn on the Graph Pad

- Understand and Use the Graph Pad

- Set Plain Blocks in the Quilt

- Set Motifs on Layer 2

- Write on Your Quilt

- Copy and Paste Motifs

- Delete Motifs

- Set Stencils on Layer 3

- Color Stencils with the Set Thread Tool

Remember to go at your own pace as you work through these lessons and e-mail us, or give us a call if you have a question. (Our contact information is on page 6.)

If you are using a laptop or touchpad, please see page 9 before starting this lesson.

Create a New Project

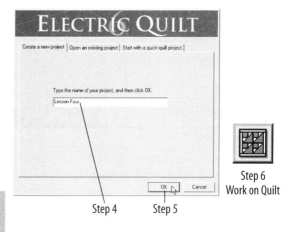

1   Double-click the **EQ6** icon on your Windows Desktop. You'll see the EQ6 splash screen play again.

2   When the Tip of the Day displays, click the **Next** button a few times and read the tips.

3   Click **Close** to close the Tip of the Day.

4   On the **Create a new project** tab of the EQ6 Project Helper, type: **Lesson Four**

Step 6
Work on Quilt

Step 4   Step 5

Notes
• If you choose to repeat this lesson, you can either delete the old Lesson Four (see 111) or give this one a slightly different name (Lesson Four – second time).

5   Click **OK**.

6   Click the **Work on Quilt** button on the top toolbar or click **WORKTABLE > Work on Quilt** on the top menu bar.

7   On the top menu bar, click **QUILT > New Quilt > Custom Set**. Custom Set quilts, as we learned in the last lesson, have one large, empty center.

Step 7

8   Click the **Layout** tab at the bottom of your screen.

9   Double-click the number for Width. Type: **30**

Step 8

10 Double-click the number for Height. Type: **30**

11 Click the **Layer 1** tab.

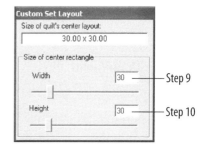

Step 9

Step 10

Step 11

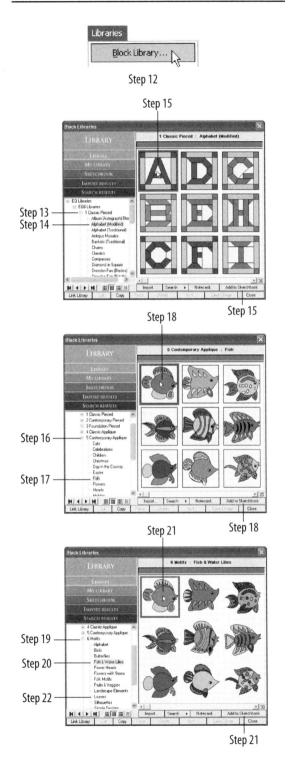

Step 12

Step 15

Step 13
Step 14

Step 15

Step 18

Step 15

Step 16

Step 17

Step 21

Step 18

Step 19

Step 20

Step 22

Step 21

Add Blocks and Motifs to the Sketchbook

12 We're going to set one of everything – blocks, motifs, and stencils – on the quilt to see how they work. On the top menu bar, click **LIBRARIES > Block Library**.

13 Drag the vertical scrollbar next to the list up until you see **1 Classic Pieced**. If it has a plus sign next to it, click the name 1 Classic Pieced.

14 Click the second style called **Alphabet (Modified)**.

15 **Click the *A* block to select it > click Add to Sketchbook three times.** You have now copied *A*, *B*, and *C*.

16 Drag the vertical scrollbar next to the list down until you see **5 Contemporary Applique**. Click the name 5 Contemporary Applique to open it.

17 Click the style named **Fish**.

18 **Click to select the first fish block > click the Add to Sketchbook button.**

19 Drag the vertical scrollbar next to the list down until you see **6 Motifs**. Click the name 6 Motifs to open it.

20 Click the style named **Fish & Water Lilies**. (Yes, there are fish here as well.)

21 **Click to select the first fish > click the Add to Sketchbook button.**

22 **Click the style named Leaves > click to select the first leaf > click Add to Sketchbook.**

Add Stencils to the Sketchbook

23 Drag the vertical scrollbar next to the list down until you see **7 Quilting Stencils**. Click the name 7 Quilting Stencils to open it.

24 **Click the style Border Stencils > click to select the second stencil Continuous Line Fish > click the Add to Sketchbook button twice.** This will add the second and third stencils from this style.

25 **Click the style Straight and Curved Lines > drag the horizontal scrollbar below the stencils to the right a little until you see stencils with wavy horizontal lines.**

26 **Position your cursor over the blocks** (without clicking) **to see the stencil names in the tooltip > find and click on Wavy Lines > click the Add to Sketchbook button three times.**

27 Click **Close** to put the Block Library away.

Understand the Sketchbook Blocks Palette

28 Setting blocks on layers and in a Custom Set quilt is different than the simple click that works for other layouts. **Click the Set Block tool.** The first thing you'll notice is that not all the blocks, motifs, and stencils you added are showing in the palette right now.

29 Inside the Sketchbook Blocks palette, click the **Motifs** tab. There are our fish and leaf motifs.

30 Click the **Stencils** tab inside the palette. There are our stencils.

31 Click back to the **Blocks** tab so we can set blocks in the quilt.

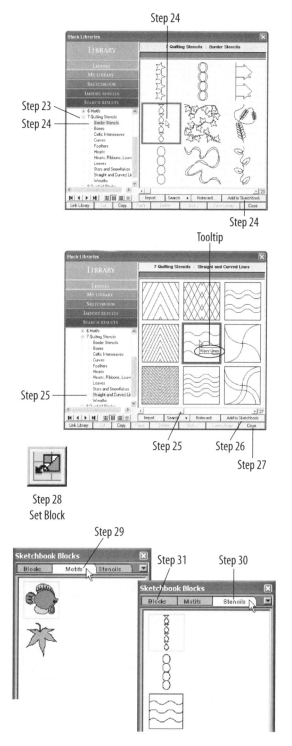

Cursor changes to a circle
with a line through it

Step 33 - Blue note

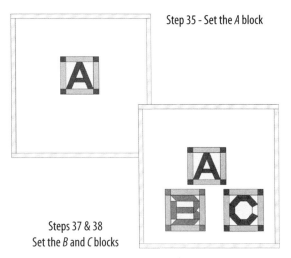

Step 35 - Set the *A* block

Steps 37 & 38
Set the *B* and *C* blocks

Step 39
Adjust

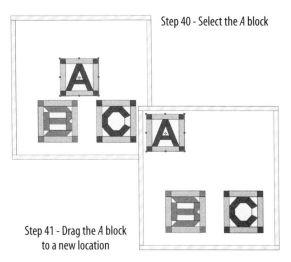

Step 40 - Select the *A* block

Step 41 - Drag the *A* block
to a new location

Set Blocks on Layer 1 of a Custom Set Quilt

32 Click the letter *A* block in the palette > position your cursor over the center of the quilt. Your cursor looks like a circle with a line through it (a "do not" sign).

33 Click once in the center of the quilt. A blue note appears saying, *Use SHIFT+drag to set a block*. Let's try that.

34 Hold down your keyboard **SHIFT** key.

35 Click and hold with the left mouse button > drag diagonally down and right to form a big box on the quilt > release the mouse button. (Laptop or touchpad users see page 9 if you're having difficulties.) The *A* block will pop from the palette into the box you formed on the quilt. Note: You are *not* dragging the block from the palette.

36 Let's try it again with a different block. **Click the *B* block in the palette.**

37 Hold down the SHIFT key on your keyboard > position your cursor inside the quilt (not on top of the *A* block) > click and hold > drag diagonally down and right > release. The *B* block will pop into the box.

38 Repeat steps 36-37 for the *C* block.

Move and Resize Blocks with the Adjust Tool

39 Once a block is set, it is very easy to move it. Click the **Adjust** tool on the right-hand toolbar.

40 Click to select the *A* block in the quilt. The block will become highlighted and has eight black squares (known as handles) around it – four on the sides and four on the corners.

41 Position your cursor in the center of the *A* block > click and hold > drag the block to a new location.

42 Try that with the *B* block. **Click to select the B block > click and hold in its center > drag it to a new location.**

43 To resize blocks, use the handles. **Click to select the C block in the quilt.**

44 **Position your cursor over a *corner* handle > click and hold on the handle > drag the handle away from the center of the block.**

45 You can also use the side handles and resize it only horizontally or vertically. **Position your cursor over the *top or bottom side* handle > click and hold on the handle > drag the handle back and forth away from and toward the center of the block.** The block will resize and become taller or shorter.

46 Repeat step 45 with the left or right side handles to see the block become wider or skinnier.

47 Let's move the *B* and *C* blocks out of the way for a little while. **Click to select the C block > click and hold in its center > drag it to the bottom-right corner of the quilt.**

48 **Click to select the B block > click and hold in its center > drag it to sit to the left of the C block** (at the bottom-middle of your quilt).

49 **Click to select the A block > click and hold in its center > drag it to sit above the other two blocks** (not overlapping).

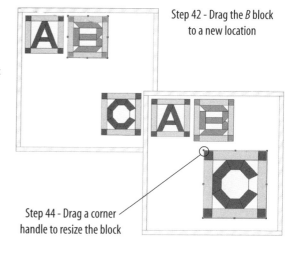

Step 42 - Drag the *B* block to a new location

Step 44 - Drag a corner handle to resize the block

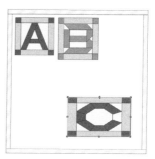

Step 45 - Use a side handle to resize the block

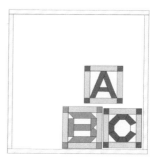

Steps 47-49
Drag all three blocks to new locations

Step 50 - Cursor changes to indicate you are in rotate-mode

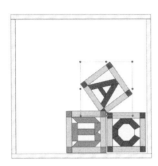

Step 51

Step 53

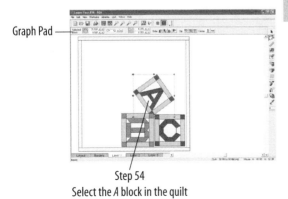

Graph Pad

Step 54
Select the *A* block in the quilt

Rotate Blocks with the Adjust Tool

50 **Click to select the *A* block > hold down your keyboard CTRL key > click in the center of the block.** The cursor changes. You are now in rotate-mode. Release the CTRL key.

51 Position your cursor over a corner handle. The cursor changes to a curved arrow. **Click and hold on the handle > drag it clockwise or counterclockwise around the center of the block.** The block will spin as you move the handle. (The select outline will disappear as you rotate.)

52 Click in an empty space in your quilt to deselect the *A* block and hide the handles.

Notes

- *To set a block,* click the Set Block tool > click the block in the palette > hold down the SHIFT key > position your cursor inside the quilt > click, hold, and drag to make a box > release.

- *To move a block with the Adjust tool,* click the Adjust tool > click the block in the quilt > click the block center and hold > drag the block to a new location > release.

- *To resize a block with the Adjust tool,* click the Adjust tool > click the block in the quilt > click and hold on a handle > drag the handle to a new location > release.

- *To rotate a block with the Adjust tool,* click the Adjust tool > click the block in the quilt > CTRL+click in its center > click and hold on a corner handle > spin the block around its center > release.

Turn on the Graph Pad

53 Let's turn on the Graph Pad. On the top menu bar, click **VIEW > Graph Pad**. A gray bar is added below the top toolbar. Using the Graph Pad and Adjust tool together help you to set, move, resize and rotate blocks precisely.

54 Right now the Graph Pad is grayed out (disabled) because nothing is selected with the **Adjust** tool. **Click the A block in the quilt to make the Graph Pad light up with numbers.**

Understand and Use the Graph Pad

55 Look at the Graph Pad. You'll see three sets of numbers followed by three sets of buttons. Each has a picture to try to help you remember what they do. The numbers are for position, rotation and size. The buttons are for stacking order, clipping at the border, and centering in the quilt. **Double-click the number for rotation.**

56 Type: **0**

57 The A block will no longer be rotated. Let's move the block with the Adjust tool and see the Graph Pad's position numbers change. **Click and hold in the center of the *A* block in the quilt > drag it to a new location in the quilt while watching the Graph Pad.** (You may move B and C at any time, if needed.)

58 Our quilt is 30" x 30". Repeat step 57 a few times to see the position numbers change when you move the block to these places:

- top-left corner of the quilt center

- bottom-right corner of the quilt center

- outside the quilt border a little bit to the left

- outside the quilt border a little bit to the top

59 You can set the block position precisely by typing in the Graph Pad. **Double-click the top number for position in the Graph Pad** (this is horizontal position).

60 Type: **0**

61 **Double-click the bottom number for position** (this is vertical position).

62 Type: **0**

63 The block is now placed precisely in the top-left corner of your quilt (not including the border). **Double-click the top number for size** (this is horizontal width).

64 Type: **30**

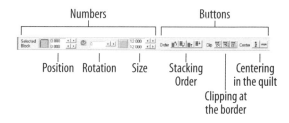

Numbers   Buttons

Position   Rotation   Size   Stacking Order   Centering in the quilt

Clipping at the border

Rotation

Step 56

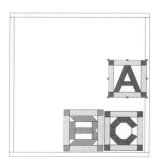

The *A* block is no longer rotated

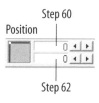

Step 60

Position

Step 62

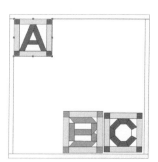

Block is positioned in the top-left corner of the quilt

Size

Step 64

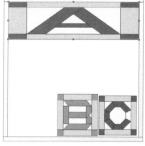

Block fills the quilt horizontally

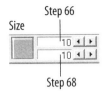

Size

Step 66

Step 68

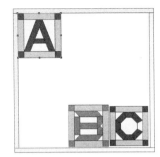

The *A* block is now 10" x 10"

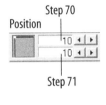

Position

Step 70

Step 71

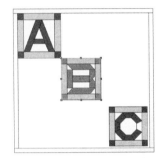

The *B* block starts at bottom-right corner of the *A* block

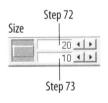

Size

Step 72

Step 73

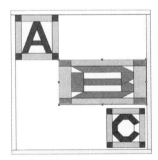

The *B* block is now 20" x 10"

Coffee Break practice quilt

65 Do you see how the block now fills the quilt horizontally? **Double-click the top number for size again.**

66 Type: **10**

67 **Double-click the bottom number for size** (this is the vertical height).

68 Type: **10**

69 **Click to select the *B* block.** The Graph Pad numbers will change to reflect how *B* is set. Let's move it.

70 **Double-click the top number for position and type: 10**

71 **Double-click the bottom number for position and type: 10**

72 Do you see how the *B* block now starts at the bottom-right corner of where the *A* block ends? **Double-click the top number for size and type: 20**

73 **Double-click the bottom number for size and type: 10**

☕ Coffee Break

Do these steps at your own pace before continuing to step 74. You've learned a lot about blocks in Custom Set quilts – now get some practice. Fill the quilt with blocks of various sizes and positions. If you like, you can match the quilt pictured at the left. If you create a different quilt, yours won't match our pictures, but that's okay.

Practice what you've learned:
1 *Set Block tool to set* – Set blocks in the quilt with SHIFT+drag.
2 *Adjust tool to move* – click, hold, and drag blocks from their center to move them or type directly in the first set of numbers on the Graph Pad.
3 *Adjust tool to resize* – click, hold, and drag handles to resize blocks or type directly in the third set of numbers on the Graph Pad.

Come back when your quilt is filled and we'll learn how to set plain blocks.

Set Plain Blocks in the Quilt

74 Click the **Add to Sketchbook** button on the top toolbar to save your ABC Custom Set quilt.

75 To set a plain block in the quilt, you need a plain block in your Blocks palette. Click the **Set Block** tool on the right-hand toolbar.

76 **Right-click inside the palette > click Add Plain Block.** An uncolored block with no piecing is added to the end of the blocks you added from the library.

77 The nice thing about Custom Set quilts is that once blocks are set, you can quickly replace them. **Click to select the plain block in the palette > click in your quilt on all the pieced blocks to replace them with plain (unpieced) blocks.** The plain block is colored off-white, so don't worry when your entire quilt turns off-white.

78 *(Optional)* Click the **Paintbrush** tool on the right-hand toolbar. **Click a pale-colored fabric to select it > click a plain block in the quilt.** Continue coloring the quilt with pale fabrics, until all the plain blocks are colored.

79 Click the **Add to Sketchbook** button on the top toolbar to save all your work on Layer 1.

Set Motifs on Layer 2

80 Click the **Layer 2** tab at the bottom of your screen. Layer 2 is intended for items you "float" on top of Layer 1.

81 **Click the Set Block tool > stay on the Blocks tab > click the *Goldie Fish* block to select it.**

Step 74
Add to Sketchbook

Step 75
Set Block

Step 76

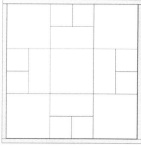

Step 77
Replace pieced blocks with plain blocks
(Your quilt may look different)

Step 78
Paintbrush

Step 79
Add to Sketchbook

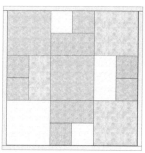

Step 78 - Color the quilt with fabric

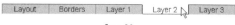

Step 80

Step 81
Set Block

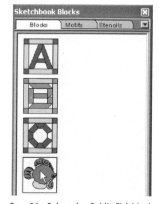

Step 81 - Select the *Goldie Fish* block

Lesson Four

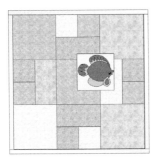

Step 82

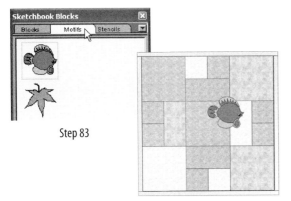

Step 83

Step 84 - Click to replace the
Goldie Fish block with the motif

Step 85
Add the Set Applique Text
button to the toolbar

Step 85
Paintbrush

Step 88 - SHIFT+drag to
form a typing box

Step 87
Set Applique Text

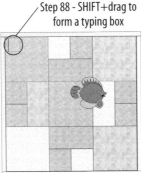

82 Set the block on Layer 2 as we have before with SHIFT+drag. **(Hold down your keyboard SHIFT key > position your cursor over the center of your quilt > click and hold > drag to make a box > release.)**

83 Do you see how the entire block (plus background) is floating above the plain blocks on Layer 1? Let's try changing this to a motif instead. **Click the Motifs tab within the palette.**

84 **Click the *Goldie Fish* motif to select it > click in the quilt on the *Goldie Fish* block to replace it.** Now you can see the difference between a block and motif: blocks have a background – motifs do not.

Write on Your Quilt

85 Motifs are not the only thing that can go on Layer 2. Do you remember how to add toolbar buttons? **Right-click on the right-hand toolbar above the Set Block tool > click Add/Remove buttons > click Set Applique Text > click outside the Add/Remove Buttons list to put the list away.**

86 Let's choose a fabric for our text – one that hasn't already been used in the quilt, so we can see what we're doing. **Click the Paintbrush tool > click a dark-colored fabric in the palette to select it.**

87 Click the **Set Applique Text** tool on the right-hand toolbar. If this is the first time you've used this tool, you will see an hourglass and it may take a moment for the Applique Text box to appear as the list fills with all the TrueType fonts installed on your computer.

88 We need to SHIFT+drag again to form a typing box. **(Hold down your keyboard SHIFT key > position your cursor over the quilt > click and hold > drag diagonally to make a box > release.** You'll see a small box with a flashing typing cursor.)

89 EQ6 is not a word processor – it doesn't know when you've misspelled something or when to put text on a new line. You need to type everything as you need it. Type: **Goldie Fish**

90 Press your keyboard **ENTER key** to start a new line.

91 Type: **has many friends**

92 If you make a mistake, press your keyboard **BACKSPACE key** until you erase the misspelling. (You can't highlight text to erase it as with a word processor.)

93 If your text extends past the right edge of the quilt, **click the Adjust tool > click the text box > click and hold in its center > drag it to the left until it fits inside. Click the Set Applique Text tool again > click the text box to select it.**

94 On the Applique Text box, click the down arrow next to the **Select typeface** box. **Click any name in the list.**

95 Now that you've chosen a typeface, use your keyboard down arrow to see some other choices.

96 Click any of the buttons across the bottom of the Applique Text box for additional formatting.

97 To set an approximate size, **drag the slider bar in the middle of the Applique Text box to the right until it reads: 3.00**. Typeface sizes vary, so if the text extends past the right edge of the quilt, try a number less than 3.00. Or use the Adjust tool to move your text. (You can also resize with the Adjust tool.)

Copy and Paste Motifs

98 **Click the Adjust tool > click the Goldie Fish motif in the quilt.**

99 Copy the selected motif by clicking **EDIT > Copy** on the top menu bar (or press **CTRL+C** on your keyboard). You won't see another fish yet. It has only been sent to the clipboard.

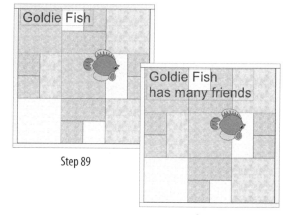

Step 89

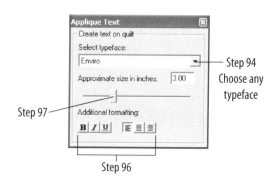

Step 91

Step 93
Adjust

Applique Text

Create text on quilt

Select typeface:

Enviro — Step 94
Choose any typeface

Approximate size in inches: 3.00

Step 97 —

Additional formatting:

B *I* U

Step 96

Step 98
Adjust

Edit

↰ Undo select block
✕ Cut   Ctrl+X
▢ Copy   Ctrl+C
▢ Paste   Ctrl+V

Step 99

Lesson Four

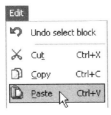

Step 100

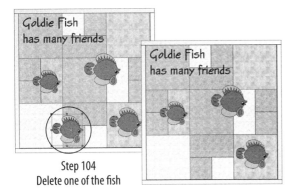

Step 104
Delete one of the fish

Step 106

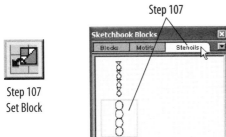

Step 107
Set Block

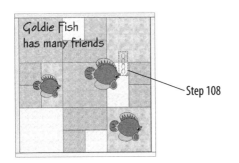

Step 108

100 Paste the fish by clicking **EDIT > Paste** (or press **CTRL+V** on your keyboard). The pasted fish is now selected.

101 Click and hold in the center of the pasted fish > drag it to another part of the quilt > drag a corner handle in toward the center to make the fish a little smaller.

102 Paste another fish by clicking **EDIT > Paste** (or press **CTRL+V** on your keyboard). Move and resize this fish as you did in step 101. All your fish can be different sizes.

103 Paste one last fish by clicking **EDIT > Paste** (or press **CTRL+V** on your keyboard). Move and resize this fish as you did in step 101.

Delete Motifs

104 Does *Goldie Fish* have one too many friends? Click a little fish with the **Adjust** tool and press your keyboard **DELETE key** (or click **EDIT > Clear**).

105 Click the **Add to Sketchbook** button.

Set Stencils on Layer 3

106 Click the **Layer 3** tab at the bottom of your screen. Notice many tools on the right-hand toolbar are grayed out. This means those tools can't be used on that layer. Only tools available on that layer are active.

107 Click the Set Block tool > click the Stencils tab (third tab) in the palette > click to select the Continuous Line Ovals stencil.

108 Hold down your keyboard SHIFT key > position your cursor inside the quilt above one of the fish > click and drag diagonally to make a tall, thin box above its head > release. You just made bubbles. If your box is drawn too thin, no stencil will appear. Try it again, making a larger box.

109 Repeat step 108 to give some of the other fish bubbles.

Color Stencils with the Set Thread Tool

110 Now we need to add the Set Thread tool to the toolbar. **Right-click on the right-hand toolbar > click Add/Remove buttons > click Set Thread > click away from the list to deselect it.**

111 Click the **Set Thread** tool on your toolbar. The palette will appear showing the thread colors from your Sketchbook.

112 Click a thread color in the palette > click *inside* a bubble on the quilt.

113 Color all the bubbles different colors, then click the **Add to Sketchbook** button.

Step 110

Step 111
Set Thread

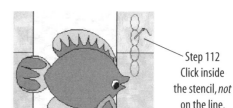

Step 112
Click inside
the stencil, *not*
on the line.

Homework

Embroidery and Photos work just like everything else we have set on layers. Embroidery goes on Layer 3 and colors like stencils with the Set Thread tool. Photos can go on Layer 2 or 3 of any quilt or can go on Layer 1 of Custom Set or Horizontal quilt layouts. Look at the picture at the right for a reminder of what can be set on each layer.

1 Click VIDEOS > Using the Quilt Tools > Set Embroidery Tool and watch. Then watch VIDEOS > Using the Quilt Tools > Set Photo Tool.
2 Go to LIBRARIES > Embroidery Library and add some designs to the Sketchbook.
3 Go to LIBRARIES > Photo Library and add some photos to the Sketchbook.
4 Add the Set Embroidery and Set Photo tools to your right-hand toolbar. (See page 302.)
5 Try setting embroidery on Layer 3 as you learned in the video with the Set Embroidery tool.
6 Try coloring the embroidery with the Set Thread tool.
7 Try setting some photos on Layer 3 as you learned in the video with the Set Photo tool.

Great job! You're finished the quilt lessons now. Review any lesson you like, then on to Lesson Five to learn about drawing!

114 Click the large **X** in the top-right corner to close EQ6 when you are finished.

Step 113
Add to Sketchbook

Layer 1

Blocks

Photos

Plain blocks of fabric

Layer 2

Motifs

Photos

Appliqué Text

Layer 3

Stencils

Photos

Embroideries

Lesson Five

Welcome to your first drawing lesson! In this lesson we are going to play with EasyDraw™ blocks from the library and draw some of our own. We'll learn to:

- Create a New Project

- Tour the Block Worktable

- Start a New EasyDraw™ Block

- Turn on the Precision Bar

- Understand and Use the Precision Bar

- Use the Grid Tool

- Edit a Library Block

- Add and Delete Lines

- Partition Arcs

- Stagger Arcs

Remember to go at your own pace as you work through these lessons and e-mail us, or give us a call if you have a question. (Our contact information is on page 6.)

If you are using a laptop or touchpad, please see page 9 before starting this lesson.

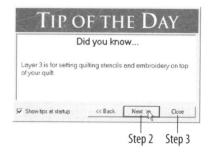

Create a New Project

1   Double-click the **EQ6** icon on your Windows Desktop. You'll see the EQ6 splash screen play.

2   When the Tip of the Day displays, click the **Next** button a few times and read the tips.

3   Click **Close** to close the Tip of the Day.

Step 2   Step 3

4   On the **Create a new project** tab of the EQ6 Project Helper, type: **Lesson Five**

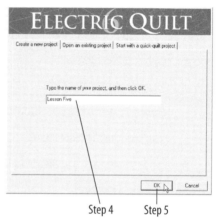

Notes
- If you choose to repeat this lesson, you can either delete the old Lesson Five (see page 111) or give this one a slightly different name (Lesson Five – second time).

5   Click **OK**.

6   Click the **Work on Block** button on the top toolbar or click **WORKTABLE > Work on Block** on the top menu bar. (Notice how the Work on Block button is now pressed in.)

Step 4   Step 5

Tour the Block Worktable
Look at the top of your screen at the menu bar.
QUILT is off the list and BLOCK is there instead because we are on the Block worktable now. So, instead of clicking QUILT > New Quilt, we click BLOCK > New Block.

Below the menu bar are the Project tools. This toolbar does not disappear when you switch worktables. If you are on the Quilt worktable, the Work on Quilt button is pressed. If you are on the Block worktable, the Work on Block button is pressed.

To the left is a toolbar of drawing tools. These change depending on the block type you choose when you click BLOCK > New Block or switch tabs.

Beside the Project and Drawing tools are rulers. These correspond with the size of the block you choose to draw. The top-left corner of the block is 0,0.

Step 6
Work on Block

Rulers

Menu Bar

Project tools

Drawing tools

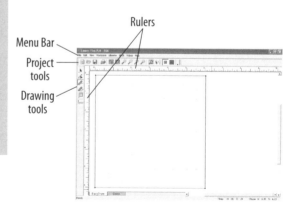

Lesson Five

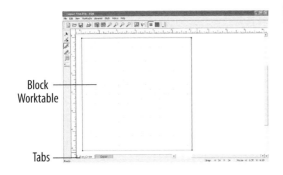

Block Worktable

Tabs

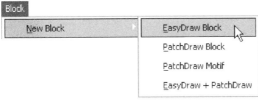

Step 7

At the bottom of the screen are tabs. Because we are on the Block worktable, these tabs changed as well. When there are two tabs, the first is for drawing and the last is for color. When there are three tabs, the first and second are for drawing and the last is for color.

In the middle of the screen is your worktable. Here you will always see a block outline or guides that you should draw within. You will also see small dots inside the block outline that are called snap points.

(Optional) Click the **Color** tab at the bottom of the screen and you'll see the drawing tools disappear from the left side of the screen and Color tools appear at the right.

Start a New EasyDraw™ Block

7   On the top menu bar, click **BLOCK > New Block > EasyDraw Block**. The EasyDraw™ tools will appear at the left and you will now have EasyDraw™ and Color tabs at the bottom.

8   Let's read how EasyDraw™ works. Turn to page 222 and read the topic called *Understanding EasyDraw™*. Pay special attention to the pictures. Come back after you read that page.

9   On the left toolbar, position your cursor over the first tool without clicking. This will show you the tool name in a tooltip.

10 Repeat step 9 for the rest of the tools on the Drawing toolbar.

11 Click the **Line** tool on the left toolbar. We're going to make a mess and make some common EasyDraw™ drawing mistakes, so we know *what not to do* and then draw real blocks.

12 Position your cursor inside the center of the block outline (not touching the edge).

13 **Click and hold to start the line > drag your cursor down and right, staying inside the block outline (not touching the edge) > release to stop the line.**

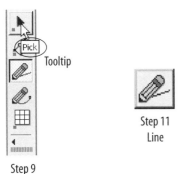

Tooltip

Step 9

Step 11
Line

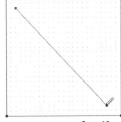

Step 12
Starting point

Step 13
Ending point

14 *EasyDraw™ Mistake #1* – lines cannot float. Lines must be connected at both ends, to either the block outline or other lines. Click the **Color** tab at the bottom of your screen. Your line will disappear because it was not connected to anything.

Step 14

Line has disappeared
on the Color tab

15 Click the **EasyDraw** tab at the bottom of your screen. The line is still gone.

16 Position your cursor over the top-left corner of the block outline on the black dot (we call this a node).

Step 16

Step 15

17 **Click and hold on the corner node to start the line > drag your cursor diagonally down and right to the opposite corner node > release when you're over the opposite corner to stop the line.**

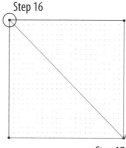

Step 17

18 Click the **Color** tab at the bottom of the screen. If you drew accurately from corner to corner of the outline, this line will stay.

19 Click the **EasyDraw** tab at the bottom of the screen. The **Line** tool should still be selected.

Step 18

20 Let's draw 3 lines that start at the bottom of the block, cross the diagonal, but don't touch the other side of the outline. (See the bottom-right picture for an example.) **Position your cursor anywhere along the bottom edge of the block outline.**

On the Color tab
the line is still there

21 **Click and hold to start the line > drag your cursor slightly over the diagonal line > release to end the line before you reach the block outline on the other side.**

Step 19

22 Repeat steps 20-21 to draw the other two lines.

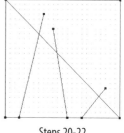

Steps 20-22

Step 23

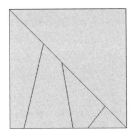

On the Color tab the
whispy ends disappear

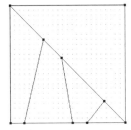

Step 24

There are three nodes
along the diagonal line

Step 25
Arc

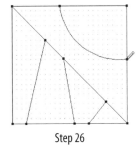

Step 26

Step 29
Add to Sketchbook

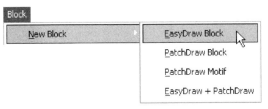

Step 30

23 *EasyDraw™ Mistake #2* – anything hanging over a line is not part of the drawing. *Remember:* only lines connected at both ends will stay. Click the **Color** tab at the bottom of your screen. The portions of the 3 lines that touch the bottom edge of the outline and the diagonal line will stay. All the "whispy" lines extending past the diagonal have disappeared.

24 Click the **EasyDraw** tab. Notice how there are now 3 nodes along the diagonal line where the other lines end.

25 On the left-hand toolbar, click the **Arc** tool. You use the same mouse movements to draw arcs as you did lines.

26 **Position your cursor anywhere on the block edge > click and hold to start the arc > drag through the block > release to stop the arc.**

27 Sometimes arcs face the wrong way as you're drawing. Use the SPACEBAR to flip them. **Position your cursor anywhere on the block edge > click and hold to start the arc > drag through the block > while dragging, press your keyboard SPACEBAR slowly a few times to flip the arc's direction. Release to stop the arc.** Be sure it touches or crosses lines in the drawing or the block edge.

28 Click the **Color** tab to see what stays and what goes.

29 *(Optional)* Click the **Add to Sketchbook** button on the top toolbar. We're finished drawing our messy block, let's draw nice ones now.

30 On the top menu bar, click **BLOCK > New Block > EasyDraw Block.**

Lesson Five

Turn on the Precision Bar

31 Just like the Quilt worktable has a Graph Pad, the Block worktable has a Precision Bar. On the top menu bar, click **VIEW > Precision Bar.**

Step 31

Understand and Use the Precision Bar

The Precision Bar is great for making quick changes to your block size, snap points, and graph paper settings.

- **Block Width, Block Height** – These numbers are your finished block size. These numbers also establish how your Block Rulers look. For example, notice how the right edge of the block outline lines up with a number on the ruler that is the same as Block Width.

- **Snaps Horizontal, Snaps Vertical** – These are your snap points. They are the dots you see inside the block outline that work like magnets in your block to pull your lines or arcs toward them.

- **Graph Paper Cells (Image, Horizontal, Vertical)** – Graph Paper is not part of your drawing, but is there to help you see where to draw if you need it. The image hides or shows the graph paper. Horizontal and Vertical establish how you want the block divided (how many cells across and down).

- The other buttons are for advanced drawing and we will cover some of them in this lesson. The majority of EasyDraw™ blocks should be drawn with the first two Snapping Options buttons pressed in as they are now.

- **Deciding Block Size and Snaps** – The settings for block size and snaps depend on the block you plan to draw. Figure out the number of equal patches across and down (let's say 3x5) and set the snaps to be a multiple thereof. Snaps could be 3x5 (you'd only be able to draw at the inch marks), 6x10 (you could split each patch in half), 12x10 (you could split each patch into fourths), and so on. For more information, see pages 223-224.

Block Width & Height   Graph Paper Cells

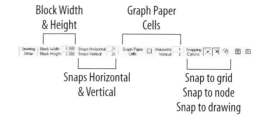

Snaps Horizontal & Vertical   Snap to grid / Snap to node / Snap to drawing

Step 32

Step 34

32 Double-click (in the Precision Bar) on the number for Block Width and type: **9**

33 Press your keyboard **TAB key** to go to Block Height. You'll see your ruler update.

34 Type: **9**

Step 36

Step 37

Step 40
Hide/show graph paper

Step 41

Step 43
Click on the
red square

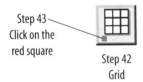

Step 42
Grid

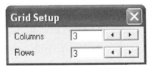

Step 43
Grid Setup box

35   Press your keyboard **TAB key** to update the size and go to Snaps Horizontal.

36   The block will be square again. Now we'll change snaps. **Type: 9 > press the TAB key.**

37   **Type: 9 > press the TAB key.**

38   This will give us snap points at every inch. You'll see the dots on the screen update. Now we'll change graph paper. **Type: 3 > press the TAB key.**

39   **Type: 3 > press the TAB key.**

40   Click the **Hide/show graph paper** button on the Precision Bar. You will see the block be divided into 3 cells across and 3 cells down.

41   *(Optional)* **Click the Color tab > look at the block > click the EasyDraw tab.** Did you see how the dots and graph are not part of your drawing? Snap points and graph paper are only there to help you draw.

Use the Grid Tool

42   The Line tool is great, but can you imagine how long it would take you to draw a 36-Patch block? Whenever you need a grid, you should use the Grid tool. Click the **Grid** tool on the left-hand toolbar.

43   Some of the tools on the Drawing toolbar have red squares in the bottom corner of their image that bring up pop-up boxes. **Click the red square in the bottom-left corner of the Grid tool button.** The Grid Setup box appears and your cursor changes to a crosshair with a grid when you move it to the block.

44   If Grid Setup is not set to 3 Columns and 3 Rows, click the left or right arrow buttons next to those numbers until each number is 3.

45 Position the center of the crosshair cursor over (or just outside) the top-left corner node of the block outline.

46 **Click and hold to start the grid > drag diagonally down and right to the opposite corner > release when you are over (or just outside) the bottom-right corner node.** Presto-chango – you just drew four lines at once to make a *Nine Patch*.

47 Click the **Add to Sketchbook** button.

48 *(Optional)* **Click the Color tab > click the Paintbrush tool > color your block > click the Add to Sketchbook button > click the EasyDraw tab > click the red square on the Grid tool.**

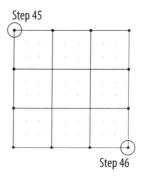

Step 45

Step 46

Step 47
Add to Sketchbook

Notes
• When you color a new block, you are telling EQ6 where you want the color. You must establish the color scheme and color groups before the CTRL and ALT keys or Spraycan tool can have any effect on your drawing.

Step 48 *(Optional)*
Color the block on the Color tab

49 Grids can be the entire block or part of the block. Let's make this block a *Double Nine Patch*. **Position your cursor over the bottom-left corner node of the block outline.**

50 **Click and hold to start the grid > drag diagonally > release when you are over the opposite corner of that square.**

51 Repeat step 50 to make grids in the remaining three corner squares and the center. If you make a mistake and drag the grid too far so it does not fit the larger *Nine Patch* square, click **EDIT > Undo** immediately on the top menu bar.

52 Click the **Add to Sketchbook** button on the top toolbar.

53 *(Optional)* **Click the Color tab.** You've created a new block, so your coloring looks jumbled because the original patches have changed. **Click the Paintbrush tool > color your block > click the Add to Sketchbook button.**

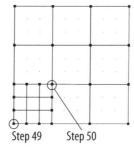
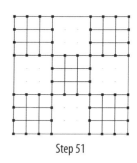

Step 49   Step 50   Step 51

Step 52
Add to Sketchbook

Step 53 *(Optional)*
Color the block

Step 54   Step 55

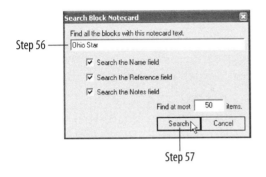

Step 56

Step 57

Step 58

Step 59
Double-click the *Ohio Star*

Edit a Library Block

54   Click **LIBRARIES > Block Library** on the top menu bar.

55   In the buttons at the bottom, choose **Search > By Notecard.**

56   Type: **Ohio Star**

57   Click the **Search** button, wait for the progress bar, then click **OK** when the results are reported. The first block is already selected.

58   Click the **Add to Sketchbook** button, then click **Close.**

59   **Click the View Sketchbook button on the top toolbar > Blocks section > double-click the *Ohio Star* block to edit it to the worktable.** The Precision Bar will update with the settings with which this block was drawn.

Add and Delete Lines

60   Click the **Line** tool on the left toolbar.

61   In the center square of the *Ohio Star* block, let's draw an X. **Position your cursor over the top-left corner of the center square.**

62   **Click and hold to start the line > drag diagonally down and right > release when you are over the bottom-right corner of the center square.**

63   **Start with your cursor over the bottom-left corner of the center square > click and hold to start the line > drag diagonally up and right > release when you are over the top-right corner of the center square.** Bravo – you have your X.

64   Click the **Pick** tool.

Step 60
Line

Step 64
Pick

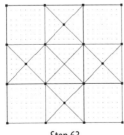

Step 63
Draw an X in the center square

65 Remember our center square? Let's delete the edges of it and leave our X in the center instead. **Click to select one of the edge lines of the center square of the** *Ohio Star.*

66 Press your keyboard **DELETE key**. (You could also click EDIT > Clear from the top menu bar.)

67 Try it again for the other three edge lines of the center square. **Click to select the line > press the DELETE key.** You now have an *Ohio Star Variation.*

68 Click the **Add to Sketchbook** button.

69 *(Optional)* **Click the Color tab > click the Paintbrush tool > color your block > click the Add to Sketchbook button.**

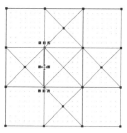

Step 65 - Select one of the center square lines

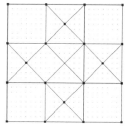

Step 66
Delete the selected line

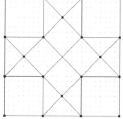

Step 67 - Delete all of the center square lines

Step 68
Add to Sketchbook

☕ Coffee Break

You've learned how to draw with the Line, Arc, and Grid tools in EasyDraw. Test yourself and see if you can draw the following:

1 BLOCK > New Block > EasyDraw Block. Use the Line tool to draw a diagonal line from corner to corner to make a *Half-Square Triangle.* Click the Color tab, color the block, and click Add to Sketchbook.

2 Click the EasyDraw tab and use the Line tool to draw the other diagonal for the block. You just turned this into a *Quarter-Square Triangle* block. Click the Color tab, color the block, and click Add to Sketchbook.

3 BLOCK > New Block > EasyDraw Block. Use the Arc tool to draw an arc around the top-left corner of the block from the same ruler mark at each edge - this makes a *Drunkard's Path* block. (Don't forget you can press the keyboard SPACEBAR to flip the arc as long as you haven't released the mouse yet.) Click the Color tab, color the block, and click Add to Sketchbook.

4 BLOCK > New Block > EasyDraw Block. Let's make a 16 Patch. Change the numbers in the Precision Bar to match (4, 4, 4, 4, 4, 4) by typing in a number and then pressing your keyboard TAB key. (Don't forget to press the TAB key after the last entry.) Click the red square on the Grid tool button. Change the Grid Setup to match that number as well (4, 4). Then drag a grid to fill the block. Click the Color tab, color the block, and click Add to Sketchbook.

Step 69 - Color the block

Half-Square Triangle

Quarter-Square Triangle

Drunkard's Path

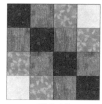

16 Patch

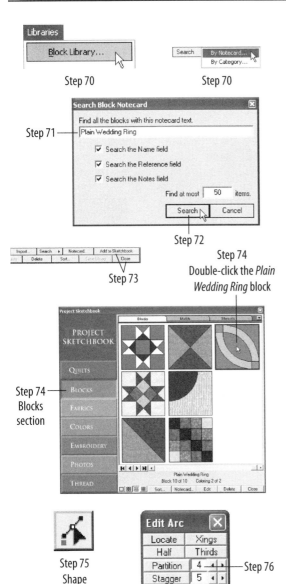

Step 70

Step 70

Step 71

Step 72

Step 73

Step 74
Double-click the *Plain Wedding Ring* block

Step 74
Blocks
section

Step 75
Shape

Edit Arc

Locate	Xings
Half	Thirds
Partition	4
Stagger	5

Step 76

Step 79
Line

Step 77 & 78 - Partition all arcs into 4 equal pieces

Partition Arcs

70 Click **LIBRARIES > Block Library**, then click **Search > By Notecard**.

71 Type: **Plain Wedding Ring**

72 Click the **Search** button, wait for the progress bar, then click **OK** when the results are reported. The block is already selected.

73 Click the **Add to Sketchbook** button, then click **Close**.

74 **Click the View Sketchbook button on the top toolbar > Blocks section > double-click the *Plain Wedding Ring* block to edit it to the worktable.** The Precision Bar will update with the settings with which this block was drawn.

75 The next tool we'll use on the Drawing toolbar is another one with a red square in the bottom corner of its image. **Click the red square in the bottom-left corner of the Shape tool button.** The Edit Arc box appears.

76 Next to Partition are a number and arrows. **Click one of the arrows next to Partition until the number reads 4.**

77 **Click an arc in the drawing to select it > click the Partition button in the Edit Arc box.** Partition splits the arc into equal pieces and puts new nodes between the sections.

78 Repeat step 77 for the other 3 arcs.

79 Click the **Line** tool on the left toolbar.

80 Position your cursor over the first new node in an outer arc.

81 **Click and hold to start the line at this node > drag in toward the center of the block to the first new node of the arc just beside it > release to stop the line on that new node.**

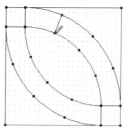

Step 81

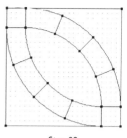

Step 82
Draw lines from node to node

82 Play "connect the dots" with the rest of the drawing by repeating steps 80-81 to draw 3 straight lines for each arc pair from node to node.

83 If you make a mistake and your line jumps to a snap point instead of a node, click **EDIT > Undo** immediately from the top menu bar. Redraw the line and try to stay on top of the nodes.

Step 84
Add to Sketchbook

84 Click the **Add to Sketchbook** button.

85 *(Optional)* **Click the Color tab > click the Paintbrush tool > color your block > click the Add to Sketchbook button.**

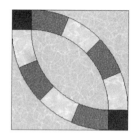

Step 85
Color the block

Stagger Arcs

86 **Click the View Sketchbook button on the top toolbar > Blocks section > double-click the *Plain Wedding Ring* block to edit it to the worktable again.**

Step 84
View Sketchbook

Step 87
Shape

87 **Click the red square in the bottom-left corner of the Shape tool button.** The Edit Arc box appears. We are going to Partition the outer arcs and Stagger the inner ones.

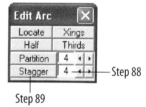

Step 89

Step 88

88 Next to Stagger are a number and arrows as well. **Click one of the arrows next to Stagger until the number reads 4.**

89 **Click an inner arc in the drawing to select it > click the Stagger button in the Edit Arc box.** Stagger splits the arc center into equal pieces, but splits the last piece in half and puts it at each end. It is like a "half-drop" style.

90 Repeat step 89 for the other **inner arc.**

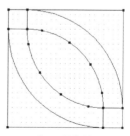

Steps 89 & 90
Stagger the inner arcs into 4

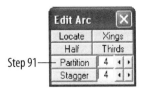

Step 91 —

Steps 91 & 92
Partition the outer arcs

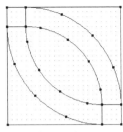

Step 93
Line

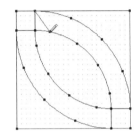

Step 95

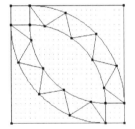

Step 96 - Draw zigzagging
lines from node to node

Step 98
Add to Sketchbook

91 Partition should still be set to 4 from our previous block drawing. **Click an outer arc in the drawing > click the Partition button.**

92 Repeat step 91 for the other **outer arc**.

93 Click the **Line** tool on the left toolbar. Now we'll draw zigzags.

94 In the top-left corner is a square (see the picture at the left). **Position your cursor over the top-right node of that square.**

95 **Click and hold to start the line at this node > drag in toward the new node of the inner arc > release to stop the line on that new node.**

96 Play "connect the dots" with the rest of the drawing by drawing from node to node between the arcs to create zigzags.

97 If you make a mistake and your line jumps to a snap point instead of a node, click **EDIT > Undo** immediately from the top menu bar. Redraw the line, staying on top of the nodes.

98 Click the **Add to Sketchbook** button.

99 *(Optional)* **Click the Color tab > click the Paintbrush tool > color your block > click the Add to Sketchbook button.**

100 Click the large **X** in the top-right corner to close EQ6.

Step 99 - Color the block

Great job! Now it's time for some homework.

Homework

1 Watch two videos on drawing. Click VIDEOS > Drawing
   Blocks > EasyDraw Blocks > EasyDraw Basics and watch.
   Then watch VIDEOS > Drawing Blocks > EasyDraw Blocks >
   EasyDraw Compass.
2 Click LIBRARIES > Block Library.
3 Click Search > By Notecard.
4 Find and add these 6 blocks to your Sketchbook:
   - *Hour Glass*
   - *Four X Star*
   - *4 Log Cabin*
   - *Twelve Triangles*
   - *Crab Apple*
   - *Basic New York Beauty*
5 Click the View Sketchbook button > Blocks section >
   double-click the block you want to draw to send it to the
   worktable.
6 Click BLOCK > Convert to Guides, and try to redraw the block
   yourself.
7 Follow the tip for each block at the right.
8 After you've drawn the block, click the Color tab and color
   the block.
9 Click Add to Sketchbook when you're done.

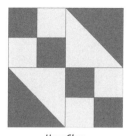

Hour Glass
Tip: Use the Grid tool set to 2x2

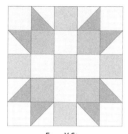

Four X Star
Tip: Use the Grid tool set to 5x5

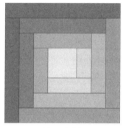

4 Log Cabin
Tip: Find the longest side
and draw it, then work
counter-clockwise around
the block drawing until you
reach the center

Twelve Triangles
Tip: Draw the outermost
diamond first, then use the
Half button on the Edit box to
continue drawing diamonds
and squares to the center

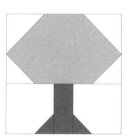

Crab Apple
Tip: Always split foundation
patterns into their sections
first (so draw the horizontal
line, then the two vertical lines
for the tree trunk), and add
the details later

Basic New York Beauty
Tip: Use the Arc tool to draw
the rings first. Then use the
Shape tool and Edit box to
Partition one arc into 5 and
Stagger the other arc into 5

Lesson Six

Welcome to your next drawing lesson! In this lesson we are going to work with PatchDraw appliqué motifs, PatchDraw appliqué blocks, and PatchDraw pieced blocks. We'll use some from the library, draw some of our own, and learn to:

- Create a New Project

- Start a New PatchDraw Motif

- Draw with the Oval and Polygon Tools

- Draw with the Freehand Tool

- Understand Patches Versus Thread

- Move and Delete Lines or Patches

- Make a Wreath

- Shape Appliqué Patches

- Verify your Sketchbook Contents

- Try Drawing a Pieced Block in PatchDraw

Remember to go at your own pace as you work these lessons and e-mail us, or give us a call if you have a question. (Our contact information is on page 6.)

If you are using a laptop or touchpad, please see page 9 before starting this lesson.

Lessons

Create a New Project

1 Double-click the **EQ6** icon on your Windows Desktop. You'll see the EQ6 splash screen play again.

2 When the Tip of the Day displays, click the **Next** button a few times and read the tips.

3 Click **Close** to close the Tip of the Day.

4 On the **Create a new project tab**, type: **Lesson Six**

Notes
• If you choose to repeat this lesson, you can either delete the old Lesson Six (see page 111) or give this one a slightly different name (Lesson Six – second time).

5 Click **OK**.

6 Click the **Work on Block** button on the top toolbar or click **WORKTABLE > Work on Block** on the top menu bar.

Start a New PatchDraw Motif

7 On the top menu bar, click **BLOCK > New Block > PatchDraw Motif**. The PatchDraw tools will appear at the left and you will now have an Applique and Color tab at the bottom. The block outline looks different than in EasyDraw™.

8 Click the **Color** tab. Nothing is there – not even a background square. That's what it means to be a motif (as we learned in Lesson Four when we set the *Goldie Fish* block versus *Goldie Fish* motif).

9 Click the **Applique** tab.

10 Let's read how PatchDraw works. Look at pages 232-233 and read the topic called *Understanding PatchDraw*. Pay special attention to the pictures. Come back after you read that page.

11 On the left toolbar, position your cursor over the first tool without clicking. This will show you the tool name in a tooltip.

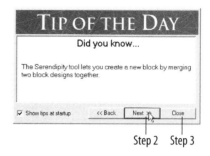

Step 2   Step 3

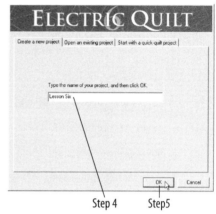

Step 4   Step5

Step 7

Step 8

Step 9

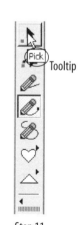

Step 11

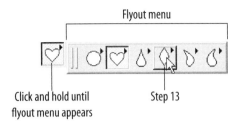

Flyout menu

Click and hold until
flyout menu appears

Step 13

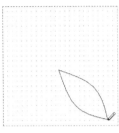

Step 15

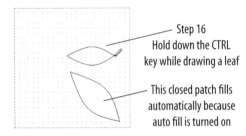

Step 16
Hold down the CTRL
key while drawing a leaf

This closed patch fills
automatically because
auto fill is turned on

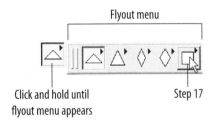

Flyout menu

Click and hold until
flyout menu appears

Step 17

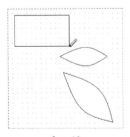

Step 18

12 Repeat step 11 for the rest of the tools on the Drawing toolbar. Notice the top two tools have red squares in the bottom corners (indicating they bring up pop-up boxes) and that the bottom two have black arrows facing out (indicating they have flyout menus with other tool options).

Draw with the Oval and Polygon Tools

13 On the left toolbar, **click and hold on the Oval tool until the flyout menu appears > click the fourth image that looks like a leaf**.

14 Let's draw a leaf. **Position your cursor in the center of the block outline guides.**

15 **Click and hold to start the leaf > drag outward from the center in any direction (watch the leaf form as you draw) > spin the leaf around the center to see how it moves > release to stop the leaf.** Closed patches automatically fill (when you have auto fill turned on) so you can easily see what is able to hold color.

16 Hold down your keyboard **CTRL key** and repeat step 15 to draw another leaf. It's ok if your patch overlaps the original leaf. The CTRL key makes it snap to increments including perfectly vertical and horizontal.

17 On the left toolbar, **click and hold on the Polygon tool until the flyout menu appears > click the fifth image that looks like a square/rectangle.**

18 **Position your cursor inside the outline guides > click and hold to start the patch > drag outward from the point you started (watch the patch form as you draw) > spin your cursor around to see how the patch reforms > release to stop the rectangular patch.** It is ok if your patches overlap.

Lesson Six

19 Hold down your keyboard **CTRL key** and repeat step 18 to draw with the square/rectangle polygon again. Notice that the orientation doesn't change, but it does try to keep it square if you drag diagonally.

20 Click the **Add to Sketchbook** button.

21 **Click the View Sketchbook button > click the Blocks section > click the Motifs tab.** Remember, if you add a PatchDraw motif to the Sketchbook, it will be added to the Motifs tab.

22 Click **Close** to put the Sketchbook away.

Draw with the Freehand Tool

23 We'll continue on top of the same drawing. Click the **Freehand** tool on the left toolbar.

24 **Position your cursor inside the outline guides > click and hold to start the freehand line > drag your cursor around as if you are drawing a letter "O" > try to end the freehand line precisely where you started it so the ending and beginning points are on top of one another > release the mouse.** If the start and end points are close "but not close enough," then click **EDIT > Undo** on the top menu bar and try this step again. You'll know you've done it correctly when the patch closes and fills. The Freehand tool smoothes the slight bumps out of your drawing so you have a smooth shape.

25 This time, draw one more freehand patch, but don't close it. **Position your cursor inside the outline guides > click, hold, and drag the cursor around to draw a letter "C" > release the mouse away from the beginning point so it doesn't close.**

Understand Patches Versus Thread

26 Click the **Color** tab.

Step 19
Hold down the CTRL key while dragging diagonally to draw a square

Step 20
Add to Sketchbook

Step 21
View Sketchbook

Step 21 - Motifs tab

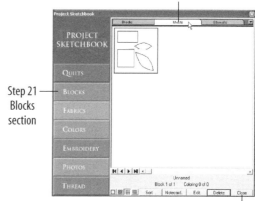

Step 21 Blocks section

Step 22

Step 23
Freehand

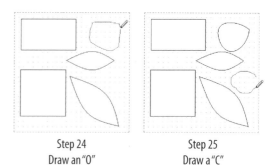

Step 24
Draw an "O"

Step 25
Draw a "C"

Step 26

Lesson Six

Steps 27 & 28
Color the leaves,
rectangle and square

Step 29
Color the "O". The "C" will not color
because it is not a closed patch.

Step 30
Add to Sketchbook

Step 31

Step 32
Pick

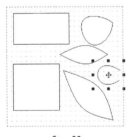
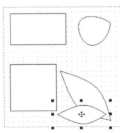

Step 33
Select the "C"

Step 36
Move one of the leaves

Step 37
Add to Sketchbook

27 Click a fabric in the palette and click both leaves.

28 Click a new fabric in the palette and click your rectangle and square.

29 **Click another fabric in the palette and click the freehand "O." Try to click the freehand "C" with that same fabric.** The "C" will not color because it is not a closed patch. PatchDraw considers it to be thread or a quilting line.

30 Click the **Add to Sketchbook** button.

Move and Delete Lines or Patches

31 Click the **Applique** tab.

32 Click the **Pick** tool at the top of the left toolbar.

33 In the drawing, click directly *on the line* of the freehand "C" to select it. You'll know it is selected when there are 8 black squares around the line and a move icon in the middle.

34 Press your keyboard **DELETE key** to delete the freehand "C."

35 Click directly on the line of one of your leaf patches to select it.

36 **Position your cursor over the move icon in the middle of the selected patch > click and hold > drag the patch to a new location within the block outline.**

37 Click the **Add to Sketchbook** button.

Notes

- **To select a line or patch** – click the Pick tool > click on the *line* of the patch.

- **To delete a line or patch** – select it first, then press DELETE on your keyboard.

- **To move a line or patch** – select it first, then line up your cursor with the move icon in the middle of the patch, and drag the line or patch to a new location.

Make a Wreath

38 Click **BLOCK > New Block > PatchDraw Motif.**

39 On the left toolbar, click and hold on the **Oval** tool until the flyout menu appears. **Click the heart shape.**

40 **Hold down your keyboard CTRL key > position your cursor inside the block outline > click and hold to start the heart > drag down to form it > release the mouse.** You'll notice the CTRL key made it draw perfectly vertical and that when you released, the patch was selected.

41 On the top menu bar, click **BLOCK > WreathMaker.** A box appears with 3 choices.

42 Under *Number of clusters,* **drag the slider bar so the number is 4.**

43 Under *Cluster spacing,* **drag the slider bar all the way to the left until the number is 0.**

44 Leave the *Resize cluster* number at its current setting (this varies according to the size of the selected patch).

45 Click **OK.** The heart will be wreathed around 4 times (number of clusters) and spaced so there is barely any room between the heart points (cluster spacing). **Click the Add to Sketchbook button.**

☕ Coffee Break

Try using WreathMaker on different patches to create appliqué wreaths. Practice with shapes oriented different ways to see how the orientation of the patch determines the resulting wreath. See pages 248-249 for examples to try.
1 BLOCK > New Block > PatchDraw Motif.
2 Click and hold on the Oval or Polygon tool and choose a closed shape from the flyout menu.
3 Click and hold in the block > drag to form the patch. (Try some with the CTRL key and others without. Try some horizontally and others vertically.)
4 The patch will become selected. Click BLOCK > WreathMaker.

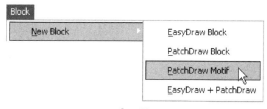

Step 38

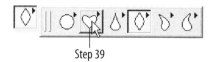

Step 39

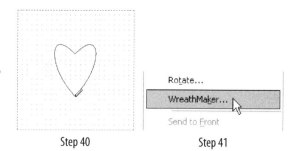

Step 40   Step 41

Step 42 —
Step 43 —
Step 44 —

Step 45

Heart wreath

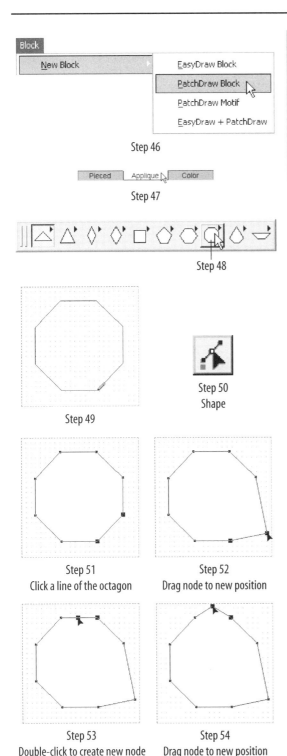

Step 46

Step 47

Step 48

Step 49

Step 50
Shape

Step 51
Click a line of the octagon

Step 52
Drag node to new position

Step 53
Double-click to create new node

Step 54
Drag node to new position

Shape Appliqué Patches

46 On the top menu bar, click **BLOCK > New Block > PatchDraw Block.** This time, you have 3 tabs instead of 2. The Pieced tab gives your appliqué a background block. The Pieced tab has new tools, which we'll play with after we learn to shape appliqué patches.

47 Click the **Applique** tab. You should recognize these tools.

48 On the left toolbar, click and hold on the **Polygon** tool until the flyout menu appears. **Click the third image from the end that looks like an octagon.**

49 **Position your cursor inside the block outline > click and hold to start the octagon > drag to form it > release the mouse so the octagon fits within the block outline.**

50 Click the **Shape** tool on the left toolbar.

51 **Click in your block on a line of the octagon.** The black squares you see between the lines are called nodes.

52 **Click and hold a node > drag it to a new position.**

53 Double-click on a line (between two nodes) to add another node.

54 **Click and hold this new node > drag it to a new position.** This is how you shape patches with straight lines.

55 Click the **Add to Sketchbook** button.

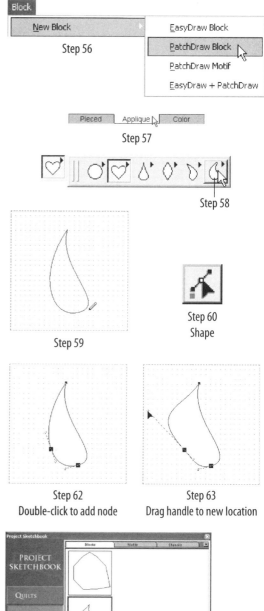

56 To shape patches with curves, let's start a new block. Click **BLOCK > New Block > PatchDraw Block** on the top menu bar.

Step 56

57 Click the **Applique** tab.

Step 57

58 On the left toolbar, click and hold the **Oval** tool until the flyout menu appears. **Click the last image that looks like a bent tear drop.**

Step 58

59 Position your cursor inside the block outline > click and hold to start the tear drop > drag to form it > release the mouse so the tear drop fits within the block outline.

Step 59

60 Click the **Shape** tool on the left toolbar.

Step 60
Shape

61 Click in your block on a curve of the tear drop. You will see black nodes again, but nodes near curves have handles (long dotted lines with hollow squares at their ends) that you use to control the curve's shape.

62 Double-click on the curve (between two nodes) to add another node. This node also has handles.

63 Click and hold in one of the hollow squares at the end of the handle (of the new node) and drag the handle to a new location. The curve will reshape as you move the handle. This is how you shape patches with curves.

Step 62
Double-click to add node

Step 63
Drag handle to new location

64 Click the **Add to Sketchbook** button.

Verify Your Sketchbook Contents

65 On the top toolbar, **click the View Sketchbook button > click the Blocks section.** You'll notice the reshaped octagon and tear drop are on the Blocks tab because they were drawn as PatchDraw Blocks.

66 Click the **Motifs** tab within the Sketchbook. You'll notice your beginning drawings and your Coffee Break wreaths are on the Motifs tab because they were drawn as PatchDraw Motifs.

67 Click the **Close** button to put the Sketchbook away.

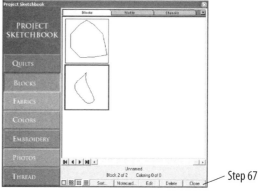

Step 67

Lesson Six

Step 68

Tooltip

Step 69

Try Drawing a Pieced Block in PatchDraw

68 Pieced blocks in PatchDraw are possible, but you need to learn the new rules. (They are opposite from what you learned with EasyDraw™.) Click **BLOCK > New Block > PatchDraw Block.** You'll be on the Pieced tab.

Notes

- **If you happen to click the block you may get blue drawing lines before you're ready to draw. Press your keyboard ESC key, or double-click, to get rid of them.**

69 On the left toolbar, position your cursor over the first tool without clicking. This will show you the tool name in a tooltip.

70 Repeat step 69 for the other tools on the toolbar.

71 You should still have the Precision Bar turned on from the Lesson Five. If you do not see the Precision Bar below the top menu and toolbar, click VIEW > Precision Bar to put a check next to it.

Step 72   Step 73   Step 74

72 **Double-click in the Precision Bar on the number for Block Width > type: 6 > press your keyboard TAB key > type: 6 > press your keyboard TAB key.**

73 The block size will update. **Click the drop down arrow next to Grid > click *Eight Point Star* in the list.** You'll see a new grid appear behind the worktable.

Click and hold until flyout menu appears

Step 75

74 **Double-click the number for Dimension 1 > type: 3 > press your keyboard TAB key > type: 3 > press your keyboard TAB key.** The dots in the grid will update.

75 On the left toolbar, click and hold on the **Polydraw** tool until the flyout menu appears. **Click the first tool (PolyLine) in the flyout.**

76 Position your cursor over the top-left corner of the block outline. (We're going to draw this top-left square.)

77 There's no "holding or dragging" for this tool, so look at the illustration to see the numbers, then **click at 1 > move to 2 and click > move to 3 and click > move to 4 and click > then back up to 1 and double-click**. The patch will fill with color if auto fill is turned on. This way you know you've successfully closed the patch.

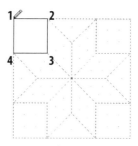

Step 77

78 *If the patch is closed but you made a mistake,* click **EDIT > Undo** on the top menu bar. *Or, if the patch isn't closed and you have blue lines at the wrong dots,* press your keyboard **ESC key** to release the drawing.

79 Try clicking in each corner of a diamond. **Click to start the patch > click each corner of the diamond > double-click the beginning point.**

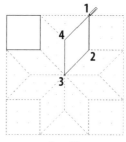

Step 79

80 We set the snaps for Dimension to be 3. This means we don't have to make patches that take up the entire square or entire diamond. We could do *Nine Patches* in the corners. **Position your cursor over the top-right corner of the block outline.** We're going to make a smaller square.

81 **Click to start the patch > move your cursor down one snap dot and click > move your cursor left to the next snap dot and click > continue clicking on each snap dot until you reach the beginning and double-click to end it.**

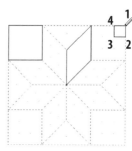

Step 79

☕ Coffee Break

Fill the entire block so there is no white space left.
Pieced blocks drawn in PatchDraw must follow these rules:
• The entire block must be filled.
• Patches cannot overlap or share lines.
• Lines cannot cross.
If you like, you can click BLOCK > New Block > PatchDraw Block to clear your current drawing and draw your masterpiece.
Click the Add to Sketchbook button once the entire block is filled.

82 Click the **X** in the top-right corner to close EQ6.

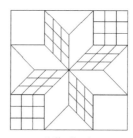

Coffee Break
Fill the block with patches

EQ6
ELECTRIC QUILT 6
Complete Quilt Design Software

Step-by-Step Reference

Quilt designed by Jean Johnson
Somerset, England

Projects

Chapter 1

A *Project* is what we call all the ingredients you save together in a file as you design a particular quilt or quilts in EQ6. While most computer files (think of Microsoft® Word documents) contain one thing (such as a letter to your Aunt Betty), a Project can contain many items. Imagine designing a Sampler Quilt. Your Sampler project file might contain dozens of blocks, colors, fabrics, plus the sampler quilts you've designed. A Memory Quilt project might include photographs, scanned fabric, and blocks you have drawn. As you design, all items in a particular project are stored temporarily in what we call a *Sketchbook*. When this Sketchbook is saved permanently on your computer's hard drive, we call the saved file a project. This chapter tells you how to save, open, delete and work with project files.

Reference

Creating a New Project

 OR

Desktop Icon   New

Step 1

1   Start **EQ6**. (Double-click the EQ6 desktop icon, or click **START > All Programs > Electric Quilt > EQ6 >EQ6**.) If you are already in EQ6, click the **New** button.

2   On the **Create a new project** tab of the Project Helper, type in any name you like.

3   Click **OK**. You will be on the quilt or block worktable ready to design. You will now see your project name on the top-left corner of your screen.

Notes

- This also works with FILE > New.

- If this is your first time using EQ6, you will see the quilt worktable. After the first time, EQ6 will open to whichever worktable you used last.

- To save your new project, see page 109.

- To open your new project after closing it, see page 107.

Step 2

This box is called the Project Helper

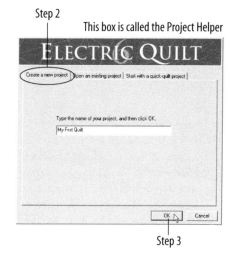

Step 3

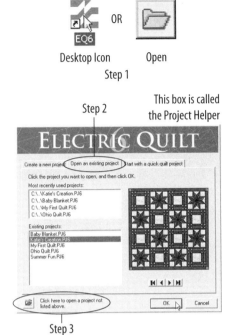

Desktop Icon   Open

Step 1

Step 2

This box is called the Project Helper

Step 3

Steps 4-5

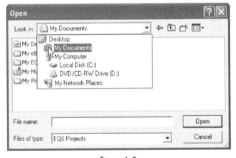

Step 6
Change the type to find EQ4, EQ5, or BlockBase projects

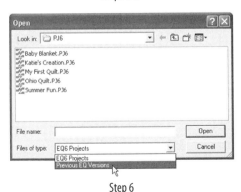

Opening a Project

You can open projects created in EQ6 or earlier EQ versions. You need to know where the project is saved on your computer.

1   Start **EQ6**. If you are already in **EQ6**, click the **Open** button.

2   Click the **Open an existing project** tab of the Project Helper. If you see the project name in any of the lists, click to select it, click **OK**, and skip to step 8.

3   If you do not see the project name in the lists, you will need to browse to find it. Click the folder in the bottom-left corner marked **Click here to open a project not listed above.**

4   Click the down arrow beside the **Look in:** box to drop the list. Click the drive the project is on.

5   Double-click the folders until you reach the one containing your project.

6   If it is a project from an earlier software version, drop the list down next to **Files of type:** and select **Previous EQ Versions**.

7   Click the name to select it, and click **Open**.

8   This project's Sketchbook will open. Select the item you want to work on and click the Sketchbook's **Edit** button.

Notes
- **Here are the default locations for previous EQ versions:**

  EQ3: My Computer > C: drive > EQ3 > prj

  EQ4: My Computer > C: drive > EQ4 > prj

  EQ5: My Computer > C: drive > My Documents > My EQ5 > PJ5

- **This also works with FILE > Open.**

- **Use this same method to open projects or bags created in other EQ software (such as BlockBase or STASH).**

- **If you can't find a project, see page 116.**

Opening a Project

Starting with a Quick-Quilt Project

EQ6 has pre-made quilts for you to use as is, or edit to make into your own.

1   Start **EQ6**. If you are already in **EQ6**, click the **Open** button.

2   Click the **Start with a quick-quilt project** tab of the Project Helper.

3   If necessary, scroll through the names to see what the quilts look like. Click on one you like, to select it.

4   Click **OK**. The Sketchbook for this project will appear. Click the Quilts section.

5   To put a quilt on the worktable, either:

  • double-click it

  • select the quilt and click the Sketchbook's **Edit** button

Notes
• If you turn off the EQ6 opening screen (Project Helper) you will no longer be able to access these quick-quilts. To turn it back on, go to FILE > Preferences > Startup (under Workspace) and put a check next to *Use EQ Project Helper dialog.*

Desktop Icon   Open
Step 1

Step 2

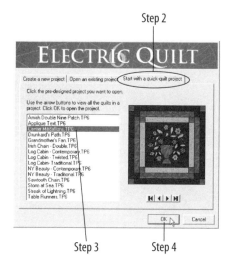

Step 3   Step 4

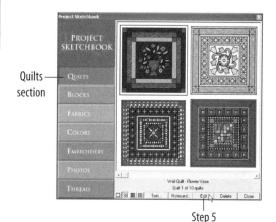

Quilts
section

Step 5
Edit button

Step 1
Add to Sketchbook

Step 3
Save

Saving a Project

Consider your project as everything you can add to the Sketchbook. If you want to see the design the next time you open the project, it needs to be added to the Sketchbook. Anything not in the Sketchbook will be lost.

Adding a New Design to the Sketchbook

1   With the new design or coloring on the worktable, click **Add to Sketchbook**.

2   Click **Add to Sketchbook** as you make new designs or modify existing designs. You can have many quilts and blocks in a project.

Saving the Project

3   Click the **Save** button. If the project is already named, the Sketchbook will be updated. If the project is unnamed, the **Save As** box will appear.

4   You want to save your project in the PJ6 folder. If necessary, drop the list down next to **Save in:** and click on **My Documents**. Double-click the folders **My EQ6 > PJ6**.

5   Type a name for the project in the **File name:** box.

6   Click **Save**. Continue to add any new designs to the Sketchbook to update the project.

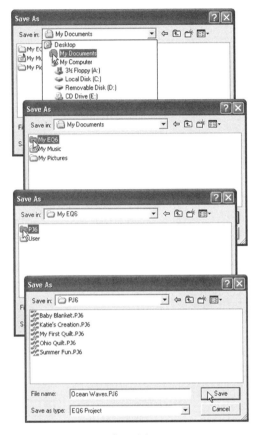

Steps 4-6

Notes

- This also works with FILE > Save.

- To open your project again, see page 107.

- When you have multiple EQ6 projects and you need to organize them, consider adding a new folder within the PJ6 folder. Use the Create a New Folder button and then continue with saving the project. Be aware that projects in subfolders will not display in the existing projects list, and will need to be opened through *Click here to open a project not listed above*. See page 107.

- To delete a design from a project, see page 122.

- To delete an entire project, see page 111.

Saving a Project

Saving a Project in a New Location

Save As is great for saving projects to other places on your computer or onto removable storage like flash drives or writeable CDs. Remember your project consists of everything in the Sketchbook. If you want to see your design again, add it to the Sketchbook. Designs not in the Sketchbook will be lost.

Step 3

1 If you want to save your project to a removable storage device (writeable CD, flash drive, etc.), be sure it is inserted or connected to your computer.

2 Make sure the EQ6 project you want to save is open.

3 Click **FILE > Save As**.

4 Click the down arrow next to **Save in:** to see the list of drive choices. Click the appropriate drive. Browse through any folders if necessary.

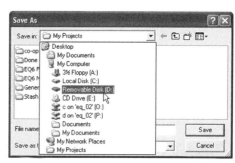

Step 4

5 Type a name for the project in the **File name:** box.

6 Click **Save**. Your project will be saved in the new location.

Notes
- To open a project from removable storage, you can either double-click the project name or use the directions on page 107 to open a project not listed above.

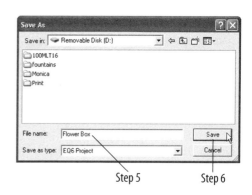

Step 5   Step 6

OR

Desktop Icon   Open
Step 1

Step 2

Step 3

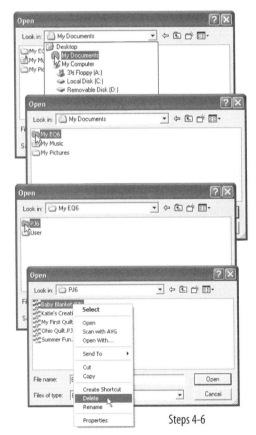

Steps 4-6

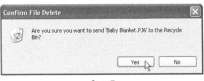

Step 7

Deleting a Named Project

1   Start **EQ6**. If you are already in **EQ6**, click the **Open** button.

2   Click the **Open an existing project** tab on the Project Helper.

3   Click the folder in the bottom-left corner marked **Click here to open a project not listed above.**

4   Click the down arrow beside the **Look in:** box to drop the list. Click the drive the project is on.

5   Double-click the folders until you reach the one containing your project. EQ6 projects are saved by default in: **My Documents > My EQ6 > PJ6.**

6   Right-click on the project name and choose **Delete**.

7   Click **Yes** if you wish to delete it and the project will be sent to the Recycle Bin.

8   Click **Cancel** to close the Open box and Cancel again to return to the worktable.

Notes

• You can also delete a project through Windows®. Go to START > My Documents > My EQ6 > PJ6. Select the project name, right-click on it and choose Delete.

• If you accidentally delete the wrong project you can recover it from the Recycle Bin. Go to your Desktop and double-click the Recycle Bin icon. Find the project and click to select it. In the column on the left, click Restore this item. The project will be sent back to the folder you deleted it from.

• Deleted projects are gone forever once you empty the Recycle Bin.

• Make sure you want to delete an entire project instead of an individual block or quilt. To delete a design from a project, see page 122.

• Don't worry if you see a deleted project name in the *Most recently used projects* list of the Project Helper. The name will be bumped off the list once other projects are opened.

Deleting a Named Project

Renaming a Project

1 Start **EQ6**. If you are already in **EQ6**, click the **Open** button.

2 Click the **Open an existing project** tab of the Project Helper.

3 Click the folder in the bottom-left corner marked **Click here to open a project not listed above.**

4 Click the down arrow beside the **Look in:** box to drop the list. Click the drive the project is on.

5 Double-click the folders until you reach the one containing your project. EQ6 projects are saved by default in: **My Documents > My EQ6 > PJ6.**

6 Right-click on the project name and choose **Rename**.

7 Type a new name. If your project ends in an extension (**.PJ6**), be sure to change the name *to the left* of the period only. Leave the extension intact.

8 Click **Cancel** to close the Open box and Cancel again to return to the worktable.

Notes

• You can also rename a project through Windows®. Go to START > My Documents > My EQ6 > PJ6. Select the project name, right-click on it and choose Rename. Type in the new name.

• Don't worry if you see the old project name in the *Most recently used projects* list of the Project Helper. The name will be bumped off the list once other projects are opened.

Desktop Icon   Open

Step 1

Step 2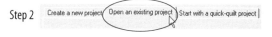

Step 3

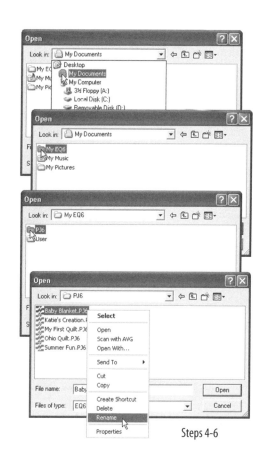

Steps 4-6

Renaming a Project

OR

Desktop Icon   Open

Step 3

Step 4

Step 5

Opening a Project Sent by E-mail

EQ6 projects sent via e-mail are sent as "attachments." You need to save the attachment to your computer before you can open it with EQ6.

1   If the attachment is an EQ6 project file (ending in .PJ6) that you are expecting from someone you know, open the attachment. (Earlier EQ versions end in PRJ, PJ4, and PJ5.)

2   If given the option, save it somewhere on your computer and remember the location you choose. You can save it with your other EQ6 projects if you like, in **My Documents > My EQ6 > PJ6**.

3   Start **EQ6**. If you are already in EQ6, click the **Open** button.

4   Click the **Open an existing project** tab of the Project Helper.

5   Click the folder in the bottom-left corner marked **Click here to open a project not listed above.**

6   Click the down arrow beside the **Look in:** box to drop the list. Click the drive the project is saved on (you chose this location in Step 2).

7   Double-click the folders until you reach the one containing your project.

8   If the project was made in an earlier version of EQ, drop the list down next to **Files of type:** and select **Previous EQ Versions**.

9   Select the project and click **Open**.

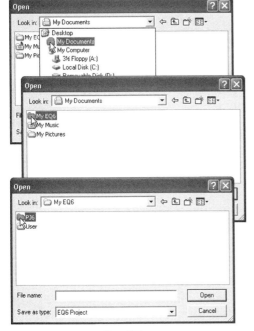

Steps 6-7

Notes
• Remember, opening unexpected attachments from people you don't know could potentially harm your computer.

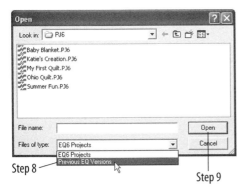

Step 8   Step 9

Sending a Project by E-mail

You can e-mail a project to someone who also has EQ6 installed. Before mailing, make the file size smaller. It's a courtesy many people appreciate, and is sometimes necessary if your e-mail account or the recipient's cannot handle large file sizes. Compressing for e-mail deletes unused items from the Sketchbook. (Unused means not used in a quilt.)

Step 1

Making a Copy of the Project (recommended, but optional)

If you plan to reduce the file size, make a copy of your project first. This way, if you drew new blocks, but forgot to set and save them in a quilt in the Sketchbook, they would not be lost forever. You would have a backup copy with the complete contents of your Sketchbook in a different project under a different name.

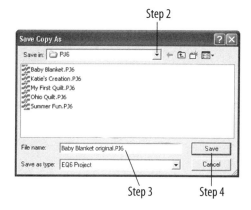

1   Click **FILE > Create Copy Project**.

2   If necessary, choose a new location for the backup copy. Drop the list down next to **Save in:** and select the drive you want. Double-click the folders until you reach the one in which you want to save the backup.

3   Type a name for the project in the **File name:** box. (You must use a new name if you're saving it in the same folder as the current project.)

4   Click **Save**. The copy will be in the location you chose and you will still be working on the current project.

Step 5

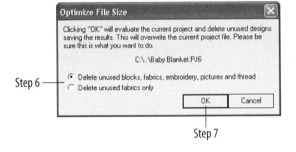

Step 6

Step 7

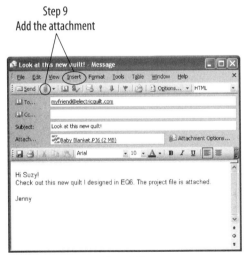

Step 9
Add the attachment

Steps 8-11

Compressing for E-mail (recommended, but optional)

Don't do this on a work-in-progress unless you make a copy of the project first. You will lose any Sketchbook contents not used in a quilt. See the Notes below for a tip about deleting quilts.

5 Click **FILE > Compress for E-mail**.

6 Put the dot next to your choice.

- **Delete unused blocks, fabrics, embroidery, pictures and thread** – anything not used in a quilt in the Sketchbook will be removed.

- **Delete unused fabrics only** – fabrics not used in quilt or block designs in the Sketchbook will be removed.

7 Click **OK** to delete unused designs and save the result. This process will overwrite the existing project file and cannot be undone. (If you made a copy of this project, as recommended, you have nothing to worry about.) Click **Cancel** to do nothing and return to the worktable.

E-mailing the Project

8 Open your e-mail account and write a new message.

9 Add an attachment. (You may see a paper clip, the menu choice INSERT > File, or the word "attach." Check with your e-mail provider on how to add attachments if you need help.)

10 Browse to find the folder where your project is saved. (Typically: My Documents > My EQ6 > PJ6)

11 Click on the project to select it and attach it to the e-mail. Type in the receiver's address, a subject line, a message, and send the e-mail.

Notes
- First remove unwanted quilts from the project to be e-mailed so the unwanted blocks and fabrics used in those quilts will be removed as well. See page 122 for how to delete items from the Sketchbook.

Searching for a Project

Misplacing things is inevitable with computers. Use these directions if you ever need to find a project that is not in the existing project list.

1   On the Windows® taskbar click **START > Search**.

2   Click **All files and folders**.

3   In the first box, type ***.PJ6** and click **Search**. (For projects created with other EQ software, see Notes below.)

4   You will see headers in the bar above the files which start appearing. The "In Folder" category will tell you where each is located.

5   You can double-click on the project in this list to open it.

6   You may want to choose **FILE > Save As** and save it in **My Documents > My EQ6 > PJ6** so it will be in the existing project list.

Notes

• When you search, you will find many projects in the program that you did not create. These "unknown" projects are needed for the default projects, backup projects, and Auto Borders in EQ6 and should not be moved or deleted. In general, do not move PJ6 projects or files out of folders in **Program Files** or C:\Program Files\Electric Quilt Company\ EQ6. If you do, you may cause the program to stop working and you will need to reinstall.

• If you are looking for projects other than those created in EQ6, try the following extensions in step 3 instead of *.PJ6:

   *.PJ5 = EQ5 project

   *.PL5 = EQ5 palette

   *.PJ4 = EQ4 project, BlockBase project

   *.BAG = STASH shopping bag

Step 1

Step 2

Step 3

Steps 4-5

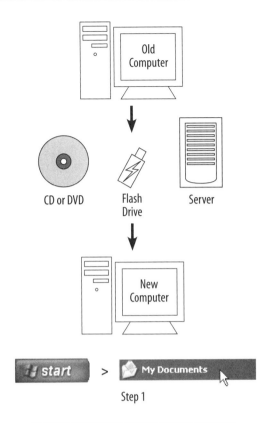

CD or DVD   Flash   Server
             Drive

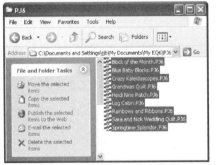

Step 1

Step 2
Select the projects you'd like to copy

Step 3

Copying Projects from One Computer to Another

To move EQ6 project files from one computer to another you need the following: 1) a computer with EQ6 installed and EQ6 project files on it, 2) a "middle man" for storing the files, and 3) another computer with EQ6 installed on it.

The "middle man" can be removable storage (like a flash drive, writeable CD, or writeable DVD) or a server. Slower methods would involve using removable storage that holds less information (like a floppy disk) or emailing yourself the projects (see pages 114-115).

You do not need to have EQ6 open to do this.

Find the Projects on the Old Computer

1   Go to the default folder for EQ6 projects by clicking **START > My Documents > My EQ6 > PJ6**.

2   Click on a project to select it. You can also use keyboard shortcuts to help you:

   • Hold down the CTRL key as you click to select scattered, individual projects.

   • Hold down the SHIFT key as you click to select a range of projects.

   • Select one item, then press CTRL+A to select all the projects in this folder.

3   Click **EDIT > Copy** on the top menu.

Copying & Moving Projects

Save the Projects to a Storage Device

4 Insert the removable storage device (writeable CD, writeable DVD, flash drive, etc.) or connect to the server you plan to use.

5 Click **START > My Computer**. Double-click the drive your storage device is in. Browse through any folders if necessary.

6 *(Optional)* Make a new folder and call it PJ6 for storing the projects. Click **FILE > New > Folder** and name it. Double-click the folder to open it.

7 Click **EDIT > Paste** on the top menu.

8 If there are any other projects lurking elsewhere on the old computer, repeat steps 1-7 for those project files. You can use the directions for searching for projects to make sure you got them all, see page 116.

9 If writing to a CD or DVD, burn the CD to make the data permanent.

Move the Projects to the New Computer

10 Insert the removable storage device into the new computer or connect to the server you used.

11 Go to the same folder you saved the files in. Click **START > My Computer**. Double-click the drive your storage device is in. Browse through any folders if necessary.

12 Click **EDIT > Select All** on the top menu.

13 Click **EDIT > Copy**.

14 Go to the new computer's PJ6 folder. Click **START > My Documents > My EQ6 > PJ6**.

15 Click **EDIT > Paste**.

Notes
- If steps 4-9 do not work for you using Windows® Explorer, try using the CD or DVD burning software that came with your burner (like Roxio Easy Media Creator® or Nero®).

Step 5

Double-click the drive

Step 6

Step 7

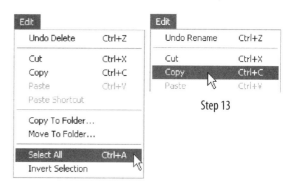

Step 13

Step 12

Step 15

Copying & Moving Projects

Quilt designed by Hélène Laparra
Clermont-Ferrand, France

Project Sketchbook

Chapter 2

Think of the Sketchbook as a notebook or paper file folder on your desk. Imagine you decide to design a Log Cabin quilt for your sister. So in EQ6 you label your notebook/file folder "Log Cabin Quilts." At first it's empty. But as you work, you gather blocks, fabrics and layout ideas and add them to the Sketchbook. When you're through designing for the day, you save your Log Cabin Sketchbook permanently on the hard drive. This is called "saving your project." The next day you open the project, see your Sketchbook full of Log Cabin designs again, and get back to work. This chapter shows you how to add items like blocks and fabrics to your Sketchbook, sort through the items, and delete any you don't want anymore. You'll also see how easy it is to name your quilts so the name shows up on printouts.

Reference

Adding Items to the Sketchbook

Every EQ6 project has its own Sketchbook. The Sketchbook is where you save your designs, kind of like a briefcase or file folder for that project. Designs and colorings added to the Sketchbook will be a part of the project the next time you open it. Designs and colorings not in the Sketchbook will be lost.

1 With the new design or coloring on the worktable, click **Add to Sketchbook**.

2 Click **View Sketchbook** to verify the new contents if you like.

Quilts section: Your new quilt will be the last quilt in the Sketchbook. Drag the scrollbar to the right to see all your quilts.

Blocks section: Click the Blocks, Motifs, or Stencils tab, depending on the item you modified. Your new block will be the last block in the Sketchbook. If you added a new coloring of a block, it will be stacked on top of the original block (up to ten colorings). Click the block, then use the **coloring arrows** to go to the end of the stack of colorings. Or right-click on the selected block and choose **Select Coloring** to see the different ways that block has been colored.

Notes
• To save a project, see page 109.

• Beginners, if you named your project when you started EQ6 or opened a named project, you do not need to worry about clicking Save after clicking Add to Sketchbook. EQ6 does an "auto-save" for you. Advanced users, if you changed this option in your Preferences, remember to click Save to make your Sketchbook changes permanent.

Step 1
Add to Sketchbook

Step 2
View Sketchbook

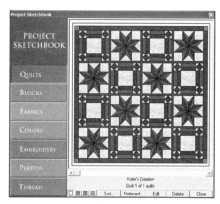

Quilts Section

Block tabs

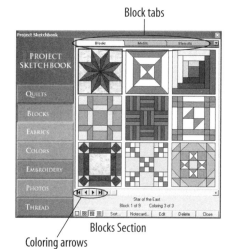

Blocks Section

Coloring arrows

Step 1
View Sketchbook

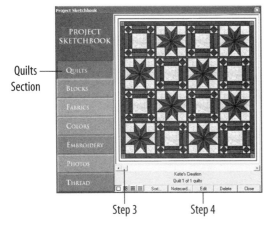

Quilts
Section

Step 3   Step 4

Step 5
Add to Sketchbook

Step 3

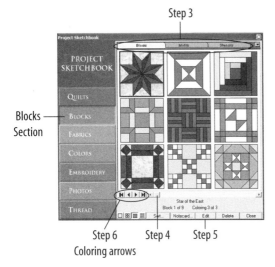

Blocks
Section

Step 6   Step 4   Step 5
Coloring arrows

Editing from the Sketchbook

You can make changes to existing designs.

1 Click **View Sketchbook**.

2 To edit a quilt, click the **Quilts** section. To edit a block, click the **Blocks** section.

Editing Quilts

3 If you do not see the quilt you wish to edit, drag the scrollbar to find it.

4 To put a quilt on the worktable, either:

- double-click on the quilt

- click the quilt once to select it, then click the Sketchbook's **Edit** button

5 Make any changes and click **Add to Sketchbook**. The new quilt will be at the end of the existing quilts.

Editing Blocks

3 Click the **Blocks**, **Motifs**, or **Stencils** tab, depending on the item you wish to edit.

4 If you do not see the block you wish to edit, drag the scrollbar to find it.

5 To put a block on the worktable, either:

- double-click on the block

- click the block once to select it, then click the Sketchbook's **Edit** button

6 Make any changes and click **Add to Sketchbook**. The new block will be at the end of the existing blocks or the new coloring will be the last of the stacked colorings for that block.

Notes

- To see block colorings, click the block to select it. Use the coloring arrows to scroll through the colorings, or right-click on the selected block and choose Select Coloring to see the different ways that block has been colored.

- The old quilt or block you edited will still be in the Sketchbook. See page 122 if you do not want to keep it.

Editing from the Sketchbook

Deleting from the Sketchbook

1   Click **View Sketchbook**.

2   **Click the section containing the item you wish to delete.** For example: To delete a quilt, click the Quilts section.

3   If you do not see the item you wish to delete, drag the scrollbar to find it.

4   **Click on the item to select it.** It will have a box around it showing it is selected.

5   If you are in the Blocks section, you can either delete a single coloring of a block or the entire block.

- *To delete a coloring*, be sure you are looking at the coloring you wish to delete. (Right-click on the block, click **Select Coloring**, then click the coloring you want to delete.)

- *To delete the entire block and all its colorings*, click the **first coloring arrow** so you are viewing the line drawing (Coloring 0).

6   Click the **Delete** button.

7   Click **Yes** if you want to delete it.

Notes

- If you are cleaning up an EQ6 project, the best order in which to delete unwanted items is quilts, then blocks, then fabrics. By deleting quilts first, any blocks or fabrics in those deleted quilts are unlinked and changed from "used" to "unused." By deleting blocks or unused block colorings next, you unlink the fabrics they were colored with. This allows you to make the project as clean as possible and the file size as small as possible. You may also want to see pages 114-115.

- To delete an entire project, see page 111.

Step 1
View Sketchbook

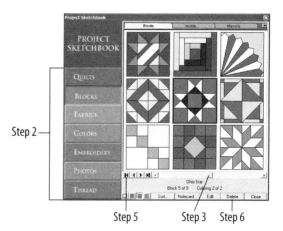

Step 2

Step 5   Step 3   Step 6

Step 7

Deleting from the Sketchbook

Step 1
View Sketchbook

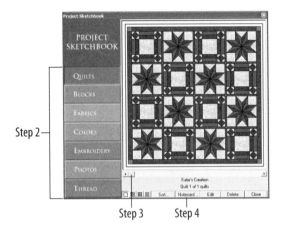

Step 2 —

Step 3   Step 4

Step 5
Name appears at the
top of printouts

Step 8

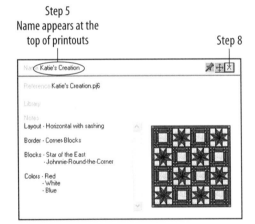

Notecard buttons

Flip   Move

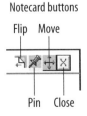

Pin   Close

Naming Quilts, Blocks & Other Sketchbook Items

Notecards are a way to name items and keep design notes. When printing, the name field of the notecard appears at the top of your printout.

1 Click **View Sketchbook**.

2 **Click the section containing the item you wish to name.** To name a quilt, click the Quilts section. To name a block, click the Blocks section.

3 If you do not see the item you wish to name, drag the scrollbar to find it.

4 **Click the item to select it > click the Notecard button.** The blinking cursor lets you know where you will begin typing.

5 Type a name for the item in the **Name** field.

6 Press your keyboard **TAB key** to move from one field to the next in the notecard.

7 Type as much as you'd like in the **Notes** field.

8 Click the **X** to close the notecard.

9 Click **Close** to put the Sketchbook away.

Notes

- Since the Name field appears at the top of the page when printing, you can change it to customize the printout. Example: *Quilt Foundry Sampler: January*

- To print notecard information, the contents need to be selected, copied, and pasted one item at a time into a word processing document and printed from that software. Try using Microsoft® Word, WordPerfect®, or Microsoft® Notepad.

- In the Sketchbook and libraries, you can move notecards out of the way or pin them to stay open as you browse. To move a notecard, click and hold on the Move icon as you drag the notecard across the screen. To pin a notecard open, click the Pin icon.

- Click the Flip icon to flip block notecards to the back side. See page 131 for more information on categories.

Naming Sketchbook Items

Sorting Items in the Sketchbook

You can sort items in any section the Sketchbook.

1   Click View Sketchbook.

2   Click the section the item is in. To sort quilts, go to the Quilts section. To sort blocks, go to the Blocks section.

3 Click the **Sort** button. A Sort box will appear.

4 To see all the items to be sorted, drag the scrollbar beneath the items.

5 You can also change the number of items that display at one time. Below the items you will see a series of display buttons with lines (or squares). Click a button with fewer lines to see fewer items. Click a button with more lines to see more items.

6   Click the items in the order you want them sorted. The first item clicked will appear first in your Sketchbook. When you click on an item, it will "disappear" from the sort box so you can't select the same item twice.

7 Continue clicking items in the order you want them to appear. Click the **Start over** button if you make a mistake.

8 Click the **Close** button if you are finished or if you want EQ6 to place the remaining items after the ones you have already sorted.

Step 1
View Sketchbook

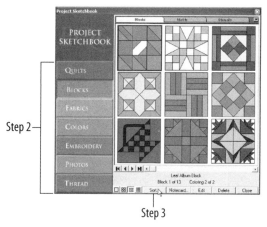

Step 3

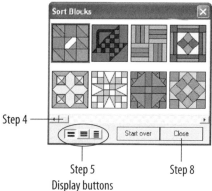

Display buttons

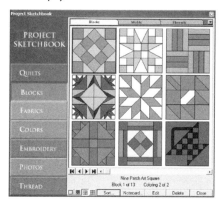

Sorted items in the Sketchbook

Libraries

Quilt designed by Lynn Majidimehr
Woodinville, Washington

Chapter 3

EQ6 comes with six separate library types containing thousands of different "ingredients" to use and re-use as you design. You can also create your own libraries. This keeps blocks you've drawn, photos you've saved or fabrics you've scanned, handy to use in any project. All the libraries work similarly, so learning one helps you understand them all. This chapter shows you what is in each library and how to use the library tools. You'll learn how to search, import, and save items in your own library.

Reference

About the Libraries

EQ6 has six libraries: Block, Fabric, Layout, Embroidery, Photo and Thread. The steps below work for any library.

1   Click **LIBRARIES > *Your Choice***. The library opens with items displayed. Notice the name *Library* on the top-left. The Library section holds blocks, fabrics, layouts, embroidery, photos and threads that come with EQ6.

Step 1

Seeing More Categories and Styles

2   Items are organized into categories. Beside the list of names **drag the vertical scrollbar down to see the different categories** (except in the Photo Library). For example, if you are in the Block Library the categories are: 1 Classic Pieced, 2 Contemporary Pieced, etc.

3   Each category has styles. **Click the plus sign next to any category name to see its styles.** For example, if you are in 4 Classic Applique (in the Block Library) you would see the styles: Birds, Butterflies, Crossing Designs, etc.

4   **Click any name to see items in that style.**

Seeing More Items in a Style

5   The number of items in each style is shown at the lower-right beside the horizontal scrollbar. If the style contains 57 items, but you only see 9, you need to scroll. **Drag the horizontal scrollbar beneath the items to the right to see more items within that style.**

6   You can also change the number of items that display at one time. Below the name list you will see a series of display buttons with squares on them. **Click a button with fewer squares to see fewer items, or one with more squares to see more items.** This is also a nice feature when viewing complex items. You can click a button with fewer squares to "zoom in" closer to see an item's detail.

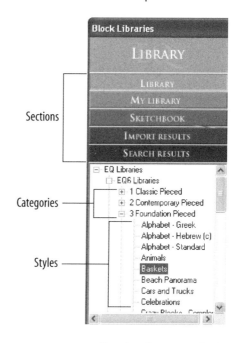

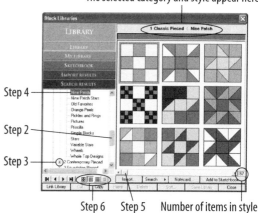

The selected category and style appear here

Number of items in style

Library - These items come with EQ6 and are always the same. You cannot "use up," delete, add to or change items in this section.

My Library - There are no items here until you add them. You can create your own library category with your favorite or most frequently used items by saving them here.

Sketchbook - This area shows what is in your current project's Sketchbook for that item type. For example, in the Block Library the Sketchbook section shows blocks you've added to the Sketchbook. In the Fabric Library the Sketchbook section shows fabrics you've added to the Sketchbook.

Import Results - When you import, your imported items will show here.

Search Results - When you search, the results will show here.

When building projects and designing use:
Add to Sketchbook

When building a My Library use:
Copy   Paste

Note for previous EQ4 and EQ5 users:
If you need something in your Sketchbook, use the Add to Sketchbook button. Do not use Copy unless creating custom My Libraries.

About the Rest of the Buttons

Each Library has five sections:
See the descriptions to the left for more details.

Each Library has these buttons:

⌗ ⊞ ⊞ ⊞ Change the number of items displayed at one time

Import... Import items from other EQ projects, or from outside files. See pages 134-135, 138 and 140.

Search ▶ Search for items in the Library. See pages 130, 131, 132, and 133.

Notecard... Name items you are saving, and keep design notes about the items (available in all sections except *Library*).

Add to Sketchbook Add items to the Sketchbook. Once they're in the Sketchbook you can use them for designing. See pages 128-129.

Link Library Link to library files in different EQ programs or from other users. See pages 136-137.

Cut   Copy Cut or copy an item you want to paste into *My Library*. See page 144.

Paste Paste a cut or copied item into *My Library*. See page 144.

Delete Delete an item (available in all sections except *Library*). See page 146.

Sort... Sort items in your desired order (available in all sections except *Library*).

Save Library Save items or changes to your *My Library*. See page 144.

Close Close the Library.

The Block Library has these buttons:

◄◄ ◄ ► ►► These coloring arrows let you view the *Library* blocks in 3 colorings: line drawing (no coloring), grayscale, or multicolor. When you take a block from the *Library*, it automatically comes with all 3 colorings.

About the Libraries

Using Items from the Library

To design with anything from a Library, you must first add it to your Sketchbook.

Step 1

Finding and Selecting Items in the Library

1   Click **LIBRARIES > *Your Choice***. Example: If you need a block, open the Block Library.

2   Click to choose the section of the library you want items from:

> **Library** – These items come with EQ6 and are always the same.
>
> **My Library** – This is empty until you add items. Use this section for original block designs, scanned fabrics, imported embroidery designs, and to organize your favorite items.
>
> **Sketchbook** – This area shows what is in your current project's Sketchbook for that item type.
>
> **Import Results** – When you import, your imported items will show here.
>
> **Search Results** – When you search, your search results will show here.

3   If you choose **Library** or **My Library**, click the category, then click the style you want to see.

4   **Click the item or items you want to use.** They will appear selected with a frame. You can also use keyboard shortcuts to help you select multiple items.

• Hold down the **CTRL key** and click on each individual item you want to select.

• Hold down the **SHIFT key** as you click to select a range of items.

• Click one item, then press **CTRL+A** to select all the items in this style.

Adding Items to your Sketchbook

5   Click the **Add to Sketchbook** button. The selected item "disappears" temporarily, showing you've added the item to your Sketchbook.

Step 4

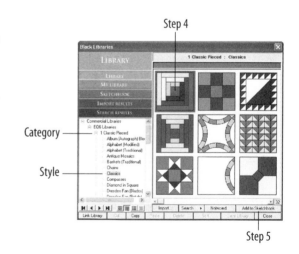

Category

Style

Step 5

To set a block (motif or stencil) into a quilt

WORKTABLE > Work on Quilt

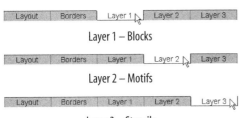

Layer 1 – Blocks

Layer 2 – Motifs

Layer 3 – Stencils

Set Block

To edit a block drawing

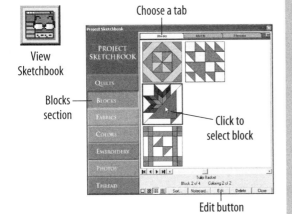

Choose a tab

View Sketchbook

Blocks section

Click to select block

Edit button

To use a thread color

WORKTABLE > Work on Quilt

Layer 3 tab

Set Thread

---

6 Click **Close** to return to the worktable.

Notes

The steps for using an item from the library depend on the item, and what you want to do with it.

- *To set a block (motif or stencil) in a quilt,* click WORKTABLE > Work on Quilt. Click the Layer 1 tab to set blocks, the Layer 2 tab to set motifs, or the Layer 3 tab to set stencils. Click the Set Block tool and then click the appropriate tab within the Blocks palette. To set a block, see page 161. To set a motif or stencil, see page 169.

- *To edit a block drawing,* click the View Sketchbook button > Blocks section > Blocks, Motifs or Stencils tab > click the block to select it > click the Edit button. You will be on the Block worktable viewing the selected block. See pages 219-264 for more about drawing.

- *To use a library quilt layout,* click the View Sketchbook button > Quilts section > scroll to find the quilt > click the quilt to select it > click the Edit button. You will be on the Quilt worktable viewing the selected quilt. To set a block in this layout, see page 161 or 169.

- *To set an embroidery design into a quilt,* click WORKTABLE > Work on Quilt > click the Layer 3 tab > click the Set Embroidery tool. (If this tool is not on your toolbar, see page 302.) To set an embroidery design on a quilt, see page 171.

- *To set a photo into a quilt,* click WORKTABLE > Work on Quilt > click the layer on which you want the photo > click the Set Photo tool. (If this tool is not on your toolbar, see page 302.) To set a photo, see page 174.

- *To use a thread color,* you first need stencils or embroidery set on Layer 3 (see pages 169 or 171). Click WORKTABLE > Work on Quilt > click the Layer 3 tab > click the Set Thread tool. (If this tool is not on your toolbar, see page 302.) To change the thread color, see page 205.

- Thread applies to any layer, any patch, open or closed, as well as embroidery.

Searching for Items by Notecard

To search in the Thread Library see page 133.

1   Open the library in which you want to search. (**LIBRARIES** > *Your Choice*.)

2   Click the **Search** button. If given two choices, choose **By Notecard**.

3   Put checks next to the fields you want to search (Name, Reference, and Notes).

4   Under **Find at most ___ items** enter a number between 1 and 999, or leave it at the default which is 50.

5   In the box at the top marked **Find all the ___ with this notecard text,** type the word or words you want to search by.

6   Click the **Search** button. After the progress bar disappears, click **OK**. You will now be viewing the Search Results section of the Library.

7   Drag the horizontal scrollbar beneath the items to see all the search results.

8   If you want to use an item from the search, **click directly on it to select it**. Click **Add to Sketchbook**. You can add as few or as many items as you want.

9   Click **Search > By Notecard** again to do a new search or click **Close** to return to the worktable.

Notes

• You will see more results if you check all 3 fields (Name, Reference, and Notes). Or, if you type part of the name instead of the full name. For instance, search for "ohio" instead of "ohio star."

• If you are searching for blocks and have BlockBase installed, be sure to put a check next to Notes. BlockBase *names* are numbers. The earliest known name for the block *(not all names)* is in the BlockBase Notes.

• Order is important when you type in more than one search word. You will get different results if you type in "Sue Sunbonnet" instead of "Sunbonnet Sue."

Step 1

Step 2

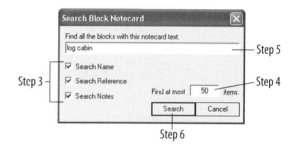

Step 5

Step 4

Step 3

Step 6

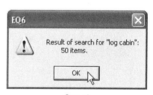

Step 6

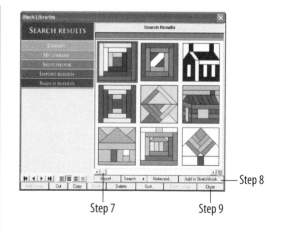

Step 8

Step 7   Step 9

Searching for Items by Notecard

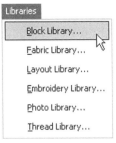

Step 1

Step 2

Step 6

Searching for Blocks by Category

Each block in the Block Library is marked according to predetermined categories. These categories are grouped into sections: Difficulty & Piecing Info, Events, Holidays, Pieced, and Appliqué.

1 Click **LIBRARIES** > **Block Library**.

2 Click **Search** > **By Category**.

3 Click any section to view the categories.

4 **Click the image next to a category name to add the category to the search.** You can add more than one. If you wish to remove a category, click the image next to the category name again, to deselect it.

5 Under **Find at most ___ blocks** enter a number between 1 and 999, or leave it at the default which is 50.

6 Click the **Search** button, then **OK**. You will now be viewing the Search Results section.

7 Drag the horizontal scrollbar beneath the blocks to see all the search results.

8 If you want to use a block from the search, **click directly on the block to select it**. Click **Add to Sketchbook**. You can add as few or as many blocks as you want.

9 Click **Search** > **By Category** again to perform a new search or click **Close** to return to the worktable.

Notes
- The blocks returned must fit into *all* the categories chosen. You can add up to 20 categories, but your results will be fewer and fewer the more you add.

- If you want to save the search results, consider copying and pasting these blocks into their own style in My Library, see page 144. For instance, if you are a beginning quilter and would like to stick to "Triangles and Rectangles," copy, paste, and save those results into a new library. Then go to that My Library each time you need a block for a new project.

Step 5

Step 4   Step 6

Selected categories
appear here

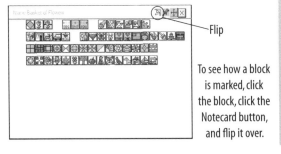

Flip

To see how a block is marked, click the block, click the Notecard button, and flip it over.

Searching for Blocks by Category

Searching for Fabrics by Color

1   Click **LIBRARIES > Fabric Library**.

2   **Click to select any fabric** (perhaps one you want to match in color) from any section (Library, My Library, etc.). You must have a fabric selected to proceed.

3   Click **Search > By Color**.

4   *To change the search color,* click the down arrow on the average color box to show your Sketchbook colors. Drag the horizontal scrollbar to see them all, then click your new color choice.

5   In the top-right you will see a list of fabric libraries linked to EQ6. You can check one or more to search. The more libraries you have checked, the longer the search will take.

6   Under **Find at most ___ fabrics,** enter a number between 1 and 999, or leave it at the default which is 50. A higher number returns more results, but takes more time.

7   Click the **Search** button, wait for the progress bar, then click **OK**.

8   Drag the scrollbar beneath the fabrics to see all the search results.

9   To use a fabric from the search, **click directly on the fabric to select it**. Click **Add to Sketchbook**. You can add as few or as many fabrics as you want.

10   Click **Search > By Color** to do a new search or click **Close** to return to the worktable.

Notes

- If you have a fabric library installed which is not showing up in the list of options, use the Link Library button in the Library section, see pages 136-137.

- To see the "average color" for any fabric, click the *Show average color* checkbox in the Fabric Library.

Step 1

Step 3

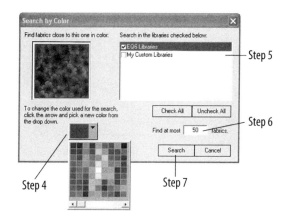

Step 5

Step 6

Step 4   Step 7

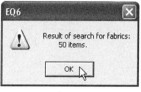

Step 7

Step 1

Step 2 - Search by Text

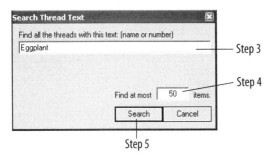
Step 3
Step 4
Step 5

Step 3 - Search by Color

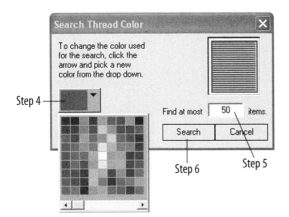
Step 4
Step 6
Step 5

Searching for Threads

You can search for threads by text or by color.

Searching by Text

1   Click **LIBRARIES > Thread Library**.

2   Click **Search > By Text**.

3   In the top box type the word or words you want to search for in the Thread Library. A name, like Eggplant, or a number like 5633 work best.

4   Under **Find at most _____ items,** enter a number from 1 to 999, or leave as is. The default is 50.

5   Click **Search**, then **OK**.

6   To use a thread from the search, click directly on the thread to select it and click **Add to Sketchbook**. Add as few or as many threads as you like.

Searching by Color

1   Click **LIBRARIES > Thread Library**.

2   **Click to select** any thread (perhaps one you want to match in color) from any section (Library, My Library, etc.).

3   Click **Search > By Color**.

4   To change the search color, click the down arrow on the color box to see your Sketchbook colors. Drag the horizontal scrollbar to see them all, then click your new color choice.

5   Under **Find at most _____ items,** enter a number from 1 to 999. The default is 50.

6   Click **Search**, then **OK**.

7   To use a thread from the search, click directly on the thread to select it and click **Add to Sketchbook**. Add as few or as many threads as you like.

Searching for Threads

Importing from Existing Projects

The import feature allows you to stay in the project you are working on and import from a different project's Sketchbook with just a few clicks. Use these same steps if you are importing fabrics from STASH shopping bags, fabrics from EQ5 palettes, blocks from BlockBase projects, or earlier EQ programs.

1   Open the library into which you want to import. (**LIBRARIES** > *Your Choice*.) Examples: If you need a group of blocks you drew in a different project, open the Block Library. If you need fabrics from a different project, open the Fabric Library.

2   Click the **Import** button. If given two choices, choose **From Project**. The Import box will appear.

3   The window has 3 important areas:

   • **Look in:** box at the top

   • White area where files and folders appear

   • **Files of type:** drop down box at the bottom

   Start by looking in the correct folder for the project from which you need to import. The default location for EQ6 projects is: **My Documents > My EQ6 > PJ6.**

4   If the file is from an earlier version of EQ software or a BlockBase project, click the arrow at the end of the **Files of type:** drop down box. Change it to **Previous EQ Versions**. If you are importing fabrics from a STASH Shopping Bag or EQ5 Palette, change the drop down box to the appropriate choice.

5   When you see the file you want to import from, click to select it.

6   Click **Open**. You will now be viewing the Import Results section of the Library.

Step 2

The default location for EQ6 projects is:
My Documents > My EQ6 > PJ6.

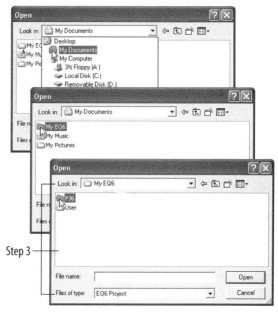

Step 3

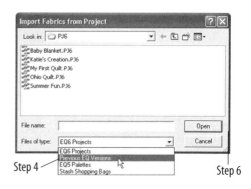

Step 4   Step 6

Importing from Existing Projects

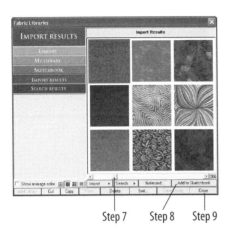

Step 7   Step 8   Step 9

7   Drag the horizontal scrollbar beneath the items to see all the import results.

8   If you want to use an imported item, **click directly on it to select it**. Click **Add to Sketchbook**. You can add as few or as many items as you want.

9   Click **Import > From Project** again to import from a different existing project or click **Close** to return to the worktable.

Notes

• If you are looking for projects made in previous versions of EQ or other EQ software, the default locations for those projects are:

EQ3 projects:
My Computer > C: drive > EQ3 > prj

EQ4 projects:
My Computer > C: drive > EQ4 > prj

EQ5 projects:
My Computer > C: drive > My Documents > My EQ5 > PJ5

BlockBase projects:
My Computer > C: drive > BB2 > bb_prj

STASH bags (Fall 1999 - Fall 2001):
My Computer > C: drive > EQ4 > Stash > bag

STASH bags (Spring 2002 - current):
My Computer > C: drive > Program Files > Electric Quilt Company > Stash > bag

My EQ5 Palettes:
My Computer > C: drive > My Documents > My EQ5 > USER

EQ's EQ5 Palettes:
My Computer > C: drive > Program Files > Electric Quilt Company > EQ5 > RES

• If you clicked BROWSE for the installation path on any of the above software programs, only you will know where to look. If you need to search for a project, see page 116.

Importing from Existing Projects

Linking Existing Libraries

Use these steps to link other EQ software (STASH, BlockBase), personal libraries from previous versions of EQ, and EQ-formatted libraries from other outside sources (friends, online challenges).

Step 1

Step 2

1   Open the library of the same type you want to link. **LIBRARIES > *Your Choice***. Example: If you want to link an outside fabric library, open the Fabric Library.

2   Click the **Link Library** button.

3   Click the **Auto Add** button to add a link for any EQ software not listed. If you have software such as BlockBase or STASH installed on this computer, the Auto Add button should find and link them automatically. If the Auto Add button does not find and link the library, you will need to add it manually.

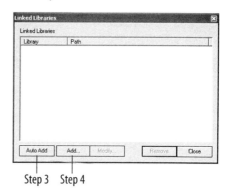

Step 3   Step 4

4   To add a library manually, click the **Add** button.

5   In the first box, **type a name for the new library**. This name will appear in the list under the Library section, so choose something that will help you identify it. Examples: ClubEQ Blocks or Foundation Pieced Blocks, not Blocks.

Step 5

Step 6

6   In the second box, you need the path to the folder containing the library files. Enter the path by clicking the **Browse** button to find it manually (recommended), type the full path in the box, or paste the full path in the box. Click **Browse**.

7   If you clicked Browse, click the plus signs next to the drives and folders until you reach the folder containing the library files. Be sure the folder is selected. Click **OK** to close the Browse for Folder box.

8   Click **OK** on the Add New Library Link box. If you mis-type the path or chose a folder with no library files, the library will not be found and you will get a message **Not a valid EQ library directory.** Change the path and click **OK** or click **Cancel** to start over.

Step 7

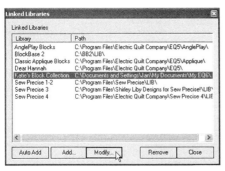

Step 9

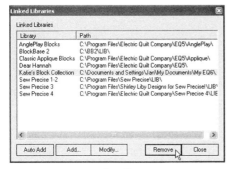

Step 10

Explorer window Address bar

Search for files

9   **Modify** allows you to change the path (not the name) of an existing item in the list. Select the library name and click the **Modify** button. Follow steps 6-8 again.

10 **Remove** allows you to take an item off the list. Select the library name and click **Remove**. At the prompt, click "yes" if you really want to delete it.

11 Click **Close** to return to the library.

12 Click **Close** again to return to the worktable.

Notes

• If you add a new library link and mis-type the name (ex. Blocs), remove it from the list and add it again.

• If you are looking for libraries to add, try going through My Computer (Windows Explorer) to find the exact location. If you have the Address bar turned on in the Explorer window, you can right-click on the path in the Address bar and choose Copy. (In Windows Explorer click VIEW > Toolbars and make sure Address bar has a check next to it.) Then when you add a new library in EQ, you don't need to browse to find the folder a second time. Just right-click in the second box and choose Paste to add the path.

• If you are having difficulty finding the files, but know they are on your computer, try doing a search through Windows. Click START > Search. Click on "All files and folders." In the first box type the file extension, then click Search. (Don't forget to type the asterisk and period.) File extensions are:

   *.blk = Block Library
   *.fab = Fabric Library
   *.qlt = Layout Library
   *.ebr = Embroidery Library
   *.pix = Photo Library
   *.thd = Thread Library

Example: To search for a Block Library you would type: *.blk

Linking Existing Libraries

Importing Image Files into the Fabric or Photo Libraries

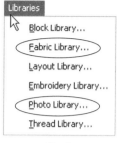

Step 1

Use these steps to import scanned fabrics for any quilt, or photos for photo-quilt projects. You can import BMP, GIF, JPEG, PNG, or TIFF files.

1   Open the library into which you want to import. (**LIBRARIES > Fabric Library or Photo Library**.) Example: To import scanned fabrics, open the Fabric Library.

2   Click **Import > From Image Files**. The Import box will appear.

Step 2

3   At the top of the box, click the down arrow beside the **Look in:** box. Go to the drive where the files are located. Double-click through the folders in the center of this box until you open the folder containing your image files.

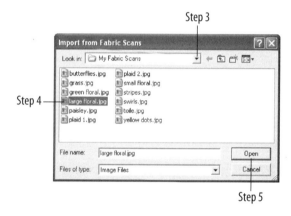

4   **Click the image files you want to import.** To select more than one:

   • Hold down the **CTRL key** and click on each individual file you want to select.

   • Hold down the **SHIFT key** as you click to select a range of files.

   • Click one file, then press **CTRL+A** to select all the files in this folder.

5   Click **Open**. You will now see the Import Results section of the Library.

6   If you want to use an imported item, **click directly on it to select it**. Click **Add to Sketchbook** if you plan to use an item in a project, or click **Copy**, if you plan to paste the item into a library. Add as many items as you want.

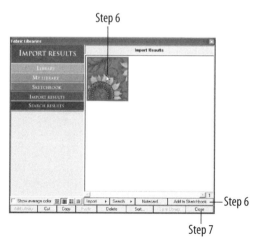

7   Click **Import > From Image Files** again to import from a different folder or click **Close** to return to the worktable.

Notes
• To color, see pages 198-199. To set a photo, see page 174.

Importing Image Files

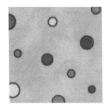 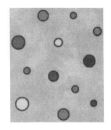

When scanning, crop the fabric to best show the repeat. Below (right) you can see how much better the fabric tiles in the quilt when it is cropped to include full circles.

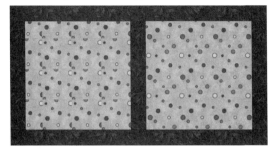

Please note:

To keep file sizes as small as possible, fabric in EQ6 "tiles" (repeats) the small fabric design you save, in order to simulate the effect of a large piece of fabric on your quilt. To make this tiling less noticeable, it is important to find your fabric's design repeat, and spend time cropping your scan at the appropriate place before importing. It's also important to keep the cropped image as small as possible. Small repeats mean small files (which is good), and large repeats mean larger files (which can make your computer run slower). Make EQ6 run most efficiently by keeping your project file sizes manageable. This means not loading in too many fabrics at once, and keeping your scanned image sizes small.

 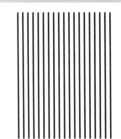

A fabric's weave can produce a moiré pattern when scanned

Use a descreening option to avoid a moiré pattern

Scanning Fabrics and Photos

Resolution for Scanned Fabrics

- **72 or 75 dpi** – all files but GIF or PNG
- **96 dpi** – GIF or PNG Files (required)

Resolution for Scanned or Digital Photos

- **72 dpi** – when you will *not* be printing from EQ6
- **150 dpi or higher** – when you will be printing from EQ6

Image Size for Fabrics

- **200 x 200 pixels** (approximately). If cropping to a rectangle to capture the design repeat, keep one dimension at 200 pixels, and let the other dimension size proportionally.

Image Size for Scanned or Digital Photos

- If you will be printing the photo from EQ6, import it in the same dimensions you'll set it and print it. For example, import a 5" x 7" photo and set it in your quilt at 5" x 7".

Other Fabric Scanning Tips

Remember: High resolution + large image sizes = large file size. Large file size = slower running EQ6.

- **Scaling** – Don't change the scale of the fabric. EQ6 will correctly scale the fabric on the block/quilt for you as long as you follow the resolution (dpi) guidelines above.

- **Preparing the Fabric** – Iron the fabric and place it as straight as possible on the scanner bed (especially with striped and checked fabric).

- **Normal vs. Photo Color** – Choose a setting such as "Normal" rather than "Photo" color, if possible.

- **Descreening** – A scanned fabric's weave can produce a moiré pattern. To avoid this, use a setting such as Descreen, or Magazine/Newspaper. Or slightly angle the fabric on the scanner bed.

- **Cropping** – The image you save is what will appear when you color in EQ6. Be sure to crop your fabric to cut out any white edge caused by the scanner bed behind the fabric.

Importing Embroidery (EXP) Files into the Embroidery Library

Only embroidery files in the EXP format can be imported into the Embroidery library.

1   Click **LIBRARIES > Embroidery Library**.

2   Click **Import > From .EXP Files**.

3   At the top of the box, click the drop down arrow beside the **Look in:** box. Go to the drive where the files are located. Double-click through the folders in the center of this box until you open the folder containing your EXP files.

4   **Click the EXP files you want to import.** To select more than one:

   • Hold down the **CTRL key** and click on each individual file you want to select.

   • Hold down the **SHIFT key** as you click to select a range of files.

   • Click one file, then press **CTRL+A** to select all the files in this folder.

5   Click **Open**. You will now see the Import Results section of the Library.

6   Drag the horizontal scrollbar beneath the embroideries to see all the import results.

7   If you want to use an imported embroidery design, **click directly on it to select it**. Click **Add to Sketchbook**. You can add as few or as many of these as you want.

8   Click **Import > From .EXP Files** again to import from a different folder or click **Close** to return to the worktable.

Notes
• EQ6 lets you control the size of the embroidery when you design. But you may not actually be able to stitch the real embroidery in that size.

Step 1

Step 2

Step 3

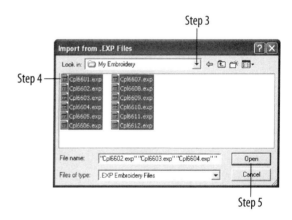
Step 4

Step 5

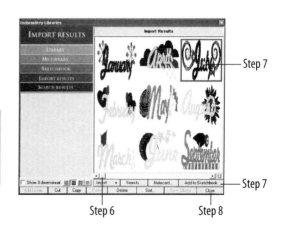
Step 7

Step 7

Step 6   Step 8

Importing Embroidery Files

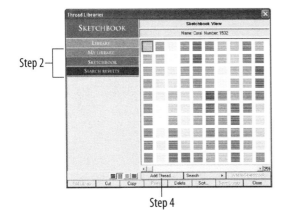

Step 2

Step 4

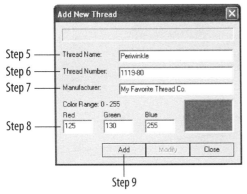

Step 5
Step 6
Step 7

Step 8

Step 9

Here is a chart of pure RGB colors. When adding thread colors, start with the closest pure color and then increase or decrease red, green, or blue to match your spool.

Black (0,0,0) Green (0,255,0) Cyan (0,255,255)
White (255,255,255) Blue (0,0,255) Magenta (255,0,255)
Red (255,0,0) Yellow (255,255,0)

Step 10

Adding Thread Colors

You can add your own thread colors to your library. Use these steps to match actual spool colors.

1 Click **LIBRARIES > Thread Library**.

2 Click the section you want to add threads to:

My Library – to add your own thread colors to your personal library.

Sketchbook – to add threads to the current project you are working on.

Search Results – to add colors temporarily to use as the base of a search for "real" threads (see page 133).

3 If you chose **My Library**, click the library name and then the style to which you want to add them. If you do not have a library created, please do this first, see page 143.

4 Click the **Add Thread** button.

5 In the first box, type the **Thread Name**. This is usually a color name like Periwinkle.

6 In the second box, type the **Thread Number**. Check the spool for the number and type it here. If you do not have a number, it is okay to leave this field blank.

7 In the third box, type the **Manufacturer** name. It is okay to leave this field blank if you do not know the manufacturer name.

8 **Enter numbers between 0 and 255** in the boxes for red, green and blue to make the thread color you want. See the chart at left for help.

9 Click **Add** when you are done.

10 If you chose **My Library** earlier, click **Save Library**. If you change styles without clicking Save Library, you will be prompted to save.

11 Click the **Add Thread** button again to add more thread colors or click Close to return to the worktable.

Adding Thread Colors

Modifying Thread Colors

Use this feature to modify thread color or to update thread names.

1 Click **LIBRARIES** > **Thread Library**.

2 Click the section of the library where the thread is located (My Library or Sketchbook sections only).

3 If you chose **My Library**, click the library name and then the style which contains the thread.

4 **Click on the thread to select it**. (You may need to scroll to find it.)

5 Click the **Add Thread** button.

6 Change the name, number, manufacturer or red/green/blue colors.

7 Click the **Modify** button to update the thread you selected in Step 4. Click **Add** to add the new version to the end of the existing threads.

8 If you chose **My Library** earlier, click **Save Library**. If you change styles without clicking Save Library, you will be prompted to save so the modification will not be lost.

9 Click to select a different thread, then click the **Add Thread** button to modify it, or click **Close** to return to the worktable.

Step 1

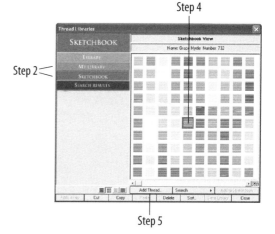

Step 4

Step 2

Step 5

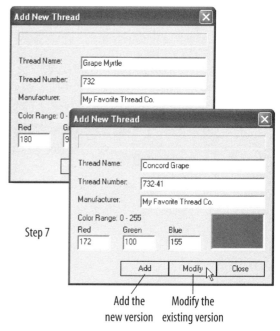

Step 7

Add the new version   Modify the existing version

Modifying Thread Colors

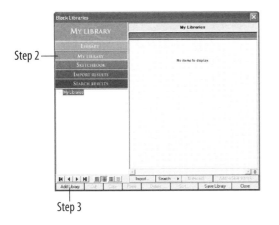

Step 2

Step 3

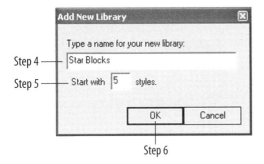

Step 4

Step 5

Step 6

Step 7

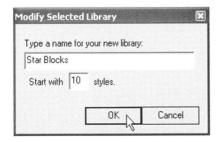

Step 8

Adding and Formatting My Library

Use custom My Libraries to store your personal designs for easy access. This feature is great for new block designs and scanned fabrics.

1 Open the library to which you want to add a My Library category. Click **LIBRARIES > *Your Choice.*** Example: If you want to add a personal library of blocks, open the Block Library.

2 Click the **My Library** section.

3 Click the **Add Library** button.

4 Type a descriptive name for the library category. Example: *Greece Trip Photos*, not *Photos*.

5 In **Start with ___ styles,** choose the number of styles (or sub-categories) for this library category. This number can be from 1 to 59 styles.

6 Click **OK** to add the new library category.

7 To format the library category and change its name or add more styles, **right-click on the name in the list and click Modify Library.**

8 Type in a new name or a new number of styles. When you're done, click **OK**.

9 Click **Close** to return to the worktable.

Notes

- If you add items to a My Library (your own personal library), they won't show up in the regular EQ6 Library. You will need to click on the My Library section to see them.

- Library and style names alphabetize themselves. When naming, consider putting numbers (01, 02, 03...) in front of the name to force the organization.

- Spaces count when alphabetizing.

- To delete an entire My Library category and all the styles it contains, you need to find the User folder. The default location is: My Documents > My EQ6 > User. Find your library (it will have the same name as in the library list, potentially with an extension), right-click it, and choose Delete. Click Yes and the library will be gone.

Adding/Formatting My Library

Adding and Saving Items in My Library

Copying the Items You Want to Add

1   Open the library to which you want to add items. **LIBRARIES > *Your Choice***. For example, if you want to add a block to a My Library, open the Block Library.

2   Click to choose the section of the library you want to copy from (Library, My Library, Sketchbook, Import Results or Search Results). If you choose Import Results (see pages 134, 138, or 140), or Search Results (see pages 130-133), follow those instructions and then return to this step.

3   **Click an item to select it.** You can also use keyboard shortcuts to help you:

- Hold down the **CTRL key** and click on each individual item you want to select.

- Hold down the **SHIFT key** as you click to select a range of items.

- Select one item, then press **CTRL+A** to select all the items in this style.

4   Click the **Copy** button (or press **CTRL+C**).

Adding and Saving the Items

5   Click the **My Library** section.

6   Click the plus sign next to the library name, then the style name you want to add these items to. (If you do not have libraries added to My Library yet, see page 143 and then return to this step.)

7   Click the **Paste** button (or press **CTRL+V**). Do not add more than 254 items to any style.

8   Click the **Save Library** button. If you change styles, without clicking Save Library you will be prompted to save the changes. Fabric limit: 254 fabrics per style.

9   Click **OK**, then **Close** to return to the worktable.

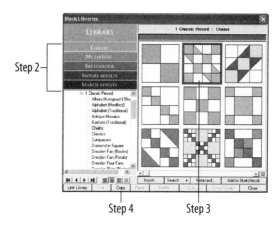

Step 2

Step 4   Step 3

The item will be pasted here

Step 5

Step 6

Step 7   Step 8 Step 9
Do not add more than
254 items to any style.

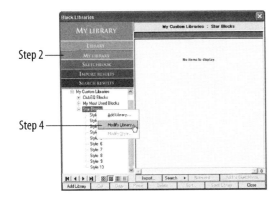

Step 2

Step 4

Step 4
Modify Library option

Renaming My Libraries and Styles

1 Open the library which contains the library category you need to rename. **LIBRARIES > *Your Choice***. For example, if you need to rename a block library category, open the Block Library.

2 Click the **My Library** section.

3 Scroll vertically through the name list to find the library or style which needs renaming.

4 You can rename the library or style in one of two ways:

- Right-click on the item and choose either **Modify Library** or **Modify Style**. In the box, type a new name for the library or style and click **OK**.

- Click once on the name to select it and click on it again to get the renaming box. (Click, pause, click.) Type a new name and then click elsewhere to deselect it.

Notes

- **If you are only changing the library or style name, you do not need to click Save Library. If you are changing the name *and* adding items to the style you *do* need to click Save Library.**

- **Library and style names alphabetize themselves. When naming, consider putting numbers (01, 02, 03...) in front of the name to force the organization.**

- **Spaces count when alphabetizing.**

Renaming My Libraries/Styles

Deleting from My Libraries

1   Open the library of the same type you want to delete from. **LIBRARIES > *Your Choice*.** For example, if you want to remove a scanned fabric, open the Fabric Library.

2   Click the **My Library** section.

3   Click the plus sign next to the library category name to open it, then click the style name containing the item or items you want to delete.

4   **Click to select all items you want to delete.** You can also use keyboard shortcuts to help you:

   • Hold down the **CTRL key** and click on each individual item you want to select.

   • Hold down the **SHIFT key** as you click to select a range of items.

   • Select one item, then press **CTRL+A** to select all the items in this view.

5   Click the **Delete** button or press your keyboard **DELETE key** to delete the selected items.

6   At the prompt, click **Yes** if you are sure you want to delete the selected items.

7   Click **Save Library.** If you change styles without clicking Save Library you will be prompted to save the changes, otherwise the items will not be deleted.

8   Click **OK**, then **Close** to return to the worktable.

Notes
• To delete an entire My Library category and all the styles it contains, you need to find the User folder. The default location is: My Documents > My EQ6 > User. Find your library (it will have the same name as in the library list, potentially with an extension), right-click it, and choose Delete. Click Yes and the library will be gone.

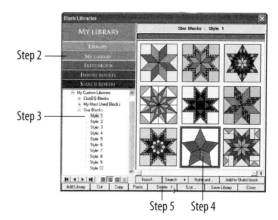

Step 2

Step 3

Step 5   Step 4

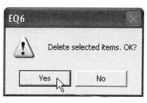

Step 6

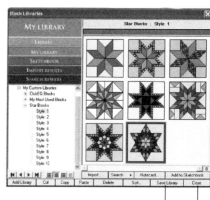

Step 7   Step 8

Quilts

Quilt designed by Linda MacDougall
Murrieta, California

Chapter 4

EQ6 has nine basic layout styles. All these styles are adjustable, so you have endless design possibilities. To create your quilt design, you fill the blank spaces with blocks, fabrics and colors. This chapter shows you how to see and choose a layout style, adjust its size and style, fill it with blocks, then vary the resulting design using flips and rotations.

Reference

Choosing a Quilt Layout

1 Click **WORKTABLE > Work on Quilt**.

2 Click **QUILT > New Quilt > *Your Choice***.

Here is a list of available layout choices:

A Horizontal layouts arrange blocks in horizontal and vertical rows. Blocks can be rectangular or square, and the layout can include optional sashing, corner blocks, and a sash border.

B On-point layouts contain square blocks tipped 45 degrees so they appear as diamonds.

C Variable Point layouts are identical to On-point, but blocks can have a different width from height.

D Baby Blocks layouts are overall grids of 3-D cubes made with equal-sided diamonds.

E Variable Blocks layouts are like Baby Blocks, but the blocks can have unequal sides and tops.

F Horizontal Strip Quilts are long horizontal pieced or unpieced strips.

G Vertical Strip Quilts are long vertical pieced or unpieced strips.

H One Patch Quilts consist of one patch repeated throughout the quilt.

I Custom Set (formerly Country Set in EQ4) layouts provide a large central area for placing blocks of different sizes. You can vary the height and width of this central area. Blocks of any size can be placed and aligned anywhere inside the center – even overlapping each other. (See Chapter 5 – page 165.)

Notes
• Your quilt's center size (without borders) will always appear at the top of the Layout box on the Layout tab.

A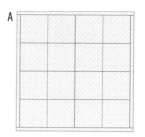

B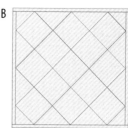

C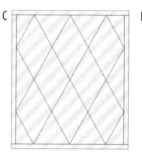

D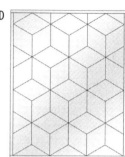

E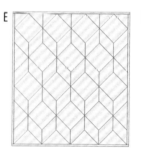

F

G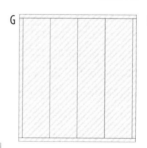

H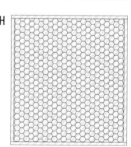

I

Quilt's center size at the
top of the Layout box

Step 1

Step 2

Making a Horizontal Quilt

1   Click **WORKTABLE > Work on Quilt**.

2   Click **QUILT > New Quilt > Horizontal**. A blank Horizontal layout will appear.

3   Click the **Layout** tab.

4   Under **Number of blocks**, click the arrows beside Horizontal and Vertical to choose the number of blocks you want. (You can also type in these boxes.)

5   Under **Finished size of blocks**, choose the block size you want. Click **Keep width and height equal** to keep your blocks square. Change the sizes in any of the following ways:

   • type a new size in the box

   • drag the slider rectangle on the line

   • click to the right or left of the slider rectangle to have the number jump in increments

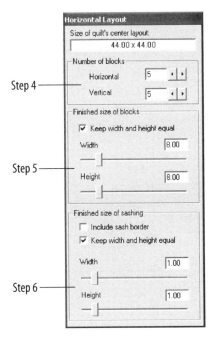

Step 4

Step 5

Step 6

6   Under **Finished size of sashing**, choose the sashing size you want. Click **Keep width and height equal** to keep your cornerstones square. For no sashing, make the sash size 0.00. The sizes can be changed the same three ways described in step 5. Click **Include sash border** if you want sashing not only between the blocks but around the outside of them.

7   Click the **Borders** tab to adjust, add, delete or insert borders, see page 185.

8   Click the **Layer 1** tab to work on the base layer of your quilt.

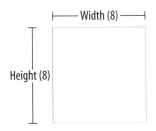

├── Width (8) ──┤

Height (8)

Notes
• To make adjustments on the Layout tab faster, you can use the keyboard TAB key to cycle between entries and type immediately.

• How blocks are measured: The width and height you input are the edges of the squares (or rectangles) you see. The sashing width is added to the left and right sides of your block. The sashing height is added to the top and bottom of your block.

Making a Horizontal Quilt

Making an On-Point Quilt

1 Click **WORKTABLE > Work on Quilt**.

2 Click **QUILT > New Quilt > On-point**.

3 Click the **Layout** tab.

4 Under **Select a style**, choose the style (either triangles in the corners or a seam).

5 Under **Number of blocks**, click the arrows beside Horizontal and Vertical to choose the number of blocks you want. (You can also type in these boxes.)

6 Under **Finished size of blocks**, choose the block size you want. You can change the size in any of the following ways:

   - type a new size in the box

   - drag the slider rectangle on the line

   - click to the right or left of the slider rectangle to have the number jump in increments

7 Under **Finished size of sashing**, choose the sashing size you want. For no sashing, make the sash size 0.00. This size can be changed the same three ways described in step 6.

8 Click the **Borders** tab to adjust, add, delete or insert borders, see page 185.

9 Click the **Layer 1** tab to work on the base layer of your quilt.

Notes

- To make adjustments on the Layout tab faster, you can use the keyboard TAB key to cycle between entries and type immediately.

- How blocks are measured: The size of blocks you input here is the diagonal edge of the on-point squares. The sashing width is added on all sides of your block.

- In this layout, your blocks will always be square. If you would rather have diamonds which can have different horizontal and vertical dimensions, use the Variable Point layout instead.

Step 1

Step 2

Triangle in corner   Seam in corner

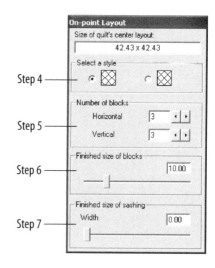

Step 4
Step 5
Step 6
Step 7

Step 1

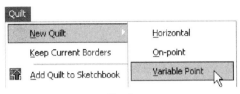

Step 2

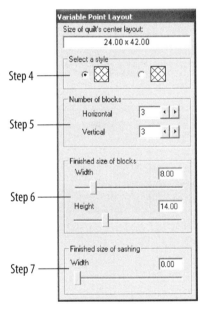

Step 4
Step 5
Step 6
Step 7

Making a Variable Point Quilt

1   Click **WORKTABLE > Work on Quilt**.

2   Click **QUILT > New Quilt > Variable Point**. A blank Variable Point layout will appear.

3   Click the **Layout** tab.

4   Under **Select a style**, choose the type of Variable Point layout style you want (either triangles in the corners or a seam).

5   Under **Number of blocks**, click the arrows beside Horizontal and Vertical to choose the number of blocks you want. (You can also type in these boxes.)

6   Under **Finished size of blocks**, choose the block size you want. You can change the size in any of the following ways:

- type a new size in the box

- drag the slider rectangle on the line

- click to the right or left of the slider rectangle to have the number jump in increments

7   Under **Finished size of sashing**, choose the size of sashing you want. For no sashing, make the sash size 0.00. This size can be changed the same three ways described in step 6.

8   Click the **Borders** tab to adjust, add, delete or insert borders, see page 185.

9   Click the **Layer 1** tab to work on the base layer of your quilt.

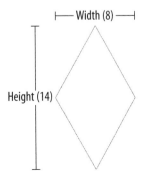

├── Width (8) ──┤

Height (14)

> **Notes**
> - To make adjustments on the Layout tab faster, you can use the keyboard TAB key to cycle between entries and type immediately.
>
> - How blocks are measured: The size of blocks you input here are NOT the edges of the Variable Point blocks you see. The width is the horizontal measurement from point to point through the block. The height is the vertical measurement from point to point through the block. The sashing width is added horizontally out on all sides of your block.

Making a Baby Blocks Quilt

1 Click **WORKTABLE > Work on Quilt**.

2 Click **QUILT > New Quilt > Baby Blocks**. A blank Baby Blocks layout will appear.

3 Click the **Layout** tab.

4 Under **Number of blocks**, click the arrows beside Horizontal and Vertical to choose the number of blocks you want. (You can also type in these boxes.)

5 Under **Finished size of blocks**, choose the block size you want. You can change the size in any of the following ways:

- type a new size in the box

- drag the slider rectangle on the line

- click to the right or left of the slider rectangle to have the number jump in increments

6 Click the **Borders** tab to adjust, add, delete or insert borders, see page 185.

7 Click the **Layer 1** tab to work on the base layer of your quilt.

Notes

- To make adjustments on the Layout tab faster, you can use the keyboard TAB key to cycle between entries and type immediately.

- How blocks are measured: The size of blocks you input is the edge length of all the sides of the Baby Blocks you see. There is no sashing for this layout style.

Step 1

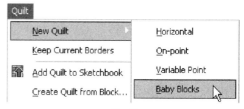

Step 2

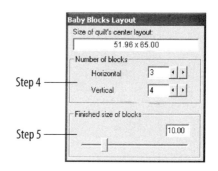

Step 4

Step 5

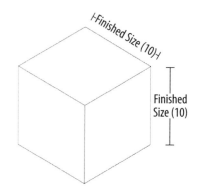

Finished Size (10)

Finished Size (10)

Making a Baby Blocks Quilt

Step 1

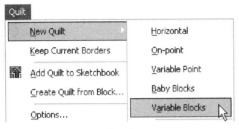

Step 2

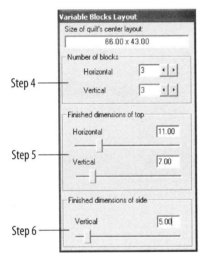

Step 4

Step 5

Step 6

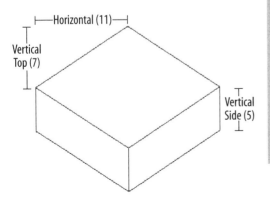

├─Horizontal (11)─┤

Vertical
Top (7)

Vertical
Side (5)

Making a Variable Blocks Quilt

1   Click **WORKTABLE > Work on Quilt**.

2   Click **QUILT > New Quilt > Variable Blocks**.
    A blank Variable Blocks layout will appear.

3   Click the **Layout** tab.

4   Under **Number of blocks**, click the arrows
    beside Horizontal and Vertical to choose the
    number of blocks you want. (You can also type
    in these boxes.)

5   Under **Finished dimensions of top**, choose the
    size you want. You can change the size in any of
    the following ways:

    • type a new size in the box

    • drag the slider rectangle on the line

    • click to the right or left of the slider rectangle
      to have the number jump in increments

6   Under **Finished dimensions of side**, choose
    the length of side you want. This size can be
    changed the same three ways described in step 5.

7   Click the **Borders** tab to adjust, add, delete or
    insert borders, see page 185.

8   Click the **Layer 1** tab to work on the base layer
    of your quilt.

Notes
• To make adjustments on the Layout tab faster, you can use
  the keyboard TAB key to cycle between entries and type
  immediately.

• How blocks are measured: The horizontal and vertical
  dimensions you input for the top are NOT the edges of
  the "top" variable block you see. Horizontal is HALF the
  horizontal measurement from point to point through the
  "top" block. Vertical is HALF the vertical measurement from
  point to point through the "top" block. Under Finished
  dimensions of side, Vertical is the edge length of that
  vertical line.

Making a Horizontal or Vertical Strip Quilt Layout

A strip quilt is made up of either horizontal or vertical rows, each of which can have its own style and width. These rows will feel similar to adjusting border styles, more so than setting up a traditional layout.

Step 1

1   Click **WORKTABLE > Work on Quilt**.

2   Click **QUILT > New Quilt >** *Horizontal Strip Quilt*, to have your strips go from left to right (horizontally). Click *Vertical Strip Quilt*, to have the strips go up and down (vertically). A blank Strip Quilt layout will appear.

3   Click the **Layout** tab.

4   Under **Select strip**, choose the strip you want to work on. You can either click directly on the strip in the quilt or use the left and right arrows to go back and forth between strips. The selected strip always appears gray in the quilt layout.

5   Once a strip is selected you can do any of the following:

   • click **Add** to add a new strip to the end of the existing strips

   • click **Delete** to remove the selected strip

   • click **Insert** to put a new blank strip in front of the selected strip

   • put a check in **Clone the selected strip** to copy the settings of the selected strip whenever you click Add or Insert

Step 2

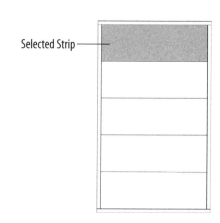

Selected Strip

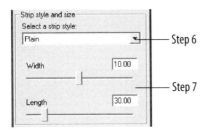

Step 6

Step 7

Step 8

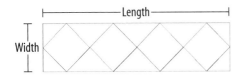

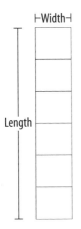

6 Under **Strip style and size**, click the down arrow on the **Select a strip style** box. Click on a style name in the list to make your choice.

7 Under **Strip style and size**, choose the strip size. The **Width** can be different for every strip, but the **Length** will be the same for all. You can change the size in any of the following ways:

- type a new size in the box

- drag the slider rectangle on the line

- click to the right or left of the slider rectangle to have the number jump in increments

8 If you choose a style which allows for blocks, then the **Number of blocks** boxes will become editable. Click the arrows beside **Along length** and **Across width** to set the number of blocks. (You can also type in these boxes.) Any number in Across width will be disabled for all styles except Checker Board.

9 Repeat steps 4-8 for each strip in the quilt.

10 Click the **Borders** tab to adjust, add, delete or insert borders, see page 185.

11 Click the **Layer 1** tab to work on the base layer of your quilt.

Notes
- To make adjustments on the Layout tab faster, you can use the keyboard TAB key to cycle between entries and type immediately.

- How blocks are measured (Horizontal Strip Quilt): The horizontal length stays the same for all strips. The vertical width can be different for each strip.

- How blocks are measured (Vertical Strip Quilt): The vertical length stays the same for all strips. The horizontal width can be different for each strip.

- The numbers for Along length and Across width determine how many blocks to add and have nothing to do with size.

- You may want to see page 157 for strip formulas for making strips with perfect squares or 90 degree angles.

Making a Strip Quilt

Choosing a Strip Style

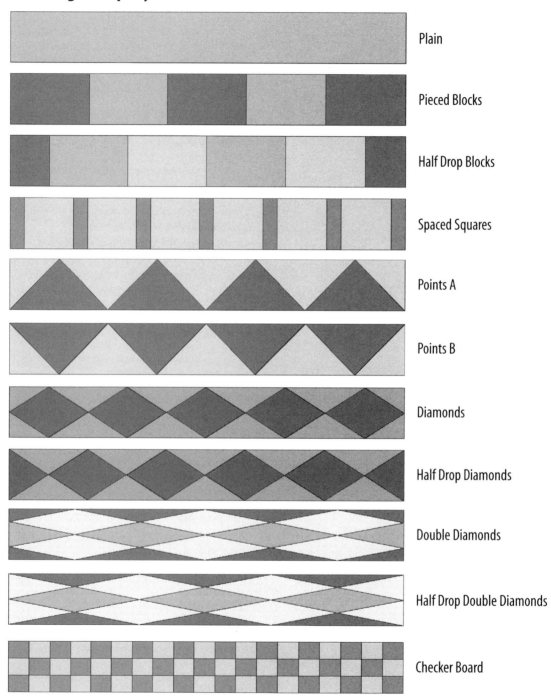

Plain

Pieced Blocks

Half Drop Blocks

Spaced Squares

Points A

Points B

Diamonds

Half Drop Diamonds

Double Diamonds

Half Drop Double Diamonds

Checker Board

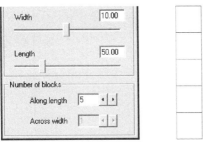

A

Example using Pieced Blocks:
10 (Strip Width) x 5 (Number of blocks) = 50 (Strip Length)

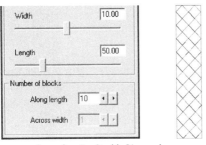

B

Example using Double Diamonds:
10 (Strip Width) x 5 (Number of blocks ÷ 2) = 50 (Strip Length)

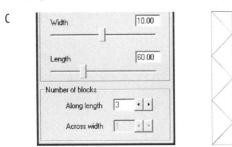

C

Example using Points A:
10 (Strip Width) x 6 (Number of blocks x 2) = 60 (Strip Length)

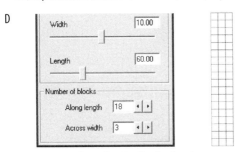

D

Example using Checker Board:
60 (Strip Length) ÷ 10 (Strip Width) = 6
6 x 3 (Blocks Across width) = 18 (Blocks Along length)

Strip Formulas

Use the formulas below when you want perfect squares or 90 degree angles in your strips.

A For Pieced Blocks, Half Drop Blocks, Diamonds, and Half Drop Diamonds

To create perfect squares or 90 degree angles:
Strip Width x **Number of blocks** = **Strip Length**

B For Double Diamonds and Half Drop Double Diamonds

To create perfect squares or 90 degree angles:
Strip Width x (**Number of blocks** ÷ 2) = **Strip Length**

C For Points A and Points B

To create triangles with a 90 degree angle:
Strip Width x (**Number of blocks** x 2) = **Strip Length**

D For Checker Board

To create perfect squares or 90 degree angles:
First divide the **Strip Length** by the **Strip Width**. Multiply that number by the number of blocks **Across width**. This will equal the number of blocks **Along length**.

Notes
- The maximum number of blocks horizontally and vertically can go from 24-100. If you can only set *Number of blocks* to 24 and need it to be higher, change it in Quilt Options. Go to QUILT > Options > All Styles (under Layout Options) and change *Maximum number of blocks horizontally and vertically* > click OK.

Strip Formulas

Cloning a Strip

To clone a strip you must have either a Horizontal or Vertical Strip Quilt layout on the screen. Cloning will copy the Layout tab settings of the selected strip and make new strips the same. This feature is great for creating consistent spacers or rows, as well as for creating Bargello quilts.

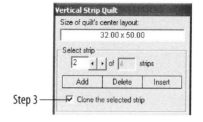

Step 3

1   Click the **Layout** tab.

2   Click in the quilt on the strip you want to clone.

3   Under **Select strip**, put a check in **Clone the selected strip**.

4   Click **Add** to put a copy of the selected strip *at the end* of the quilt.

Click **Insert** to put a copy *in front of* the selected strip.

A blank (empty) strip with the same settings as the cloned strip will be added or inserted. You will need to set blocks into and recolor this empty strip on Layer 1, because EQ considers the cloned strip a "new" strip.

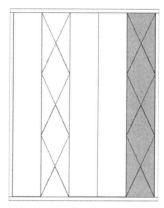

Step 4
Add puts a copy of the selected strip at the end of the quilt

Notes

• When you want a quilt of only one strip style, use the Delete button to delete all strips except one. Set the style and sizes for the single strip and clone it until the desired quilt size is achieved.

• To quickly set up a strip quilt with two alternating strips, delete all but two strips in the quilt. Set the styles and sizes for each strip and put a check in "Clone the selected strip." Select the first strip and click Add. Now alternate between the left arrow (next to Selected strip) and the Add button (just below it) to quickly add the alternating strips.

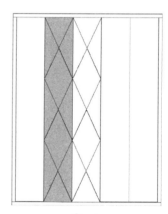

Step 4
Insert puts a copy in front of the selected strip

Click the left arrow and the Add button repeatedly to quickly add alternating strips

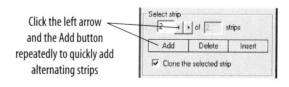

Step 1

Step 2

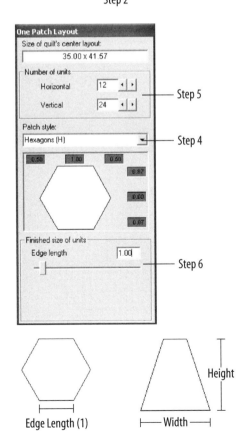

Edge Length (1) ⊢— Width —⊣

Making a One Patch Quilt

1   Click **WORKTABLE > Work on Quilt**.

2   Click **QUILT > New Quilt > One Patch Quilt**.
    A blank One Patch layout will appear.

3   Click the **Layout** tab.

4   Under **Patch style**, click the down arrow on the
    Patch style box. Click a style name in the list to
    choose your patch type.

5   Under **Number of units**, click the arrows for
    Horizontal and Vertical to set the number of
    patches. See the EQ6 Help Contents if you
    question how patches are counted.

6   Under **Finished size of units**, choose the size
    you want. For some styles you choose Width
    and Height, and for others, Edge length.
    Change the size in any of the following ways:

    • type a new size in the box

    • drag the slider rectangle on the line

    • click to the right or left of the slider rectangle
      to have the number jump in increments

7   Click the **Borders** tab to adjust, add, delete or
    insert borders, see page 185.

8   Click the **Layer 1** tab to work on your quilt.

Notes
• To make adjustments on the Layout tab faster, you can use
  the keyboard TAB key to cycle between entries and type
  immediately.

• How blocks are measured:
  Edge length is the length of a side of a hexagon/octagon.
  Height is the vertical measurement through the patch from
  the lowest point to the highest.
  Width is the horizontal measurement through the patch
  from the furthest left point to the furthest right.

• You may want to see page 200 for information on the new
  EQ6 Paintbrush coloring options.

Making a One Patch Quilt

Making Custom Patches in a One Patch Quilt

Custom patches start like other patch styles, but you can change their shape. Custom patches have light gray "glides," which run horizontally or vertically from the patch corners (see step 7 picture). Pull on the glides to make the shape. (These glides do not appear on the quilt, just on the One Patch Layout box.)

Step 1

1 Click **WORKTABLE > Work on Quilt**.

2 Click **QUILT > New Quilt > One Patch Quilt**. A blank One Patch Quilt layout will appear.

3 Click the **Layout** tab.

4 Under **Patch style**, click the drop down arrow to choose either **Custom** or **Custom (Glide)**. They are the first and last choices in the list.

Step2

5 Under **Number of units**, click the arrows beside Horizontal and Vertical to choose the number of blocks you want. (You can also type in these boxes.) See the EQ6 Help Contents if you question how patches are counted. It may not be obvious.

6 Under **Finished size of units**, choose the size you want for Width and Height.

7 Position your cursor over one of the gray glides in the display beneath **Patch style**. Click, hold, and drag the glide to a different position. When you release the mouse, the patch will fill the quilt.

8 Click the **Borders** tab to adjust, add, delete or insert borders, see page 185.

9 Click the **Layer 1** tab to begin coloring your Custom One Patch.

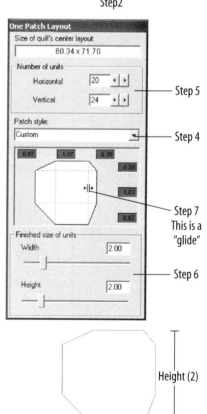

Notes
- How blocks are measured: Height is the vertical measurement through the patch from the lowest point to the highest. Width is the horizontal measurement through the patch from the furthest left point to the furthest right.

Step 1
Set Block

Step 2

Step 2
Click the colored block you want to set

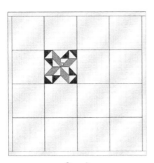

Step 3

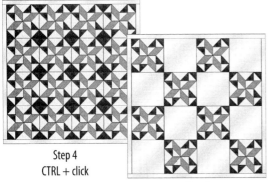

Step 4
CTRL + click

Step 4
ALT + click

Setting Blocks into a Quilt Layout

To set blocks you need a block in your Sketchbook, and a quilt layout on the screen, see pages 128-129 and 148.

These instructions are for layouts other than One Patch and blank Custom Set quilts. You can only set fabric and color in One Patch quilts (not blocks). For Custom Set, see Chapter 5 (page 165).

1   **Click the Set Block tool > click a block in the palette**.

2   *(Optional)* **Right-click on the block > choose Select Coloring > click the colored block you want to set**. (You will see only a line drawing if your block has not been colored.)

3   Click a block space on your quilt. The selected block will pop into the quilt.

4   *(Optional)* Hold down the **CTRL key** as you click to set the block into all spaces on that layer. Or, hold down the **ALT key** as you click to set blocks into alternate spaces on that layer. Some layouts require more than one click to fill.

5   *(Optional)* Click in a sash, corner block, border block, or border strip. The selected block will stretch to fit the space.

Notes

• Blocks cannot be set into mitered borders.

• To replace one block with another, just set the new block on top of the old. You do not need to erase or delete the block.

• To remove a block immediately after you've set it, choose EDIT > Undo. Or, click on it with the Erase Block tool.

• When you color a block, your coloring is stacked on top of the block drawing – up to 10 different colorings. This avoids having a new block form each time you recolor and save. To see all colorings on a block, see step 2. See page 204 for more on how colorings work.

• To set a plain block, click the block space with the Erase Block tool, then use the Paintbrush tool to color it with a fabric or color.

Setting Blocks in a Quilt Layout

Erasing a Block

You can use the Erase Block tool to erase blocks in any quilt.

Step 2
Erase Block

1   Click the layer tab on which you originally set the block you want to erase.

2   Click the **Erase Block** tool.

3   Click on the block in the quilt. The block will disappear, leaving a blank space in your quilt.

4   *If you are on the Layer 2 tab or Layer 3 tab, or are using a Custom Set quilt,* the Erase Block tool does not "delete" motifs or stencils. It will leave a blank block outline. To remove the blank block, click the **Adjust** tool, click on the block, and press your keyboard **DELETE key**.

Step 3 ——

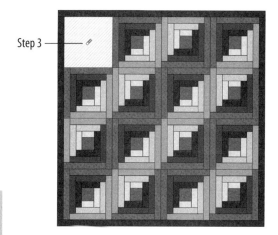

Notes

- If you change your mind after erasing, click EDIT > Undo to restore the block. This must be done immediately after erasing, before you click anywhere else.

- CTRL+click erases *every* block in your quilt.

  ALT+click erases *alternate* blocks in your quilt.

  On some complex quilt layout styles, you'll need to repeat these steps to erase alternates or all.

- Erasing is not really necessary since it's quicker to just replace a "wrong" block with a "right" block in one step by clicking the new block on top of the old.

- To set a plain block, click the block space with the Erase Block tool, then use the Paintbrush tool to color it with a fabric or color. For Custom Set quilts, see page 170.

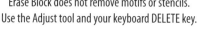

Step 4
Erase Block does not remove motifs or stencils.
Use the Adjust tool and your keyboard DELETE key.

Step 4
Adjust

Symmetrical block

Asymmetrical block

Step 1
Rotate Block

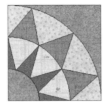

Original Block

1 click - 90 degrees

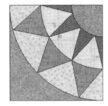

2 clicks - 180 degrees

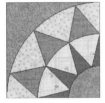

3 clicks - 270 degrees

4 clicks - 360 degrees
(Back to original)

Step 1
Flip Block

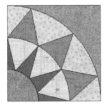

Original Block

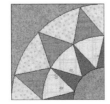

1 click -
Flips block horizontally

Rotating or Flipping Blocks

The Rotate Block and Flip Block tools work on all blocks (including motifs and stencils) set in the quilt. The block being rotated of flipped must be asymmetric (not the same on all sides) to notice a rotation or flip.

Rotating Blocks

Go to the layer on which you set the block (or motif or stencil).

1 **Click the Rotate Block tool > click any asymmetrical block in the quilt**. It will rotate 90 degrees clockwise with each click. If you click too quickly, your click may not register, so click again.

2 Click **Add to Sketchbook** to save your quilt with any rotations you like.

Flipping Blocks

Go to the layer on which you set the block (or motif or stencil).

1 **Click the Flip Block tool > click a block in the quilt**. It will flip (mirror) horizontally (from left to right) with each click.

2 Click **Add to Sketchbook** to save your quilt with any flipped block arrangement you like.

Notes

- CTRL+click rotates *every* block in your quilt on that layer.

  ALT+click rotates *alternate* blocks in your quilt on that layer (Layer 1 only).

- Rotating and flipping works on sashes and borders as well as the main body of the quilt.

- Your rotation is not limited to 90 degrees in a Custom Set layout, or on Layer 2 or 3, see pages 176-177.

- These tools do not work on photos, embroidery or text. Instead, see pages 176-177.

Creating Fast Designs with Symmetry

The Symmetry tool automates flipping and rotation on all blocks simultaneously. It works on Layer 1 for all layouts, but works best with a Horizontal layout with no sashing, as in the example. ***Be sure to choose asymmetrical blocks, which are not the same on all sides.***

Start with a quilt on your screen (see page 149) and blocks in your Sketchbook (see page 128).

1 **Click the Set Block tool > click any asymmetrical block in the Blocks palette**.

2 Hold down your keyboard **CTRL key** and click a block space on your quilt. The selected block will pop into every block space in the quilt. (You can combine different blocks in your quilt and still use the Symmetry tool.)

3 Click the **Symmetry** tool.

4 Hold down your keyboard **CTRL key** and click on the quilt. There are 16 different symmetries built into the tool, so you can click 16 times to see all the variations.

5 Click **Add to Sketchbook** to save any quilt design you like.

Notes

- If your quilt design doesn't change as you click, check your block. It must be asymmetric (not the same on all sides) in color or design, to make symmetries noticeable.

- Some layouts require more than one CTRL+click to fill. If it takes more than one CTRL+click to set blocks into the layout chosen, then it will also take the same number of times to CTRL+click when using the Symmetry tool.

- If you replace rotated blocks, the new blocks will also be rotated. To turn this feature off, go to QUILT > Options > Setting Blocks (under Tool Options) and uncheck *Maintain the block rotation from the current quilt when replacing blocks* > click OK.

Symmetrical block

Asymmetrical block

Step 1
Set Block

Step 2
CTRL+click to fill every block space in the quilt

Step 3
Symmetry

A few examples of the 16 possible symmetries

Quilt designed by Kathleen Potvin
Andrews, Indiana

Custom Set Quilts
and Layers 2 & 3
Chapter 5

There are times when the design you've imagined doesn't seem to fit any layout available in EQ6. When your quilt requires a special layout, then it's time for Custom Set. Custom Set gives you a large blank layout space. There, you can set any blocks, in any sizes, any place on the quilt; rotating them at any angle you want. To multiply your design possibilities, you can use Layers 2 and 3. While Layer 2 is typically used for floating appliqué elements on your quilt, and Layer 3 is for quilting stitches, this chapter will suggest other uses. It will also explain exactly how to use the versatile tools in Custom Set and Layers 2 and 3.

Reference

Using Layers and the Graph Pad

Layers

Every quilt you create has 3 layers. Whether you decide to use all 3 is up to you.

Typically, Layer 1 is used for blocks, Layer 2 is used for appliqué motifs (such as leaves, flowers, or text that you "float" on top of your pieced quilt), and Layer 3 is for thread (quilting stencils and embroidery). Photos can go on any layer.

Graph Pad

The Graph Pad is a necessity when working with Custom Set quilts, Layer 2, or Layer 3. The Graph Pad gives you control of a block's size, position, and rotation, among other things. It appears as an extra bar across the top of your screen, below menus and toolbars. To add the Graph Pad to your screen, click **VIEW > Graph Pad**.

Changes to blocks, motifs, and stencils are made using the **Adjust** tool. You will not see the Graph Pad numbers or buttons until you select an item with the **Adjust** tool.

Position

The first set of numbers denotes the position. These are in X and Y coordinates. The top number is for horizontal position; the bottom for vertical position. These numbers tell EQ6 where to put the top-left corner of your block in relation to the upper-left corner of the quilt center (border not included). On the Graph Pad there is a small block outline with a little white square denoting what point you are positioning. If you rotate a block, this small outline changes as well. See pages 176-177.

Rotation

The second part of the Graph Pad denotes rotation. The item's position can be rotated a full 360 degrees, from -180 to 180. See pages 176-177. (The Rotate Block tool only rotates the design within the block, and doesn't affect the block position on the quilt.)

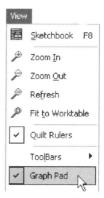

Click to put a check next to Graph Pad on the VIEW menu

Adjust

The Graph Pad appears below the
Project toolbar at the top of the screen

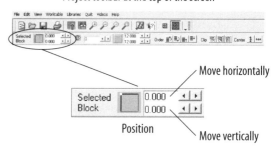

Move horizontally

Position

Move vertically

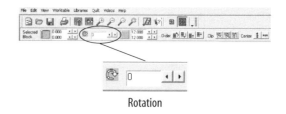

Rotation

Using Layers and the Graph Pad

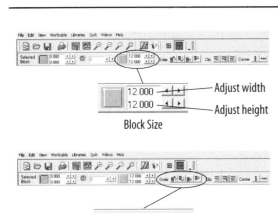

Adjust width
Adjust height

Block Size

Order - One Block Selected

Clip - One Block Selected

Center - One Block Selected

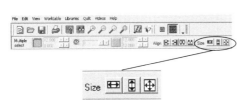

Align - Multiple Blocks Selected

Size - Multiple Blocks Selected

Block Size

The third part of the Graph Pad denotes the size. The top number is for the width, the bottom for the height. If you rotate a block, these numbers do not change. See pages 176-177.

Graph Pad Buttons

The Graph Pad buttons change depending on the number of blocks selected at once. *To select one block,* click it with the Adjust tool. *To select multiple blocks,* click the block you want to be your anchor (the block that all other blocks need to follow) and then SHIFT+click the other blocks.

Order – One Block Selected

Order controls the layering or stacking order of items on this layer. Although your blocks or motifs can be side by side, you may want them to overlap in some instances. Use these buttons to send the selected block to the front, up one, down one, or to the back. See page 179.

Clip – One Block Selected

The clipping tools are used for controlling how your blocks behave with respect to the borders. Use these buttons to let the block extend past the quilt and its borders, clip the block to remain within the quilt, or clip the block to remain within the borders. See page 180.

Center – One Block Selected

You can center the selected block horizontally or vertically within the quilt. Click both buttons if you want it centered exactly in the center of the quilt. See page 181.

Align – Multiple Blocks Selected

These buttons align the lefts, rights, tops, or bottoms of the selected blocks, in relation to the first block selected. See page 182.

Size – Multiple Blocks Selected

These buttons make the selected blocks the same width, height, or both, in relation to the first block selected. See page 183.

Using Layers and the Graph Pad

Making a Custom Set Quilt

Custom Set can be filled with large and small blocks together in one quilt. This layout style starts out as a large blank space that you can fill with any blocks, any size, anywhere on your quilt.

Step 1

All other layout styles have shortcuts for filling the layout quickly. No shortcuts are possible with Custom Set, because anything goes! Create the layout by setting each individual block exactly as you want it.

1   Click **WORKTABLE > Work on Quilt**.

2   Click **QUILT > New Quilt > Custom Set**. A blank Custom Set layout will appear.

3   Click the **Layout** tab.

4   Under **Size of center rectangle**, choose the size you want for width and height. You can change the size in any of the following ways:

- type a new size in the box

- drag the slider rectangle on the line

- click to the right or left of the slider rectangle to have the number jump in increments

5   Click the **Borders** tab to adjust, add, delete or insert borders. See page 185.

6   Click the **Layer 1** tab to work on the base layer of your quilt.

Step 2

Step 4

Notes

- To make adjustments faster, you can use the keyboard TAB key to cycle between entries and type immediately.

- Making a Custom Set quilt is much easier with the Graph Pad turned on. To learn how to use the Graph Pad, see page 166.

- Please refer to pages 169 and 176-177 for more on setting and manipulating blocks in a Custom Set quilt.

Step 2
Set Block

Step 2

Step 3

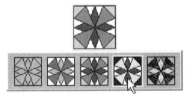

Step 3
Select the block with the coloring you want to use

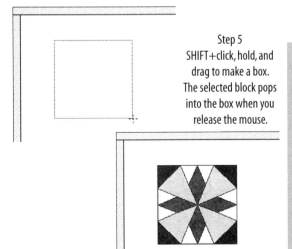

Step 5
SHIFT+click, hold, and drag to make a box. The selected block pops into the box when you release the mouse.

Setting Blocks, Motifs and Stencils

Begin with a quilt layout (see page 148) and blocks, motifs, or stencils in your Sketchbook (see page 128).

1   Click the **Layer 1** tab to set blocks in a Custom Set quilt. Click **Layer 2** to set appliqué motifs in any quilt. Click **Layer 3** to set stencils or embroidery in any quilt.

2   **Click the Set Block tool > inside the palette click the tab the design is on (Blocks, Motifs, or Stencils) > click the design to select it**.

3   *(Optional)* **Right-click on the block > choose Select Coloring > click the colored block you want to set**.

4   Hold down the **SHIFT key** on your keyboard and move your cursor over the center of the quilt.

5   Click and hold as you drag diagonally on the quilt to make a box. (Don't worry about size or position now. See pages 176-177.) The selected block will pop from the palette into the box when you release the mouse. (Laptop/touchpad users see page 9 if you're having difficulties.)

6   To delete a block, click the Adjust tool, click the block in the quilt, and press your keyboard DELETE key.

Notes

• You can adjust block size, position, rotation, and more with the Adjust tool and Graph Pad. See pages 176-177.

• Custom Set gives you a blank canvas to work on. If you would rather have "guides" behind your Custom Set quilt to help you see where to set blocks, try setting your blocks in Layer 2 over a Horizontal quilt instead. Change the Horizontal layout to have 2" or 3" blocks and a large number of blocks horizontally and vertically. Set the blocks in Layer 2 and drag out blocks to cover the squares. You will still want to use the Adjust tool to make the size and position precise.

Setting Blocks, Motifs, Stencils

Setting Plain Blocks in a Quilt

1   **Click the Set Block tool > right-click inside
     the Sketchbook Blocks palette > click Add
     Plain Block**. A plain square will appear in your
     Blocks palette. It is already selected and ready to
     be set.

2   Hold down the **SHIFT key** on your keyboard
     and move your cursor over the center of the
     quilt where you want the plain block.

3   Click and hold as you drag diagonally to make a
     box on the quilt. The plain block will pop from
     the palette into the quilt when you release the
     mouse. (To move or resize, see pages 176-177.)

4   **Click the Paintbrush tool > click a fabric
     or color in the Fabrics and Colors palette >
     click the plain block** you just set on your
     quilt to color it. When you add your quilt to the
     Sketchbook, the plain block's color will become
     a coloring of the plain block in the palette.

Notes

• To set plain blocks in layouts other than Custom Set, it is
  best to erase what is there with the Erase Block tool, then
  color the empty space with the Paintbrush tool.

• When you color a block, your coloring is stacked on top of
  the block drawing – up to 10 different colorings can stack
  on the same block. This avoids having a new block form each
  time you color any patch on the quilt. To see all colorings
  on any block, right-click on the block (in the Blocks palette
  or Sketchbook) > choose Select Coloring. You can also use
  the coloring arrows found on the Palette and Sketchbook
  beneath the blocks to page through the various colorings.
  See page 204 for more information on block colorings.

Step 1
Set Block

Step 1

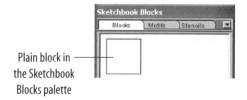

Plain block in
the Sketchbook
Blocks palette

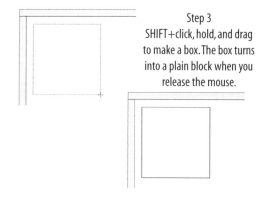

Step 3
SHIFT+click, hold, and drag
to make a box. The box turns
into a plain block when you
release the mouse.

Step 4
Paintbrush

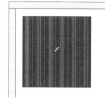

Click the plain
block to color it

Setting Plain Blocks in a Quilt

Step 3
Set Embroidery

Step 4
Click, hold, and drag to set an embroidery design

Draft Quality   3 Dimensional

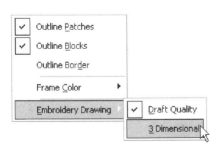

Change the embroidery display to 3 dimensional

Setting Embroidery in a Quilt

Embroideries must be set on Layer 3. To set embroidery on your quilt, you need an embroidery design in your Sketchbook (see pages 128 or 140) and the Set Embroidery tool on your toolbar (see page 302).

1 Start on the Quilt worktable with a quilt on the screen.

2 Click the **Layer 3** tab.

3 **Click the Set Embroidery tool > click the embroidery design in the palette**.

4 **Hold down your keyboard SHIFT key > position your cursor over the quilt where you want to place the embroidery > click and hold as you drag diagonally to make a box > release the mouse**. The selected embroidery will pop from the palette into the box when you release the mouse. Don't worry about size or position now. See pages 176-177.

Notes
- The embroidery designs included with EQ6 cannot be digitized. They are only images of the real digitizable designs. The digitizable designs are sold and copyrighted by the embroidery manufacturers. Contact the manufacturer listed on the notecard for specific information regarding the actual digitizable embroidery.

- Please note that EQ6 will let you manipulate the designs to a greater extent than you may be able to sew them. When you purchase the actual designs, they will always stitch as rectangles in a precise size.

- To print an individual embroidery design, see page 282.

- Use the Thread tool to recolor embroideries, see page 205.

- Embroidery is displayed in draft quality by default. To change to 3-Dimensional, right-click on the quilt > point to Embroidery Drawing > click 3 Dimensional, to check it.

- The Rotate and Flip tools do not work on embroideries. To rotate an embroidery, see pages 176-177.

Setting Embroidery in a Quilt

Writing on Your Quilt

EQ6 is not a word processor, but it lets you "write" on your quilt. You can print appliqué text as templates to get the patterns for each letter.

1   **Click the Paintbrush tool > click a fabric or solid color you want for your text > click Layer 2 > click the Set Applique Text tool**. (If, on Layer 2, you do not see the Set Applique Text, add it to your toolbar, see page 302.)

2   It may take a few moments for the box to appear. Once the **Applique Text** box appears, under **Select typeface**, click the down arrow to drop down your list of font choices. These are the TrueType fonts installed on your computer.

3   **Click on any typeface, to select it**. (You can always change the typeface later.)

4   Drag the size slider bar to set a starting size. (You can change the size later.) This size is approximate (font sizes vary depending on the style). Rely on how the text looks on your quilt.

5   Choose any additional formatting options you want: bold, italics, underlining, and alignment. Be aware all choices you make will apply to all words in the same text box.

6   **Hold down your keyboard SHIFT key > point your mouse cursor at the quilt > click and hold as you drag diagonally to make a box > release the mouse**. A text box forms. Don't worry about the size of the box because it resizes to a small box which enlarges when you type.

7   Start typing and you'll see your text. The text won't wrap, so to make a new line of text, press your keyboard **ENTER key**. You control how long each text line is, and how many lines there are. While the Applique Text box is still up, you can resize or choose a different font (see steps 2-4 above) and your font will change on the quilt.

Step 1
Paintbrush

Step 1
Set Applique Text

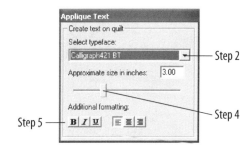

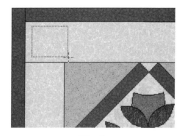

Step 6
SHIFT+click, hold, and drag to make a box.

Step 7

Step 8
Adjust

Click, hold, and drag the text box to a new location

Step 9
Adjust

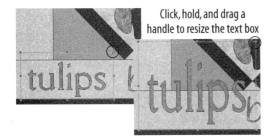

Click, hold, and drag a handle to resize the text box

Each word above is in a separate text box, allowing different typefaces to be used for each one

8 *To move the text box,* **click the Adjust tool > click the text box to select it > click and hold in the center of the text box as you drag it to a new location.**

9 *To resize the text box,* **click the Adjust tool > click the text box to select it > click and hold on a handle of the text box and drag the handle to a new location.**

Notes

- All text in one box will have the same format. To make letters or words different styles than the rest of the text they must be in their own separate text boxes. You must have a *new* text box for each different typeface, size, format or text color.

- To change the text after it has been deselected, click the Set Applique Text tool, click the text box to reselect it, and resize or choose a different font as described in steps 2-5.

- To recolor, use any of the color tools. Recoloring one letter will recolor all letters in the same text box.

- To quickly align or size multiple text boxes, see pages 182-183.

- The Rotate and Flip tools do not work on text boxes. To rotate a whole text box, you will need to use the Adjust tool and/or Graph Pad, see pages 176-177. Finish editing before rotating. You will lose any changes made with the Adjust tool if you try to edit you text again with the Set Applique Text tool.

- Text prints only as templates and all letters in the selected box will print together. Remember to be on Layer 2, click the text box with the Select tool and click "Use size from quilt." See pages 274-275 if you only want to print one letter.

- You can't highlight or copy and paste text. You can only copy and paste entire text boxes (with the Adjust tool).

- Some font styles require special formatting (bold, italics). If this formatting is removed, the text may disappear. See the EQ6 Help Contents for more help.

- To preview font styles, use a word processing program, like Microsoft Word, by choosing FORMAT > Font.

Writing on Your Quilt

Setting Photos in a Quilt

You can set a photo on Layers 2 or 3 of any quilt, but only on Layer 1 of a Horizontal or Custom Set layout. To set photos in your quilt, you need a photo in your Sketchbook (see pages 128 or 138) and the Set Photo tool on your toolbar (see page 302). Photos can come from the Photo Library or be imported. Import photos at the same proportion as the block space you plan to set the photo into. So, if you know you want to make your photos square on your quilt, crop them in your photo program to make them square before importing them into EQ6.

Setting Photos on Layer 1 of a Horizontal Layout

1   Start with a horizontal quilt.

2   Click the **Layer 1** tab.

3   **Click the Set Photo tool > click the photo in the Sketchbook Photos palette**.

4   Click the block space on the quilt. The photo will fill the block space.

Setting Photos on Custom Set or Layers 2 or 3

1   Start with any style quilt.

2   Click the layer tab on which you want to set a photo. (Layer 1 (Custom Set only), 2 or 3)

3   **Click the Set Photo tool > click the photo in the Sketchbook Photos palette**.

4   **Hold down your keyboard SHIFT key > position your cursor over the quilt where you want the photo > click and hold as you drag diagonally to make a box > release the mouse**. (Laptop/touchpad users see page 9 if you're having difficulties.) The photo will pop into the box. Don't worry about size or placement yet, see pages 176-177.

> **Notes**
> • Photos must be set as squares or rectangles. They will not clip to fit triangles, for example.
>
> • Photos can be rotated on Custom Set, Layers 2 or 3 only, using the Adjust tool. See pages 176-177.

Step 3
Set Photo

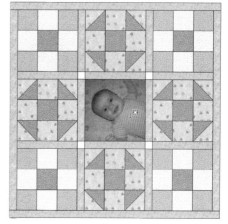

Step 4
On Layer 1, click the block space

Step 4
On a Custom Set quilt, or Layers 2 or 3,
SHIFT+click, hold, and drag to make a box

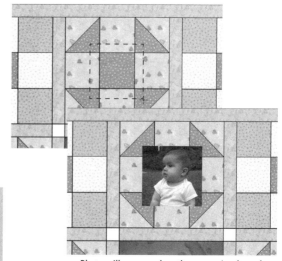

Photo will appear when the mouse is released.
Adjust size and position with the Adjust tool.

Step 2

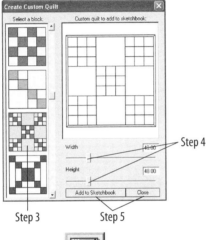

Step 3   Step 5

Step 4

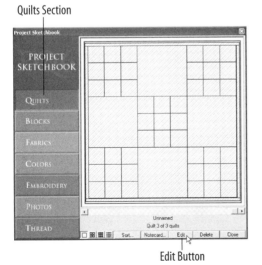

Step 6
View Sketchbook

Quilts Section

Edit Button

Creating a Quilt from a Block

EQ6 can turn a block into a quilt layout, but the block *must have only horizontal and vertical lines.*

1   Start with blocks in your Sketchbook and the Sketchbook closed.

2   Click **QUILT > Create Quilt from Block**. Under **Select a block**, Sketchbook blocks with only horizontal and vertical lines will be shown in a column. At the right, you will see a quilt layout, made from the selected block.

3   You may need to drag the vertical scrollbar to see all the blocks. **Click any block to see it shown as a layout.**

4   Drag the Width and Height sliders or type in the boxes to set the Custom Set quilt size. (Choose a size proportional to the block's grid.)

5   Click the **Add to Sketchbook** button to add the quilt layout to the Sketchbook. Add as many quilts as you'd like. Click **Close** when finished.

6   To use the layout, **click View Sketchbook > click the Quilts section > find and click the quilt layout > click the Edit button**. Your layout is ready to fill with blocks and color.

Notes

• Add new layouts to your My Library, see pages 143-144.

• Here are three ways to resize your new Custom Set layouts:

1) QUILT > Options > under Layout Options click All styles > make sure "Don't resize content of layers when resizing quilt" is *not* checked > OK. When you change the numbers on the Layout tab, the blocks will size proportionally together, still filling the quilt.

2) QUILT > Options > under Layout Options click All styles > make sure "Don't resize content of layers when resizing quilt" *is* checked > OK. When you change the numbers on the Layout tab, the blocks will keep their current sizes and stay in the upper-left corner of the quilt.

3) Skip all the Quilt Options and just use the Adjust tool and Graph Pad to set the block sizes, see pages 176-177.

Creating a Quilt from a Block

Moving, Resizing, Rotating, and Skewing Blocks

Begin with a quilt layout and blocks set on Layer 1 of a Custom Set quilt or Layers 2 or 3 of any quilt layout, see page 169.

1   Click the Layer tab on which the block is set. (Blocks are on **Layer 1** of a Custom Set quilt. Motifs and text are on **Layer 2**. Stencils and embroidery are on **Layer 3**).

2   Click the **Adjust** tool.

3   **Click on the block in the quilt to select it**. It will have a dotted box around it with little black squares at the sides and corners. These squares are "handles" and are used to modify the block.

Using the Handles of the Selected Block

4   *To move the block* – position your cursor inside the dotted box so your cursor looks like a cross with arrows. Click and hold as you drag the block to a new location.

To resize the block – position your cursor over one of the handles so your cursor looks like a double-ended arrow. Click and hold as you drag the handle to a new location. The selected block will resize as you move the handle.

To rotate the block – hold down your keyboard **CTRL key** and click in the center of the block. Position your cursor over one of the corner handles. Click and hold the corner handle as you move it around the center of the block. The block will spin around its center and stop when you release the mouse button.

To skew the block – hold down your keyboard **CTRL key** and click in the center of the block. Position your cursor over one of the side handles (watch for your cursor to change to two parallel lines). Click and hold as you slide the side handle up/down or left /right to a new position. The selected block will reshape itself as you move the side handle.

Step 2
Adjust

Moving a Block (click in the center and drag to new location)

Cursor becomes a cross with arrows

Resizing a Block (click and drag handle)

Cursor becomes a double-ended arrow when held over the handles

Cursor

Rotating a Block (CTRL + click and spin handle)

Cursor becomes a circle with an arrow on one end when held over the corner handles

 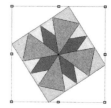

Skewing a Block (CTRL + click and slide side handle)

Cursor becomes two parallel lines when held over the side handles

Step 5

Using the Graph Pad with the Selected Block

5 If you do not see the Graph Pad at the top of your screen below the toolbars or menus, click **VIEW > Graph Pad** on the menu bar.

6 If you want to type directly in a box, highlight the text first and then type to replace it. You can use the **TAB key** on your keyboard to go from box to box in the Graph Pad and the text will automatically highlight for you.

7 *To move the block* – use the arrows next to the first set of numbers or type directly in the boxes to change the position. These are in X and Y coordinates starting from the top-left corner of the quilt center (borders not included). On the Graph Pad there is a small block outline with a little white square denoting what point you are positioning.

   To resize the block – use the arrows next to the third set of numbers or type directly in the boxes to change the size.

   To rotate the block – use the second section of the Graph Pad to change the rotation. Rotations go from -180 to 180 degrees. Use the arrows or type directly in the boxes to change the rotation. If you want to type a negative rotation, go first to a negative number using the left arrow, then highlight the numbers after the negative sign and type.

   To skew the block – you cannot skew a block using the Graph Pad. Please see Step 4 "To skew the block."

8 Click outside of the dotted selection box to deselect the block.

Move the block   Resize the block

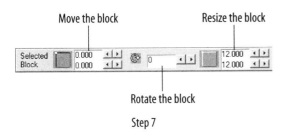

Rotate the block

Step 7

Notes

- If you don't like the changes you made, click EDIT > Undo.

- Flipping a block works the same way for all quilt styles and layers, see page 163. You cannot flip embroideries, photos, or appliqué text.

Move, Resize, Rotate, Skew

Copying & Pasting or Deleting Blocks

Begin with a quilt layout and blocks set on Layer 1 of a Custom Set quilt or Layer 2 or 3 of any layout, see page 169.

Step 2
Adjust

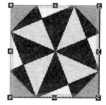

Step 3
Click the block to select it

1 Click the Layer tab on which the block is set. (Blocks are on **Layer 1** of a Custom Set quilt. Motifs and text are on **Layer 2**. Stencils and embroidery are on **Layer 3**.)

2 Click the **Adjust** tool.

3 **Click the block in the quilt to select it.**

4 *To copy and paste the block* – choose **EDIT > Copy**, then **EDIT > Paste** if using the menu. Or, **Press CTRL+C, then CTRL+V** on your keyboard to do the same thing. The pasted block is still selected, so you can click and hold in its center, and drag to move it (see pages 176-177).

To delete the block – choose **EDIT > Clear** from the menu or press your keyboard **DELETE key**.

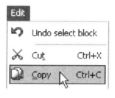

Step 4
Copy & Paste

The pasted block will appear down and to the right of the original block

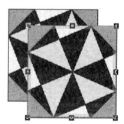

Notes
- You can also add buttons to your toolbar for Cut, Copy, and Paste, see page 301. Then, once a block is selected with the Adjust tool, you can use the toolbar buttons instead of the menu or your keyboard. Cut will work similarly to Delete; the item will disappear and go to your clipboard, but you can choose whether you want to paste it or not.

Step 4
Delete

Toolbar buttons

Cut   Copy   Paste

Copying & Pasting or Deleting

Step 2
Adjust

Step 3

Initial stacking order

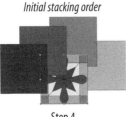

Step 4
Click block to re-stack

Send to Front   Send Up

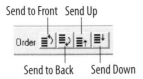

Send to Back   Send Down

Stacking Blocks

Begin with a quilt layout and blocks set on Layer 1 of a Custom Set quilt or Layer 2 or 3 of any layout, see page 169.

You can layer blocks simply by moving them on top of one another, but they may not overlap in the order you like. To change the stacking order you must have the Graph Pad turned on.

1 Click the Layer tab on which the block is set. (Blocks are on **Layer 1** of a Custom Set quilt. Motifs and text are on **Layer 2**. Stencils and embroidery are on **Layer 3**.)

2 Click the **Adjust** tool.

3 Be sure the Graph Pad is turned on. Click **VIEW > Graph Pad** if you do not see it below the top menu and toolbars.

4 **Click the block in the quilt** you want to re-stack.

5 Click any of the four **Order** buttons on the Graph Pad to change the stacking order.

A Send to Front will make the selected block the top-most block.

B Send to Back will make the selected block the lowest block.

C Send Up will move the selected block up one in the stacking order.

D Send Down will move the selected block down one in the stacking order.

Notes
• This technique is great for appliqué motifs stacked in the corners of borders that need to overlap.

A

Send to Front

B

Send to Back

C

Send Up

D

Send Down

Stacking Blocks

Clipping Block Designs at the Border

Begin with a quilt layout and blocks set in Layer 1 of a Custom Set quilt or Layer 2 or 3 of any layout, see page 169.

You will not notice any change in blocks set in the center of your quilt. Blocks must be at the edge of the quilt center or overlapping a border to notice the clipping.

1   Click the Layer tab on which the block is set. (Blocks are on **Layer 1** of a Custom Set quilt. Motifs and text are on **Layer 2**. Stencils and embroidery are on **Layer 3**.)

2   Click the **Adjust** tool.

3   Be sure the Graph Pad is turned on. Click **VIEW > Graph Pad** if you do not see it below the top menu and toolbars.

4   **Click the block in the quilt** you want to clip.

5   Click any of the three **Clip** buttons on the Graph Pad to change the way your blocks behave at the borders.

   Do not clip will allow the block to hang over and past the quilt's outer border.

   Clip to border of quilt will clip the block at the outer edge of the quilt.

   Clip to center rectangle of quilt will clip the block to stay within the quilt center (stop before the borders).

Notes
• This technique works well for stencils set on Layer 3 of on-point quilts that need to be over the quilt blocks, but not over the borders.

Step 2
Adjust

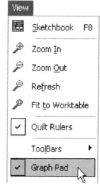

Step 3

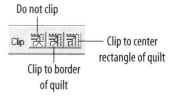

Do not clip

Clip

Clip to center
rectangle of quilt

Clip to border
of quilt

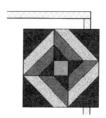

Do not clip

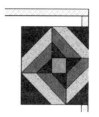

Clip to border of quilt

Clip to center
rectangle of quilt

Step 2
Adjust

Step 3

Center vertically

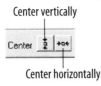

Center horizontally

Original block position

Center vertically

Center horizontally

Center both vertically and horizontally

Centering Blocks

Begin with a quilt layout and blocks set in Layer 1 of a Custom Set quilt or Layer 2 or 3 of any layout, see page 169.

1   Click the Layer tab on which the block is set. (Blocks are on **Layer 1** of a Custom Set quilt. Motifs and text are on **Layer 2.** Stencils and embroidery are on **Layer 3.**)

2   Click the **Adjust** tool.

3   Be sure the Graph Pad is turned on. Click **VIEW > Graph Pad** if you do not see it below the top menu and toolbars.

4   **Click the block in the quilt** you want to center.

5   Click one or both of the **Center** buttons on the Graph Pad:

   Center vertically will space the block equally between the top and bottom of the quilt center. It will not change its horizontal position.

   Center horizontally will space the block equally between the left and right sides of the quilt center. It will not change its vertical position.

   Clicking both will put the center of the block in the exact center of the quilt.

Notes
• These tools are great for when you are starting a custom set quilt with a center medallion block.

Centering Blocks

Aligning Blocks

Begin with a quilt layout and blocks set in Layer 1 of a Custom Set quilt or Layer 2 or 3 of any layout, see page 169.

When using the Align buttons, *you need to start with one block that is set in the correct position.* This block will be your anchor. All other blocks you select will move according to your anchor's position.

1 Click the Layer tab on which the blocks are set. (Blocks are on **Layer 1** of a Custom Set quilt. Motifs and text are on **Layer 2**. Stencils and embroidery are on **Layer 3**.)

2 Click the **Adjust** tool.

3 Be sure the Graph Pad is turned on. Click **VIEW > Graph Pad** if you do not see it below the top menu and toolbars.

4 **Click on your anchor block.** (The anchor block is the one positioned correctly, to which you want to align the other blocks.)

5 Hold down the **SHIFT key** on your keyboard.

6 **Click on the remaining blocks** you want to align with your anchor block.

7 Release the **SHIFT key**.

8 Click one of the four **Align** buttons on the Graph Pad:

Align Lefts will make the selected blocks line up with the left side of the anchor block.

Align Rights will make the selected blocks line up with the right side of the anchor block.

Align Tops will make the selected blocks line up with the top of the anchor block.

Align Bottoms will make the selected blocks line up with the bottom of the anchor block.

Notes
• This technique is great for lining up quilting stencils and for lining up rows of blocks in a Custom Set quilt.

Step 2
Adjust

Step 3

Click anchor block

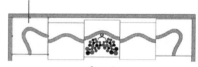

Step 4

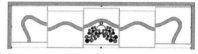

Step 6
Select remaining blocks while holding down the SHIFT key

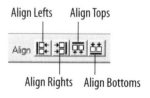

Align Lefts   Align Tops

Align Rights   Align Bottoms

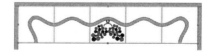

Step 8
Click one of the Align buttons
(The Align Tops button was used in this example)

Aligning Blocks

Step 2
Adjust

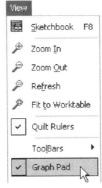

Step 3

Click anchor block

Step 4

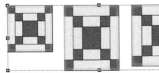

Step 6 - Select remaining blocks
while holding down the SHIFT key

Same Width   Same Size

Same Height

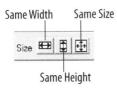

Same Width

Same Height

Same Size

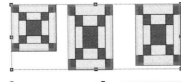

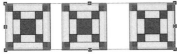

Using the Same Size Buttons

Begin with a quilt layout and blocks set in Layer 1 of a Custom Set quilt or Layer 2 or 3 of any layout, see page 169.

When using the Same Size buttons, *you need to start with one block that is the correct size.* This block will be your anchor. All other blocks you select will size according to your anchor.

1   Click the Layer tab on which the blocks are set. (Blocks are on **Layer 1** of a Custom Set quilt. Motifs and text are on **Layer 2**. Stencils and embroidery are on **Layer 3**.)

2   Click the **Adjust** tool.

3   Be sure the Graph Pad is turned on. Click **VIEW > Graph Pad** if you do not see it below the top menu and toolbars.

4   **Click on your anchor block**. (This is the block that is sized correctly.)

5   Hold down the **SHIFT key** on your keyboard.

6   **Click on the remaining blocks** you want to size according to your anchor block.

7   Release the **SHIFT key**.

8   Click one of the three **Size** buttons on the Graph Pad:

   Same Width will make the selected blocks the same horizontal width as the anchor block.

   Same Height will make the selected blocks the same vertical height as the anchor block.

   Same Size will make the selected blocks the same width and height as the anchor block.

Notes
• **This technique is great for creating Custom Set quilts where your blocks are still in rows and columns, but sometimes need to be the same height and different widths or vice versa.**

Using the Same Size Buttons

Showing and Hiding Quilt Layers

As you design, you may want to isolate the layers in order to clearly see which items are on which layer of your quilt. If so, follow the directions below to add special icons to your layer tabs, which will allow you to choose which layers to display and which to hide.

Step 1

1   Click **QUILT > Options > View Settings** (under Tool Options).

2   Under Layer Icons, click to put a check next to **Provide icons to show and hide quilt layers**.

3   Click **OK**.

4   Next to each layer tab name you will now see a light bulb icon for changing the visibility.

> *To hide a layer,* **click the icon next to the layer you want to hide.**

> *To see a hidden layer,* **click the icon to view it again.**

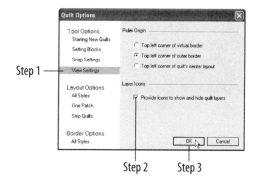

Step 1 · Step 2 · Step 3

Notes
- Items on Layer 1 will show as a transparency when Layer 1 is hidden.
- Showing and hiding layers does not impact fabric yardage. The items on those other layers are still there, even if you cannot see them.

Step 4

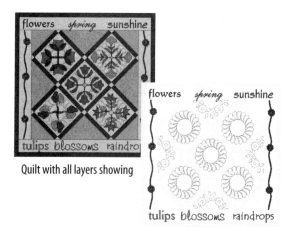

Quilt with all layers showing

Quilt with Layer 1 hidden to better see the appliqué and stencils

Quilt designed by Jo Moury
Haymarket, Virginia

Borders

Chapter 6

The border tools in EQ6 allow you great flexibility. You can build your own custom borders from scratch, choosing from 22 styles. Or you can use the Set Auto Borders tool to set pre-designed borders with a click. This chapter tells you how to use all the border styles and tools.

Reference

Choosing a Border Style

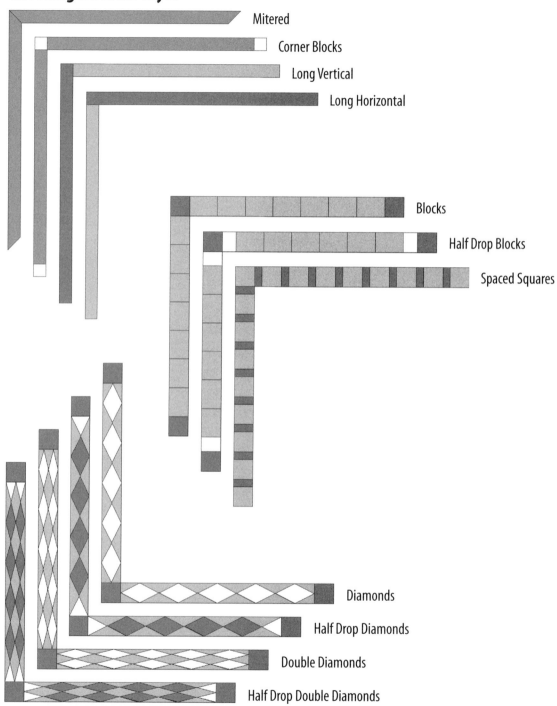

Mitered

Corner Blocks

Long Vertical

Long Horizontal

Blocks

Half Drop Blocks

Spaced Squares

Diamonds

Half Drop Diamonds

Double Diamonds

Half Drop Double Diamonds

Choosing a Border Style

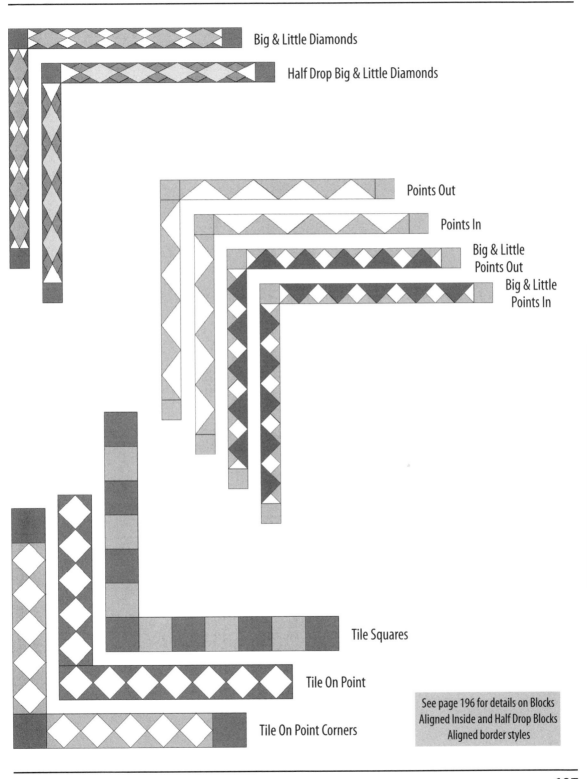

Big & Little Diamonds

Half Drop Big & Little Diamonds

Points Out

Points In

Big & Little
Points Out

Big & Little
Points In

Tile Squares

Tile On Point

Tile On Point Corners

See page 196 for details on Blocks
Aligned Inside and Half Drop Blocks
Aligned border styles

Choosing a Border Style

Making a Quilt Border

Start with a quilt on the worktable, see page 148.

1   Click the **Borders** tab. The Borders box will appear. All quilt layouts have one Long Horizontal border by default. So, the first step is to either resize this border or choose a new border style.

Border Style and Size

2   Under **Select a border style,** click the down arrow to display the choices. Drag the vertical scrollbar to see all the style names.

3   **Click any style to select it.** You can also press your keyboard up or down arrow to scroll through the list. Notice the border on your quilt changes as the style name changes.

4   To change a border size, click, hold and drag the Left, Top, Right, or Bottom slider bars one at a time. Each side can be sized independently. Or, to size them all at once to the same width, click the **All** box under **Lock size adjustments**. To make only the left and right borders adjust together, click **L+R**. To make only the top and bottom borders adjust together, click **T+B**. See page 190 for more information on locking.

Blocks in Border

The Blocks in border number boxes are only active for styles with block spaces.

5   If the number boxes are active, click the left and right arrows to select the block number you want. (In some border styles, only one number box can be changed.)

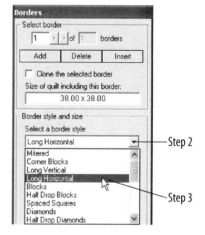

Step 2

Step 3

Step 4

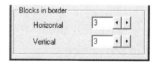

Step 5

Notes

• Each border can be a different size, but all four borders must be the same style. For a trick that gives the effect of making each border a different style see pages 194-195.

• You can set blocks into all border spaces except Mitered borders. Blocks will stretch or skew to fit the border space.

Making a Quilt Border

Before

Step 2
Adding a border

After: Long Horizontal border
added to the outside of quilt

Before

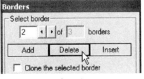

Step 2
Deleting a border

After: Diamond border
has been deleted

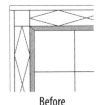

Before

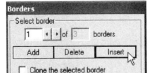

Step 2
Inserting a border

After: Long Horizontal
border inserted in front of
the Mitered border

Adding, Deleting, or Inserting a Border

Begin with a quilt layout on your screen. If you have not done this already, see page 148.

1 Click the **Borders** tab. The Borders box will appear.

2 *To add a border* – click the **Add** button on the Borders box. A blank, Long Horizontal border with 1.00" sides will be added around the outside of your quilt.

To delete a border – position your cursor directly over the quilt and click on the border you wish to delete. The border turns gray, showing it is selected. Click the **Delete** button on the Borders box. The selected border will disappear.

To insert a border – position your cursor directly over the quilt and click on the border you wish to insert another border *in front of.* Click the **Insert** button on the Borders box. A Long Horizontal border with 1.00" sides will be added in front of the border you selected.

Notes

- **To add or insert a border the same size and settings as another border on your quilt see how to clone a border on page 191.**

- **The default border style for new borders is Long Horizontal, unless you change it. Go to QUILT > Options > Starting New Quilts (under Tool Options) > change the drop down for *Default border style* > click OK.**

- **If you added or inserted a border, you can now change the border style and size, see page 188.**

Add, Delete, or Insert a Border

Sizing Borders Quickly by Locking

You can lock all border sides together, so changing one changes them all. Begin with a quilt layout with at least one border on your screen. If you have not done this already, see pages 148 and 188.

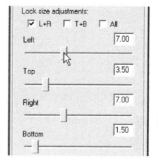
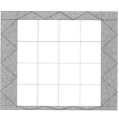

Step 3
Click *L+R* to lock the left and right borders

1   Click the **Borders** tab. The Borders box will appear.

2   **Click in the quilt on the border** you wish to change. The border turns gray, showing it is selected.

3   Under **Lock size adjustments, click to put a check next to the option(s)** you would like to lock. (**All** overrides your choices in **L+R** and **T+B**.)

The lock options are as follows:

L+R will lock the left and right sides of the border. They can still be independent from T+B.

T+B will lock the top and bottom sides of the border. They can still be independent from L+R.

All will lock all sides of the border.

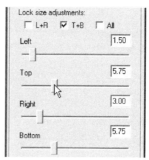
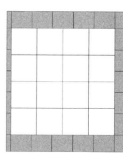

Step 3
Click *T+B* to lock the top and bottom borders

4   **Click, hold, and drag a slider bar** to size the locked borders together.

Notes
· If it is hard to get the size you want by dragging the slider bar, try these alternate ways of adjusting the size:

1) Double-click in a size box, type a size, then click the slider rectangle. All locked borders will change to the new size.

2) Position your cursor over the slider line to the left or right of the slider rectangle and click on the line. The size of all locked borders will change in increments.

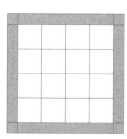

Step 3
Click *All* to lock all the borders

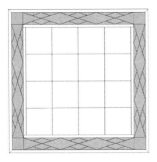

Step 2
Click to select the border you want to clone

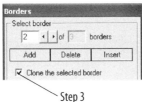

Step 3
Click to check *Clone the selected border*

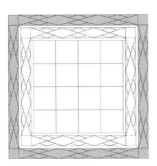

Cloned border added to the outside of the quilt

Cloning a Border

Begin with a quilt layout with at least one border that you want to clone on your screen. If you have not done this already, see pages 148 and 188.

1   Click the **Borders** tab. The Borders box will appear.

2   **Click in the quilt on the border you wish to clone.** The border turns gray, showing it is selected.

3   If there is not a check next to the **Clone the selected border** checkbox, click to put a check there. (Find it beneath the Add, Delete, and Insert buttons).

4   To put a copy of the selected border around the *outside of the quilt*, click the **Add** button. Or, to insert a border *in front of* the selected border, click the **Insert** button. A blank border with the same settings as the cloned border is added to or inserted in your quilt.

Notes
- If you clone a border, you will need to recolor or add blocks to it. EQ considers the cloned border a "new" border.

- If you want to keep your current border style, but change the layout style of the inside of your quilt, see page 193.

Cloning a Border

Step 1
Set Auto Borders

Using the Set Auto Borders Tool

Start on the Quilt worktable with the quilt to which you want to add auto borders. It must have at least one border on it to change. See pages 148 and 188.

1   Be on the **Layer 1** tab. Click the **Set Auto Borders** tool. (If you do not have the Set Auto Borders tool on your toolbar, see page 302.) The **Auto Borders** palette appears.

2   Under **Select a style,** click the down arrow to display choices. Drag the vertical scrollbar to the end of the list to see all the choices. **Click to select the style of your choice.**

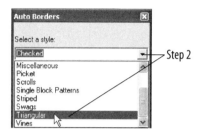

3   Drag the horizontal scrollbar (beneath the borders) to see them all. **Click to select a border.**

4   **Click the border on your quilt.** The border will fill with the auto border you selected.

5   Click the **Borders** tab.

6   *(Optional)* Drag the Left, Top, Right, or Bottom scrollbars to make the border wider or narrower.

7   *(Optional)* Under **Blocks in Border**, use the left and right arrows to change the number of blocks in the border.

8   Click the **Layer 1** tab to continue designing.

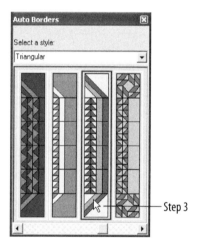

Step 3

Notes

- Auto Border blocks work just like other blocks. If you don't like them in the quilt, click a different block (or Auto Border style) on top of them.

- On the Borders tab, do not change *Border style* or your automatic border will disappear from the quilt. You can only change Width or Blocks in border.

- On the Layer 1 tab, you can color your border quickly with the Paintbrush tool and CTRL+click.

- If you like using EQ6's other border styles, but do not fill them with blocks, try using the Single Block Patterns style instead. These set as one long block and print in one pattern instead of many separate ones.

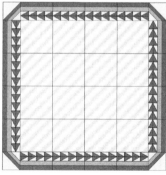

Step 4 - Click on quilt border

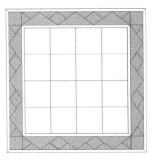

Original quilt and borders

Step 1

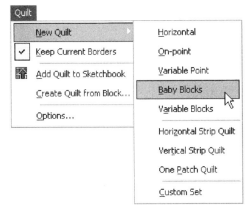

Step 2
Start a new quilt

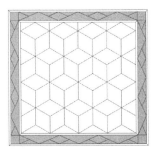

New quilt with same border styles as the original

Keeping Borders when Changing Layouts

If you have a quilt with a series of borders you like, you can reuse these borders on another quilt. When you switch to a new layout, you won't lose your current border settings, but the blocks, fabrics, or colors will erase from the border.

Start on the Quilt worktable and have the quilt with the borders you like in front of you, see pages 148 and 188.

1 Click **QUILT > Keep Current Borders** to put a check next to it. (The menu will close, so you will not see the check until the next time you use the **QUILT** menu.)

2 Now click **QUILT > New Quilt > and choose a new layout style**. You will see the new quilt layout style, with the same border style as your previous layout.

3 Set blocks (see pages 161 or 169) and color the quilt and borders (see pages 198-199) as you like.

Notes
• The Keep Current Borders option will stay turned on (have a check next to it) until you click on it again to turn it off.

Keep Borders / Change Layouts

Making Each Side a Different Style

To make one border that appears to have different styles on each side, you actually make four separate borders eliminating 3 sides on each. This is easier than it sounds.

To work on borders, you must be on the Quilt worktable and have the quilt you want to add borders to on the screen, see page 148.

1   Click the **Borders** tab. The Borders box will appear.

2   Look at the boxes under **Lock size adjustments**. Click to remove any checks so that all boxes are *unchecked*. Now each border side can be sized independently.

3   If your quilt started with a 1.00" Long Horizontal border, use this border. Otherwise, click **Add.**

Bottom Border

4   Click, hold and drag the Left, Top, and Right slider bars (not the Bottom) one at a time all the way to the left, so that size is 0.00. This eliminates all but the bottom side.

Left Border

5   Click the **Add** button. This adds a small Long Horizontal border all around your quilt.

6   Click, hold and drag the Top, Right and Bottom slider bars (not the Left) one at a time one at a time all the way to the left, so that size is 0.00. This eliminates all but the Left side from your second border.

Top Border

7   Click the **Add** button.

8   Click, hold and drag the Left, Right and Bottom slider bars (not the Top) one at a time all the way to the left, so that size is 0.00. This eliminates all but the Top side from your third border. Your Bottom and Left borders will still appear, since they are part of your first and second borders.

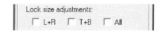

Step 2
Remove all checks under Lock size adjustments

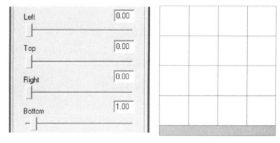

Step 4

Step 5

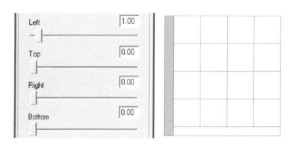

Step 6

Step 7

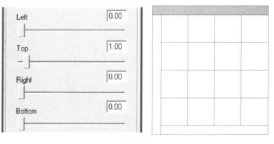

Step 8

Make Each Side a Different Style

Step 9

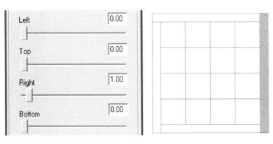

Step 10

Right Border

9   Click the **Add** button.

10   Click, hold and drag the Left, Top and Bottom slider bars (not the Right) one at a time all the way to the left, so that size is 0.00. This eliminates all but the Right side from your fourth border. Your Top, Bottom and Left borders will still appear, since they are part of your first, second and third borders.

Modify Sizes, Styles and Number of Blocks

11   Click directly on a border in the quilt to select it.

12   Under **Select a border style,** click the down arrow to display border style choices and click on a name to select it. If your selected style has blocks, click the **Blocks in border** arrows to choose the number of blocks.

13   Three sides will be set to 0.00. *If you need to change the size of the selected border*, modify the side that is NOT set to 0.00.

14   Repeat steps 11-13 for the remaining sides.

Notes

- Use a similar method to make a quilt with a "pillow covering" top border which is different than the sides and bottom borders. Or, eliminate the top border altogether.

- Depending on the order you add the borders you can get Log Cabin-like or Court House Steps-like borders.

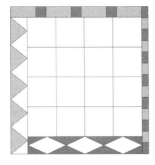

Example quilt with each border side a different style and size.
Border Settings:
Left: Points In, 5.25"
Top: Spaced Squares, 3.25"
Right: Blocks, 2.00"
Bottom: Diamonds, 5.25"

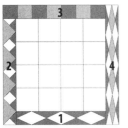

Borders added in Log Cabin order

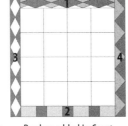

Borders added in Court House Steps order

Make Each Side a Different Style

Understanding "Aligned" Borders

EQ6 has two new border styles found at the bottom of the border style list. These styles need a bit more explaining than the others.

When you want two adjacent borders to have rectangular blocks lined up exactly with one another, try setting the inner border as you like and using an Aligned style on the outer border. **Set the number of blocks in the border (Horizontal and Vertical) to be the same for both borders**.

Blocks Aligned Inside

The two example quilts on the right have a Blocks style border with 4 blocks (gray). **Example A** has the outer border also set to the Blocks style. The blocks in the outer border do not line up with the blocks of the inner border. **Example B** has the outer border set to the Blocks Aligned Inside style. Notice that in the Blocks Aligned Inside style you actually get two "extra" blocks along each side that line up with the corner blocks of the inner border.

This works with other border styles as well. **Example C** shows a quilt with a Points In border. The blocks in the adjacent Blocks Aligned Inside border line up with the triangles of the inner border.

Try these border styles with Blocks Aligned Inside: Corner Blocks, Blocks, Half Drop Diamonds, Half Drop Double Diamonds, Big & Little Diamonds, Half Drop Big & Little Diamonds, Points In, Big & Little Points Out, Big & Little Points In, and Tile Squares.

Half Drop Blocks Aligned

The Half Drop Blocks Aligned style works the same way. It is simply a "half-drop" style of the Blocks Aligned Inside border style. See **Example D**.

Try these border styles with Half Drop Blocks Aligned: Corner Blocks, Half Drop Blocks, Diamonds, Double Diamonds, Big & Little Diamonds, Half Drop Big & Little Diamonds, Points Out, Big & Little Points Out, and Tile On Point Corners.

Blocks Aligned Inside style on the Borders palette

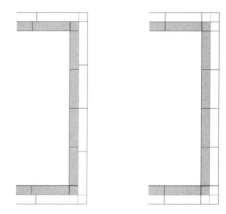

Example A
Border blocks do NOT line up when both are set to Blocks

Example B
Border blocks DO line up when 2nd border is set to Blocks Aligned Inside

Example C
Points In border (gray) and a Blocks Aligned Inside border

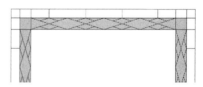

Example D
Half Drop Big & Little Diamonds border (gray) and a Half Drop Blocks Aligned border

Coloring

Quilt designed by Carola Forsberg
Vargarda, Sweden

Chapter 7

EQ6 lets you color on the Block or Quilt worktable, using any of six different coloring tools. You'll have hundreds of solid colors and thousands of fabrics to choose from. You can also import your own fabric scans and create new color palettes. Several tools help you fine-tune your design by fussy-cutting or rotating fabric, or adding outlines of colored thread around patches. One feature even makes dramatic color changes with each click of the mouse. All of the ways you can use colors and fabrics on your blocks and quilts are described in this chapter.

Reference

Coloring and Recoloring

Once you have drawn a block, or set a block in a quilt layout, you can color it with fabrics or solid colors. If you don't have a quilt set with blocks yet, see pages 148 and 161.

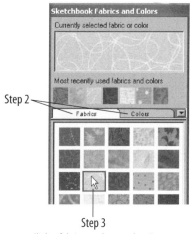

A Block on the Block worktable

1   Click the **Color** tab. The **Paintbrush** tool is now automatically selected, and the Fabrics and Colors palette appears. (If you find lines or patches missing from your drawing, this indicates drawing errors. See the Notes on page 199.)

2   Click the **Fabrics** tab in the palette to see the fabric prints or the **Colors** tab to see the solid colors. Use the scrollbar along the bottom to see all the swatches.

3   **Click a fabric or color to select it > click a patch in your block** to color it with the selected fabric or color. (If your whole block colors or you cannot color a patch, see the Notes on page 199.)

4   To recolor, click a different fabric or color in the palette and click the patch again. The patch will be newly colored.

Step 2

Step 3
Click a fabric or color to select it

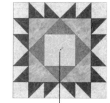

Original block   Newly colored patch

A Quilt on the Quilt worktable

1   Click the **Paintbrush** tool.

The steps below use the Paintbrush tool's *One Dot Brush* (one of five Paintbrush styles on the Quilt worktable), which is automatically selected for you unless you have previously chosen another Paintbrush style.

To see all the styles, click the Paintbrush tool and hold down the mouse button until the flyout menu appears, displaying the five brush styles. Click to select the *One Dot Brush,* then continue with the steps below.

2   Click the **Fabrics** tab within the palette to see the fabric prints or the **Colors** tab to see the solid colors. Use the scrollbar along the bottom to see all the swatches.

Click and hold on the tool to see the flyout menu

One Dot Brush   Step 1
                                 Paintbrush

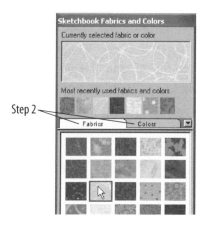

Step 2

Original quilt

Newly colored patch

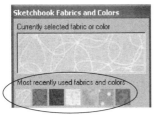

Shortcut: Click any *most recently used fabric* on the palette to use it again in the quilt

3 Click a fabric or color in the palette to select it > click a patch in your quilt, block, or border to color it with the selected fabric or color.

4 To recolor, click a different fabric or color in the palette and click the patch in the quilt again. The patch will be newly colored.

Notes

- Your *Most recently used fabrics and colors* will appear on the Fabrics and Colors palette. You can click any most recently used fabric at the top to use it again.

- Coloring errors are caused by drawing errors. Each drawing style has its own requirements which, if not met, can cause drawing errors. See pages 220, 222, and 232-233.

  - EasyDraw tab (of EasyDraw™ blocks or EasyDraw + PatchDraw blocks) – If you do not see one of your lines, or the whole block colors at once, you have a line that is not connected properly in the drawing. Click the EasyDraw tab, use the Zoom In tool and check that your lines are connected properly to each other and to the block outline.

  - Pieced tab (of PatchDraw blocks) – If you are unable to color all of the background, then you may have misdrawn patches or not filled the background completely. Use the Pick tool and your keyboard DELETE key to delete bad patches and redraw them and any missing patches with the PolyLine or PolyArc tools, see pages 238-239.

  - Appliqué tab (of any type except EasyDraw™ blocks) – If you cannot color one of your patches and it only appears as lines on the Color tab, then your patch is not closed. Use the Zoom In and Shape tools to check that the nodes of that patch are connected and rejoin them. If you cannot see one of your patches, it's possible it is hiding behind a larger patch that is directly on top of it. Send the larger patch to the back to change the layering order, see page 250.

- To color your quilt quickly, use the other color tools, see pages 201-203.

Coloring and Recoloring

Using the Coloring Tools

The best way to learn what each tool does is to try it out. If any of these tools are not on your toolbar, see pages 302 or 303.

Paintbrush tools

The Paintbrush tool works patch by patch in the quilt. There are five brush styles on the Quilt worktable. To see them all, press and *hold down* the Paintbrush tool until the flyout menu appears. Click the brush style of your choice.

One Dot Brush (default Paintbrush style)
- *Click* – paints one patch at a time with the selected fabric.
- *CTRL+click* – paints the same patch in all matching blocks.
- *ALT+click* – paints the same patch in all alternate matching blocks.

(Try using ALT and CTRL for coloring One Patch quilt layouts.)

The other four brush styles work similarly. Position your cursor over the quilt. Click and hold as you drag the brush across the quilt. A line draws, indicating the brush path. Release the mouse to see all patches touched by this path change to the selected color. (Note: You may be surprised to find patches you did not expect to color were touched by the brush path. Zoom-in before coloring so you can clearly see the brush path as you color. Use the One Dot Brush to recolor patches you did not intend to color.) The following four styles are especially useful for coloring One Patch quilt layouts.

Freehand Brush
- Paints a freehand line of color

Line Brush
- Paints a straight line of color

Rectangle Brush
- Paints a rectangular outline of color

Oval Brush
- Paints an oval outline of color

Click and hold on the tool to see the flyout menu

Paintbrush
(One Dot Brush)

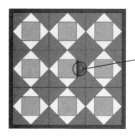

Click - colors one patch

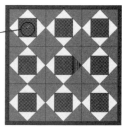

CTRL+click - colors the same patch in all matching blocks

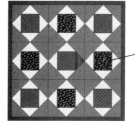

ALT+click - colors the same patch in alternate blocks

Freehand Brush   Line Brush   Rectangle Brush   Oval Brush

Example using the Line Brush

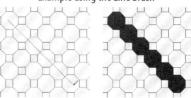

Drag a path across the quilt   Release the mouse to see the colored patches

Using the Coloring Tools

Spraycan

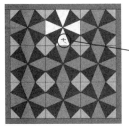

Click - sprays all similarly-colored patches in a block or motif

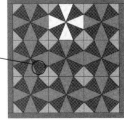

CTRL+click - sprays all similarly-colored patches in all blocks or motifs

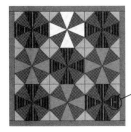

ALT+click - sprays all similarly-colored patches in every other block or motif

Swap All Colors

All similarly-colored patches across the entire quilt, including borders, have been swapped

Spraycan tool

The Spraycan tool works block by block in the quilt. Select the fabric you want from the palette. Click on a fabric in a block to "spray" all the similarly colored patches in the block with the new fabric.

- *Click* – sprays all similarly-colored patches in one block or motif with the selected fabric.

- *CTRL+click* – sprays all similarly-colored patches in all blocks or motifs on the quilt.

- *ALT+click* – sprays all similarly-colored patches in alternate blocks or motifs on the quilt.

Notes
- With the Spraycan tool, you choose your *fabric* first, then click to change the patch color.

- With the EQ4 Spray tool, you choose your *patches* first, then change that fabric in the Fabrics palette to a different color. This lets you try out color after color while the quilt patches are still selected.

Swap All Colors tool

The Swap All Colors tool works color by color across the entire quilt and all its layers. It will change all patches of a given fabric or color in your quilt to the new fabric or color, regardless of what layer you are on. In other words, use the Swap All Colors tool to change the yellow patches, all over your quilt, to green.

- Click to change a fabric in the entire quilt (all layers) to the selected fabric.

Notes
- If you wish to "swap" the colors on one layer but not the other, use the Spraycan tool while holding down your keyboard CTRL key.

- With the Swap tool, you choose your fabric first, then click to change that color on all layers. With the EQ4 Swap tool, you click on the quilt to select all matching colors on that layer (not all layers), then change that fabric in the palette to a different color. This lets you try out color after color while the quilt patches are still selected.

Eyedropper tool

Use this tool to find a fabric that you've already used in the quilt. After you have clicked the color in the quilt, EQ6 will automatically switch you to the last color tool used. When using the eyedropper, make sure you are using it on Layer 1 to "pick up" a color from a block, or on Layer 2 to "pick up" a color from a motif.

- Click on a fabric or color in the quilt to find it in the palette.

Eyedropper

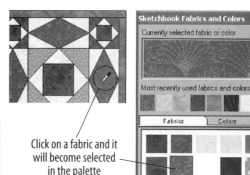

Click on a fabric and it will become selected in the palette

Notes
- **You can also find recently used fabrics in the palette, by clicking on any swatch in the row of *Most recently used fabrics and colors*.**

Fussy Cut tool

This tool lets you slide fabrics around to center motifs precisely, making your block look perfect on the screen.

- Click and hold in a block or quilt patch colored with fabric and drag the mouse to choose what part of the fabric you see. The fabric "moves" in the patch as you drag the mouse. Release the mouse when you're done fussy cutting.

Fussy Cut

Notes
- **You can also use the keyboard arrow keys to fussy cut fabric.**

Block before fussy cutting   Block after fussy cutting

Random Recolor tool

With the Random Recolor tool you can switch your entire quilt back and forth from fabrics to solid colors, and even shift the colors randomly or by hue, saturation, or brightness with a click.

- Add your current quilt to the Sketchbook first. Then, click on the quilt with the Random Recolor tool. The changes you see will depend on the options you have selected. See pages 215-218 for more discussion of this tool and options.

Random Recolor
See pages 215-218 for more details

EQ4 Spray

First, click on the quilt to select your patches

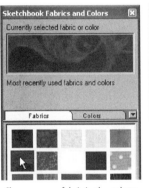

Choose a new fabric in the palette

The patches fill with the selected fabric

EQ4 Spray tool

With the EQ4 Spray tool, first you choose the patches in the quilt you want to change, then click a fabric in the palette. This lets you audition color after color while the quilt patches are still selected.

- *Click* – selects all similarly colored patches in one block or motif. Then click a fabric or color in the palette to change the patches.

- *CTRL+click* – selects all similarly colored patches in all blocks or motifs. Then click a fabric or color in the palette to change the patches.

- *ALT+click* – selects all similarly colored patches in alternate blocks (not motifs). Then click a fabric or color in the palette to change the patches.

EQ4 Swap tool

The EQ4 Swap tool will change all patches of a given fabric on one layer in your quilt to the new fabric.

- Click in the quilt to select a fabric or color you want to replace, then click a new swatch in the palette to replace it. Continue to click on fabrics or colors in the palette to swap colors in the quilt, if desired. Click a new tool, or click away from the quilt, to make the change permanent.

EQ4 Swap

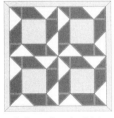

Click to select the fabric

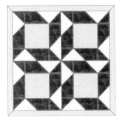

Click in palette to see fabric change in the quilt

Rotate Fabric
See pages 212-213 for more details

Notes

- With the EQ4 Swap tool, you click the *color* in the quilt you want to replace, then click a fabric in the palette. This lets you audition color after color while the patches are still selected. But this tool only works on one layer at a time.

- With the Swap All Colors tool, you choose your *fabric* first, then click in the quilt to change that fabric or color on all layers.

Rotate Fabric tool

The Rotate Fabric tool lets you rotate fabric patch by patch in the design or to align it to an edge of a patch. For example, rotate stripes to make them vertical instead of horizontal. See pages 212-213.

Using the Coloring Tools

Understanding Block Colorings

When you recolor and add a quilt to the Sketchbook, each block coloring is stacked up to 10 times to save space in the palette. You see only the selected coloring.

Step 1
Set Block

Step 1
Select Coloring

See Stacked Colorings with Select Coloring

1   On the Quilt worktable, **click the Set Block tool > click a block in the Blocks palette > right-click on it > choose Select Coloring**. You'll see a strip showing all the colorings.

2   Click on any coloring to display it in the palette.

Step 2
Select a coloring

See Stacked Colorings with the Coloring Arrows

1   **Click View Sketchbook > click the Blocks section > click a block to select it**. Or, on the Quilt worktable, click the **Set Block** tool and select a block.

2   Use the coloring arrows, found at the bottom of the Blocks palette and the Sketchbook, to page back and forth among the colorings:
   • **First arrow** – moves to the front (line drawing)
   • **Second arrow** – moves back one
   • **Third arrow** – moves forward one
   • **Last arrow** – moves to the last coloring

Step 1
View Sketchbook

3   Below the blocks in the Sketchbook, the number of colorings and which one you're viewing are displayed. For example, 2 of 5.

To Split Stacked Colorings

1   Right-click a block in the palette or Sketchbook and choose **Select Coloring**.

2   Click the coloring where you want to start the split.

3   Right-click the block again and click **Split Coloring**.

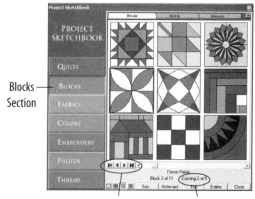

Blocks Section

Coloring arrows   Coloring 2 of 5

If You Do Not Want Colorings Stacked

If you prefer to have a new block form each time you color and recolor a block, click **FILE > Preferences > General (under Project Properties) > change Maximum number of colorings per block to 1 > click OK**.

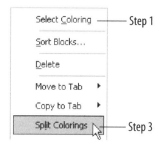

Select Coloring ——— Step 1

Split Colorings ——— Step 3

Click and hold on the tool to see the flyout menu

Brush Thread | Spray Thread | Swap Thread | Step 2 Set Thread

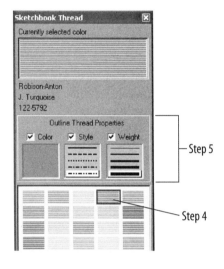

— Step 5

— Step 4

Quilt stencil before

Quilt stencil after

Close-up of stitches

Close-up of stitches

Using the Set Thread Tool

To use the Thread tools, you must have the Set Thread tool on your toolbar (see page 302) and thread in your Sketchbook (see page 128).

The Thread tools are used to change the thread color on quilting stencils and embroideries, and to color block and patch edges around blocks and motifs.

1   Click the Layer tab on which the design is set. (Blocks are on **Layer 1** of any quilt. Motifs and text are on **Layer 2**. Stencils and embroidery are on **Layer 3**.)

2   **Click and hold down the mouse button on the Set Thread tool until the flyout menu appears** displaying the three Thread styles:

- **Brush Thread** – changes thread color one section at a time. Use CTRL+click to change color in all identical designs.
- **Spray Thread** – changes thread color in one block, motif, or stencil.
- **Swap Thread** – changes thread color over the entire quilt.

3   **Click the thread tool you want to use**.

4   **Click to select a thread color in the palette**.

5   *(Optional)* Under Outline Thread Properties, check the boxes to change color, style, and/or weight. You must have at least one checked.

- **Color** – check this and click a color below to change the thread color
- **Style** – check this and select a style to change the line style from solid to dashed
- **Weight** – check this and select a thickness to change the line weight (thread width)

6   **Click any patch** in your block, motif or stencil, or any thread in your embroidery.

Notes
- The Brush Thread and Spray Thread are available on the Block Worktable as well as the Quilt Worktable. Changes to thread color on the Block Worktable will be saved with the block when you click the Add to Sketchbook button.

Sorting Fabrics or Colors

Sorting fabrics or colors arranges them in the order you want, letting you put your favorites up front in the palette.

Sorting Fabrics or Colors Manually

1   Be on the Quilt worktable, **Layer 1** tab OR be on the Block worktable, on the **Color** tab.

2   Click the **Paintbrush** tool.

3   Inside the Fabrics and Colors palette, click the **Fabrics** tab to sort the fabrics or the **Colors** tab to sort the colors.

4   *Fabrics* – **Right-click over the swatches > click Sort Fabrics**.

   Colors – **Right-click over the swatches > point to Sort Colors > click Manual**.

5   **Click the swatches in the order you want them sorted**. The first swatch clicked will appear first in your palette. When you click on a swatch, it will "disappear" from the Sort box so you won't select the same one twice. Use the display buttons to see more or fewer swatches at a time.

6   Continue clicking swatches in the order you want them to appear. Click the **Start over** button if you make a mistake.

7   Click the **Close** button if you are finished or if you want EQ6 to place the remaining swatches in their current order after the ones you have already sorted.

Step 2
Paintbrush

Step 4
On Fabrics tab, right-click over the swatches and click Sort Fabrics

Step 4
On Colors tab, right-click over the swatches, point to Sort Colors, click Manual

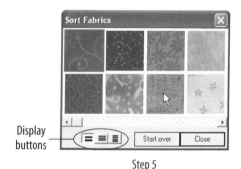

Display buttons

Step 5
Click on the fabrics in the order in which you want them to appear

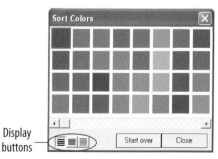

Display buttons

Step 5
Click on the colors in the order in which you want them to appear

Sorting Fabrics or Colors

Step 2
Paintbrush

Step 2
Click Automatic

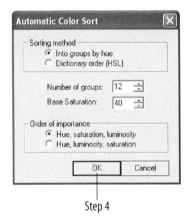

Step 4

To unsort colors, right-click in the palette,
point to Sort Colors and then click Unsort.

Sorting Colors Automatically

1   Be on the Quilt worktable, **Layer 1** tab OR be
    on the Block worktable, on the **Color** tab.

2   **Click the Paintbrush tool > click the Colors
    tab within the palette > right-click over
    the swatches > point to Sort Colors > click
    Automatic**. The Automatic Sort Colors box
    appears.

3   Choose from the following options:

    • **Into groups by hue** – Hue is another word
      for what we think of as color. In common use,
      hue is identified by color names like red,
      orange, yellow, etc.
        • **Number of groups** – Choose from 6 to 20
          groups for dividing the current colors.
          (Available in: *Into groups by hue*)
        • **Base Saturation** – Determines how much
          gray is added. The allowable values are from
          40 to 160. (Available in: *Into groups by hue*)
    • **Dictionary order** – Sets the tooltip to display
      HSL values. The H (hue) values for each color
      swatch will start with the smallest and
      increase. In other words, the first color swatch
      will have a low number for H like 8, and the
      last color swatch will have a high number for
      H like 240.
    • **Hue, saturation, luminosity** – Saturation
      is the strength or purity of the color. High
      saturation is pure and vivid, whereas low
      saturation is grayer, muted and subdued.
    • **Hue, luminosity, saturation** – Luminosity
      is the lightness or amount of white in the
      color. The palest shade of a given color or hue
      will have a luminescence value of 240.

4   Make your choices in step 3 and click **OK**.

Unsorting Fabrics or Colors

To unsort fabrics, follow steps 1-7 on the previous
page to click them back in their original order.

To unsort colors, **right-click on the swatches >
point to Sort Colors > click Unsort**.

Adding New Solid Colors

If you can't find the solid colors you need for your block, you can create your own.

Step 1
Paintbrush

1   From **Layer 1** of the Quilt worktable or the **Color** tab of the Block worktable, click the **Paintbrush** tool.

2   Inside the palette, click the **Colors** tab.

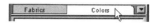

Step 2

3   Place the cursor over a color swatch (don't click). You will see an RGB number appear. The number is different for every swatch and represents the amount of red (R), green (G), and blue (B) in that color. The palette can range from black (R:0 G:0 B:0) to white (R: 255 G: 255 B: 255). Every combination (over 2,700,000) does not exist in the Sketchbook/ palette, but can be made.

Step 3
See the RGB tooltip

4   **Click any color swatch to select it.**

5   Right-click on the swatch and click **Add Colors**. A standard Windows Color box appears with 48 basic colors.

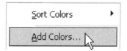

Step 5

6   Click **Define Custom Colors**.

7   If the box expands past the edge of your screen, move it to the left. To do this, click and hold on the title bar at the top of the box, then drag the box to the left until it fits on your screen.

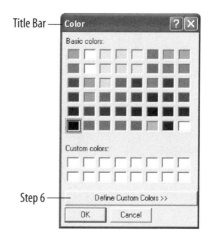

Title Bar

Step 6

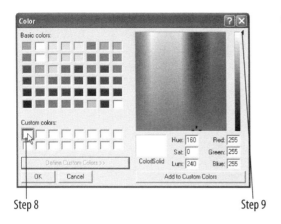

Step 8   Step 9

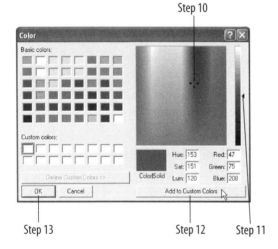

Step 10

Step 13   Step 12   Step 11

8   Under *Custom colors*, **click the top-left white square**. (You must select the boxes in order from left to right before you modify the color or it will not work as expected. Start in the top-left square, fill the top row, then start in the bottom-left square and fill the second row.)

9   At the far right is a thin, vertical bar with a black triangle. Drag the triangle up or down to the middle of the bar.

10   In the large colorful square, **click near the color you want to make**. Below you will see the Color/Solid box show the color you selected. Click elsewhere in the large colorful square and watch the Color/Solid box update as you slide it around.

11   On the vertical bar at the right, **drag the arrow up or down to make the selected color lighter or darker.**

12   When you see a color in the Color/Solid box that you like, click the **Add to Custom Colors** button at the bottom.

13   If you are finished adding colors, click **OK**.

If you would like to add another color, start at step 8 again and select the white box just to the right of the last square you filled. Once you fill the top row, start in the bottom-left square and fill the second row. You can add 16 colors at a time.

Notes
• You can manually type in any RGB (0-255) or HSL (0-240) number. Do steps 1-8, then double-click the number for Red or Hue so it turns shaded and type the new number. Press the TAB key and type the next number, then press the TAB key and type the last number. Click Add to Custom Colors if you like the new color, then go to step 13.

Adding New Solid Colors

Adding Shades & Tints or Tones

You can add shades (dark values) and tints (light values) of a selected color to your EQ6 color palette.

Step 1
Paintbrush

Tones are pure colors to which gray has been added. This determines how saturated (pure) a color is. The more gray, the less saturated it is (like earthtones). You can also add a range of tones to your EQ6 colors.

1   From **Layer 1** of the Quilt worktable or the **Color** tab of the Block worktable, click the **Paintbrush** tool.

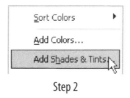

Step 2

Step 2

2   Inside the Fabrics and Colors palette, **click the Colors tab > click a color you want to modify > right-click and click Add Shades & Tints** (if you want it lighter or darker) **OR click Add Tones** (if you want to make it more gray). You'll see a range of values.

3   *(Optional)* You can add or remove swatches from the range and make 4-16 colors.

   To insert a new color, click the swatch you want to insert in front of and click the **Insert** button.

   To remove a color, click the swatch and click the **Remove** button.

4   Click the **Add to Sketchbook** button to add this range to your EQ6 color palette. Your added colors will be at the end of the current palette.

   Click **Cancel** to close the window without adding shades & tints or tones.

Step 3   Step 3
Insert   Remove

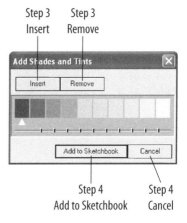

Step 4   Step 4
Add to Sketchbook   Cancel

Step 3   Step 3
Insert   Remove

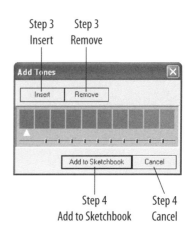

Step 4   Step 4
Add to Sketchbook   Cancel

Notes

- If you don't want your new colors at the end of the palette you can sort your color swatches, see pages 206-207.

- You can also make Shades and Tints by using Add Grades. Mix the selected color with white or black, see page 211.

- You can also make Tones by using Add Grades. Mix the selected color with any gray, see page 211.

Step 1
Paintbrush

Step 2

Title Bar

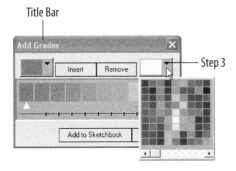

Step 3

Step 4   Step 4
Insert   Remove

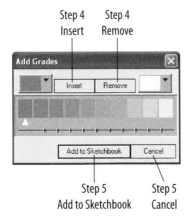

Step 5   Step 5
Add to Sketchbook   Cancel

Adding Grades

Adding Grades lets you mix one color with another.

1   From **Layer 1** of the Quilt worktable or the **Color** tab of the Block worktable, click the **Paintbrush** tool.

2   Inside the Fabrics and Colors palette, **click the Colors tab > click a color you want to mix > right-click and choose Add Grades**. You will see a box appear with two colors at the top. The color on the left will be the color you selected.

3   If you want to change the color on the right, first move the whole Add Grades box to the left. To do this, click and hold on the title bar at the top of the box and drag the box to the middle of your screen. Now, **click the down arrow beside the color you want to change > click another color from the picker**. (To see all the colors, drag the bottom scrollbar.) The color on the right and the graded colors below will change.

4   *(Optional)* When you're mixing colors you can add or remove swatches from the range. You can have 4-16 colors.

    To insert a new color, click the swatch you want to insert in front of and click the **Insert** button.

    To remove a color, click the swatch and click the **Remove** button.

5   Click the **Add to Sketchbook** button to add this range of colors to your EQ6 color palette. Your added colors will be at the end of the current palette.

    Click **Cancel** to close the window without adding grades.

Notes
• If you don't want your new colors at the end of the palette you can sort your color swatches, see pages 206-207.

• Add tints by mixing with white. Add tones by mixing with any gray. Add shades by mixing with black.

Adding Grades

Rotating Fabrics

The Rotate Fabric tool lets you rotate fabric in several different ways on the quilt. (Don't confuse it with the Rotate tool, which rotates blocks in the quilt.) To use the Rotate Fabric tool you must have fabric in a quilt on the Quilt worktable. If you do not have this, see pages 128, 148, 161, and 198-199.

1   Click the layer tab where the fabric is that needs rotating.

2   Click the **Rotate Fabric** tool. If the Rotate Fabric tool is not on your toolbar, see page 302.

3   **Click on the circle next to Simple, Advanced or Align to edge**, to select your rotating style. (See Rotating Styles below.)

4   **Click any fabric in the quilt or block** to rotate it according to the style you selected.

Simple Rotating Style

A simple quarter turn rotation
Click the fabric to rotate it 90 degrees clockwise with each click. Four clicks will return the fabric to the original orientation.

• CTRL+click = rotates in all blocks

• ALT+click = rotates in alternate blocks

Advanced Rotating Style

A custom rotation
Choose the starting angle of rotation (0 – 359); this impacts the first click only. Choose the number of rotations (1-16) you want within 360 degrees for future clicks. You can either enter any number (1-16) or divide 360 degrees by the degree you want the fabric to rotate by and enter that number.

Example 1:
Starting angle: 10 degrees
Number of rotations: 8 (360 degrees ÷ 45 = 8)
click 1: 55 degrees (10 + 45)
click 2: 100 degrees (10 + 45 + 45)
click 3: 145 degrees (10 + 45 + 45 + 45)
And so on. It will take 8 clicks to rotate 370 degrees (360 degrees + the initial 10 degrees).

Step 2
Rotate Fabric

Step 3

Simple Rotating Style

Original

1 Click - 90 degrees

2 Clicks - 180 degrees

3 Clicks - 270 degrees

4 Clicks - 360 degrees

Advanced Rotating Style - Example 1

Original

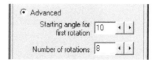

Example 1 settings

1 Click - 55 degrees

2 Clicks - 100 degrees 3 Clicks - 145 degrees

Rotating Fabrics

Advanced Rotating Style - Example 2

Original

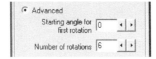

Example 2 settings

1 Click - 60 degrees

2 Clicks - 120 degrees

3 Clicks - 180 degrees

Align to Edge Rotating Style

Align to Edge settings

Alignment edge marker

Original

Click 1

Click 2 - rotates 90 degrees

Click 3 - rotates 90 degrees more

Example 2:
Starting angle: 0
Number of rotations: 6 (360 degrees ÷ 6 = 60)
click 1: 60 degrees
click 2: 120 degrees (60 + 60)
click 3: 180 degrees (60 + 60 + 60)
And so on. It will take 6 clicks to rotate 360 degrees.

- CTRL+click = rotates in all blocks

- ALT+click = rotates in alternate blocks

Align to Edge Rotating Style
Aligns the design of fabric to the patch edge
Click a patch to see a line appear along the patch's long edge. The fabric will rotate to align along that edge. Click in the center of the patch to rotate the fabric 90 degrees each time with respect to the alignment edge. You can change the alignment edge in the patch, if you:

- Click on the **Move alignment edge** arrow in the palette, OR

- **SHIFT+click** in the patch.

This option works on one patch only, not multiple patches in the quilt. Therefore, CTRL and ALT do not affect other patches.

Example:
To rotate the fabric 90 degrees from the alignment edge, you can just click.
click 1: finds the long edge and rotates the fabric along that edge
click 2: rotates the fabric 90 degrees more
click 3: rotates 90 degrees more
And so on.

> **Notes**
> - **The Rotate Fabric tool does not work on One Patch quilts.**

Changing the Default Palette

The fabrics, colors, and threads you start with in every EQ6 project are in the *default project*. You can choose different *defaults* that will then appear each time you open EQ6 and start a new project.

1   **Click View Sketchbook > click the Fabrics, Colors, or Threads section > click an item and click Delete > click Yes to delete it.**

2   Click **Close** when you have deleted all the items you do not want in your new projects.

3   Click **LIBRARIES > Fabric or Thread Library**. For colors, see Adding New Solid Colors see pages 208-209.

4   Click to select any fabrics or threads, then click **Add to Sketchbook**. Add as many as you'd like from any section or category. See page 128 if you need help using the libraries.

5   Click the **Sketchbook** section to check and approve your choices. If you want to add more fabrics or threads to the Sketchbook, repeat step 4. If you want to remove items, select the item and click **Delete**.

6   Click **Close** when you're finished.

7   When you are ready to make your new default palette, click **FILE > Save Palette as Default > OK**. Your new palette will now appear each time you start a new project.

Or, click **Cancel** to do nothing, and return to the worktable. The original EQ6 default palette will not change when you start a new project.

Notes
• Once you've changed the palette, you can revert back to the original "default palette" by clicking FILE > Preferences > Restore (under Workspace), then click to put a check next to *Include original fabrics, colors and thread*. Click the Restore Default Settings button, then OK. Your palette will revert to the original EQ6 palette (and toolbars and dialog boxes will revert to their original settings and positions).

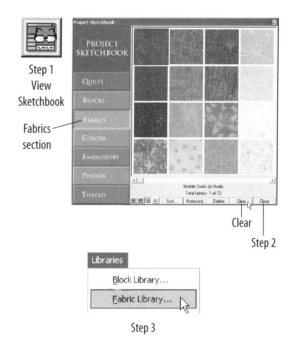

Step 1
View
Sketchbook

Fabrics
section

Clear

Step 2

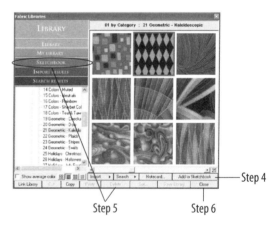

Step 3

Step 4

Step 5   Step 6

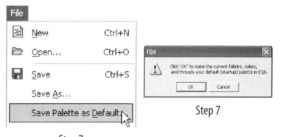

Step 7

Step 7

Changing the Default Palette

Step 2
Add to Sketchbook

Step 3
Random Recolor

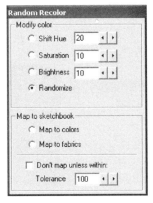

Step 4

Using the Random Recolor Tool

Testing out new colorations of the same quilt has never been this fun. With the Random Recolor tool you can switch your entire quilt back and forth from colors to fabrics, and even shift the colors randomly, by hue, saturation, or brightness.

1 You must be on the Quilt worktable with a colored quilt on the screen. The quilt can be colored with solid colors or fabrics.

2 Click **Add to Sketchbook** to keep your current quilt in case you don't like the recolored version.

3 Click the **Random Recolor** tool. If the Random Recolor tool is not on your toolbar, see page 302.

4 Choose your option from the choices described on the following pages.

5 **Click directly on your quilt as many times as you like.**

6 The new colors will not be your Sketchbook colors. They are mathematical variations of the originals.

 • Click **Map to Colors** to change the quilt's colors to the closest colors in the Sketchbook.
 • Click **Map to Fabrics** to change the quilt's colors to the closest fabrics in the Sketchbook.

7 Click **Add to Sketchbook** whenever you find a version you want to keep.

Original quilt

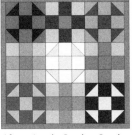

After using the Random Recolor tool set to Randomize

Step 6

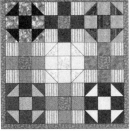

After clicking Map to Fabric

Step 7
Add to Sketchbook

Notes
 • The Random Recolor tool does exactly what it says – it randomly recolors the quilt. You may find after a few clicks you would like to try a different option instead of the one you chose. To go back to your original quilt (which you added to the Sketchbook in step 2), click View Sketchbook > find and click the quilt > click the Edit button.

Modifying Color with the Random Recolor Tool

Before you begin, see page 215. In EQ6, *Modify color* sends the current colors through a calculation and returns different colors. If your quilt is colored with fabrics they will be replaced by the average color of that fabric. Remember to Map to Colors or Fabrics after any modifications.

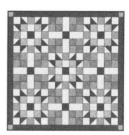

Original quilt

Shift Hue (-40 to +40)

Colors are identified by their hue. Hue is what makes something red, or green, or blue. If you think of a color wheel (or putting a rainbow in a circle), this is how Shift Hue works in EQ6. You can click a long time because you're going in a circle. The higher the number, the more dramatic the change will be.

Set Hue to 0 and click on your quilt.
The only change you will notice is that fabrics will be replaced by solid colors.

Set Hue to a negative number and click on your quilt.
Watch your colors go around the color wheel one way with each click.

Set Hue to a positive number and click on your quilt.
Watch your colors go around the color wheel the opposite way with each click.

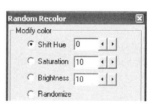

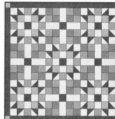

Shift Hue set to 0 – fabrics change to solid colors

Saturation (-20 to +20)

Saturation is the purity of color. High saturation is very rich in color, low saturation looks washed out. Saturation is changed by adding or subtracting gray. While hue change is circular, saturation is not. This means saturation will stop, because eventually the quilt cannot get any grayer or purer. The higher the number, the more dramatic the change will be.

Set Saturation to 0 and click on your quilt.
You will notice the fabrics will be replaced by solid colors and may be slightly toned down.

Set Saturation to a negative number, click on the quilt.
Your quilt will become grayer with each click.

Set Saturation to a positive number and click on the quilt.
Most of the colors in your quilt will become richer.

Shift Hue set to -40   Shift Hue set to 40

Saturation setting

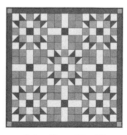

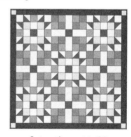

Saturation set to -20   Saturation set to 20

Brightness setting

Brightness set to -20

Brightness set to 20

Brightness (-20 to +20)

Brightness is the intensity of a color. A high brightness would have a lot of white; a low brightness would have more black. Like saturation, a color is either bright or not. Because brightness is not circular, eventually brightness will stop since you can't make the quilt any darker or lighter. The higher the number, the more dramatic the change will be.

Set Brightness to 0 and click on your quilt.
You will notice the fabrics will be replaced by solid colors.

Set Brightness to a negative number and click on the quilt.
Your quilt will become darker with each click.

Set Brightness to a positive number and click on the quilt.
Your quilt will become lighter with each click.

Randomize

Choosing randomize will replace all the colors in the quilt with a different solid color from the current Sketchbook palette. EQ6 will keep track of the colors used and try to prevent duplicating them (see Notes below). The more colors you have in your Sketchbook the better the results.

Randomize setting

Example results of using Randomize

Notes
- When you use Shift Hue, Saturation or Brightness and choose a number close to zero, your changes will be gradual. If you choose a number farther away from zero, the changes will be quite drastic.

- When you choose Randomize, EQ6 will try to avoid duplicating the colors in the quilt. But, sooner or later, the color differences may "collapse" and some patches will be colored with the same solid color. Use the Paintbrush tool to recolor them again in different colors, if necessary.

Modify Color / Random Recolor

Mapping to the Sketchbook with the Random Recolor Tool

When you modify colors with the Random Recolor tool, the resulting colors are not in the Sketchbook. You must map the modified colors to colors or fabrics in the Sketchbook before you continue to work on the quilt. Before you begin, see pages 215-217.

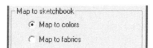

Map to Colors

Map to Colors

This feature will replace each fabric or color with the closest color in the current palette. If a fabric is being replaced, closeness means closest to the fabric's average color. If "Don't map unless within" is checked, a replacement will only be made if within the tolerance chosen. See *Tolerance* below.

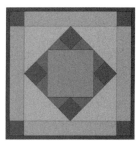

Original quilt with fabrics   After choosing Map to Colors

Map to Fabrics

This feature will replace each color with the closest fabric in the current palette. Closeness for colors is compared to a fabric's average color. Once again, if *Don't map unless within* is checked, a replacement will only be made if within the tolerance chosen. See *Tolerance* below.

Map to Fabrics

Tolerance (0 to 500)

Tolerance is the "trade-off" between the accuracy of a replacement and the number of replacements. To require a Tolerance when mapping, be sure there is a check in the checkbox and that the tolerance value has been adjusted.

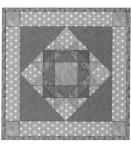

Original quilt with solid colors   After choosing Map to Fabrics

Notes

- When only using colors, try a combination of the Random Recolor tool and Add Shades & Tints, Add Tones, or Add Grades so EQ6 will have many colors from which to replace.

- Don't forget to color all parts of your quilt. The Random Recolor tool does not change erased or uncolored areas filled with hatching lines.

- Suggestion: Put a check next to Don't map unless within, and set the Tolerance somewhere between 100 and 200. Put the dot next to Map to Fabrics and click on the quilt to replace your colors accurately. Then go to the Fabric Library and find fabrics similar to the ones not replaced.

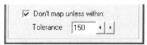

Tolerance setting keeps your mapping accurate.
Example: If you have 300 solid colors and 10 fabrics in your Sketchbook, and choose *Map to Fabrics*, some of your solid colors may be mapped to the same fabric because there are no fabrics in the Sketchbook that are a close match.

Quilt designed by Daphne Stewart
Sunnyside, Washington

Drawing

Chapter 8

EQ6 has two very different drawing styles: EasyDraw™ and PatchDraw. Pieced blocks can be drawn with either style; appliqué blocks require using PatchDraw. When you first start drawing, you may feel overwhelmed with choices and tools. But with practice, each drawing method will become more familiar. We encourage you to study the information in this chapter as well as Lesson Five, Lesson Six, and the program's Help files. For there are many drawing options you may well not discover on your own. This chapter is split into three sections; one for each drawing style and directions that work for both. It gives you basic information about each style, "rules" you need to follow for success, along with many drawing tips.

Reference

Understanding Block Types

	EasyDraw™ Blocks	PatchDraw Blocks	PatchDraw Motifs	EasyDraw + PatchDraw
Tabs	EasyDraw, Color	Pieced, Applique, Color	Applique, Color	EasyDraw, Applique, Color
(Pieced or plain) Background square and block outline permanent	Yes	Yes- on Pieced tab	No background square or outline	Yes- on EasyDraw tab
Block can have appliqué patches	No	Yes- on Applique tab	Yes- on Applique tab	Yes- on Applique tab
Appliqué motifs with no background square	No	No	Yes	No
Copy, paste, rotate, and move	Lines	Patches- on both tabs	Patches	Lines- on EasyDraw tab Patches- on Applique tab
Edit pieced blocks	Yes- draw new lines over existing drawing, or delete lines	Yes- delete old patches, then redraw with Polydraw tools to fill holes completely	No	Yes- draw new lines over existing drawing, or delete lines on EasyDraw tab
How do I know if I've drawn incorrectly?	EasyDraw tab- 1) lines disappear, 2) color bleeds into other patches	Pieced tab- unable to color all of background Applique tab- unable to color patches or color bleeds into background patches	Applique tab- unable to color patches or color bleeds into background patches	EasyDraw tab- 1) lines disappear, 2) color bleeds into other patches Applique tab- unable to color patches or color bleeds into background patches
Most common drawing mistakes	EasyDraw tab- 1) lines floating, 2) lines do not cross each other, 3) lines do not touch block outline	Pieced tab- 1) patches are overlapping, 2) patch lines cross themselves (like a figure-eight), 3) the background is not filled completely and has holes Applique tab- 1) patches are not closed, 2) patch lines cross themselves (like a figure-eight), 3) patches are missing lines because they cannot share lines with other patches	Applique tab- 1) patches are not closed, 2) patch lines cross themselves (like a figure-eight), 3) patches are missing lines because they cannot share lines with other patches	EasyDraw tab- 1) lines floating, 2) lines do not cross each other, 3) lines do not touch block outline Applique tab- 1) patches are not closed, 2) patch lines cross themselves (like a figure-eight), 3) patches are missing lines because they cannot share lines with other patches
Print Block or Templates	Yes	Yes	Yes	Yes
Print Rotary Cutting Chart or Foundation Pattern	Only if drawn to be rotary cuttable or foundation pieceable	Only if drawn to be rotary cuttable or foundation pieceable	No	Only if drawn to be rotary cuttable or foundation pieceable
Layer of quilt on which it is typically set	Layer 1- as a pieced block, Layer 3- as a quilting stencil	Layer 1- as a pieced block, Layer 3- as a quilting stencil	Layer 2- as an appliqué motif, Layer 3- as a quilting stencil	Layer 1- as a pieced block, Layer 3- as a quilting stencil

Quilt designed by Robert Ignaszak
Waukesha, Wisconsin

EasyDraw™ Blocks

Section A

EasyDraw™ is one drawing method you can use for drawing simple pieced blocks. This "pencil and paper" drawing style lets you draw straight and semi-circular lines to subdivide a square or other rectangle into patchwork sections. You must draw so that all line segments connect to one another and touch the edge. In return, EQ6 automatically creates complete closed patches for you. This chapter will show you how to use all of the EasyDraw™ tools.

Reference

Understanding EasyDraw™

EasyDraw™ is just like drawing with a pencil and graph paper. **The rule is: as long as the lines connect to one another, or to the edge of the block, you can fill the patches they create with color.** Any segments breaking the rule will disappear or cause color to bleed through multiple patches.

You can see from the picture at the top that it is not necessary to think in terms of outlining all sides of a patch. You are not required to draw one triangle patch, draw a second triangle exactly the same size (as in PatchDraw) to create the block. Instead, you draw one line and EQ does the rest. That's why it's called *Easy*Draw™.

EasyDraw™ is great for creating traditional and foundation pieced blocks. In addition to the Line and Arc tools, you have a Grid tool for drawing all the lines of the selected grid in one stroke and a Shape tool that can create more dots (nodes) for you to snap lines to. Through a combination of these tools, you can draw everything from Nine Patches to Compasses, New York Beauties, and more.

To see examples of blocks drawn using EasyDraw™, **go to LIBRARIES > Block Library > click the Library section > look at any of the blocks in 1 Classic Pieced, 2 Contemporary Pieced, or 3 Foundation Pieced.**

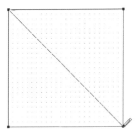

Draw a diagonal line to divide the block into two triangles.

EQ understands the drawing and creates the templates that make up the block.

Good – All lines touch, creating a pieceable block.

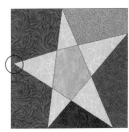

Bad – If we bump the left point off the block outline, the lines still touch, but the left side cannot be easily pieced and color will bleed.

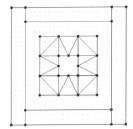

Although this may be a beautiful block, the center is not connected to the block outline.

The Log Cabin border will be all that remains.

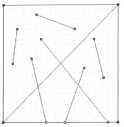

Lines floating or extending past an existing line will disappear.

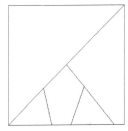

Only lines connected to the outline or each other will remain.

Step 1
Work on Block

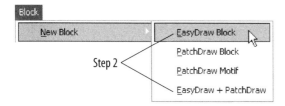

Step 2

Step 3
BLOCK > Drawing Board Setup

Change width and height

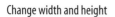

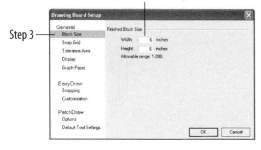

Step 3

Step 4

Change snap points

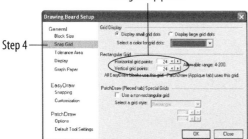

Drawing an EasyDraw™ Block

Starting the Block

1 Click **WORKTABLE > Work on Block**, or click the **Work on Block** button.

2 Click **BLOCK > New Block > EasyDraw Block** to start a block with just a pieced layer, or **EasyDraw + PatchDraw Block** to start a block that can have appliqué motifs floated above it.

Verify Block Size, Snap Points & Graph Paper

Steps 3-5 are somewhat optional, but it is important to know how to change them if needed.

3 *Block Size* – Click **BLOCK > Drawing Board Setup > Block Size** (under General) to double-check the finished block size. **Width** and **Height** determine your rulers. Double-click in the box and type a new size to change it.

4 *Snap Points* – Click **Snap Grid** (under General), verify the numbers for horizontal and vertical grid points. Double-click in the box and type a new number to change them. These should be a *multiple of your block size*. For example,

- **If you are working in inches and your block size is 6" x 6",** you should set both your horizontal and vertical snaps points to:
  6 (snap every inch, 6 x 1 = 6),
  12 (snap every 1/2 inch, 6 x 2 = 12),
  24 (snap every 1/4 inch, 6 x 4 = 24),
  48 (snap every 1/8 inch, 6 x 8 = 48), etc.

- **If you are working in centimeters and your block size is 15x15cm,** you should set both your horizontal and vertical snaps points to:
  15 (snap every cm, 15 x 1 = 15),
  30 (snap every 0.5cm, 15 x 2),
  75 (snap every 2mm, 15 x 5 = 75),
  150 (snap every mm, 15 x 10 = 150), etc.

- **If your block is a rectangle at 6" x 10",** you should set your snaps to be multiples of each number. Snaps would be 6 x 10, 12 x 20, etc.

5   *Graph Paper* – Click **Graph Paper** (under General).

- Click the checkbox next to **Show graph paper** to choose whether or not you want to see it.

- To change its color, click the down arrow next to **Graph paper color** and click on a color in the list.

- You can also set the number of cells that appear on the block. Double-click in the box and type a new number to change either **Number of cells wide** or **Number of cells high** (allowable values are from 2 to 48).

Show graph paper checkbox

Change graph paper color

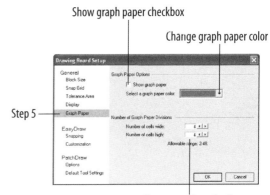

Step 5

Change number of cells

Using the EasyDraw™ Tools

6   Use any of the EasyDraw™ tools to draw or modify your block:

- **Pick tool** – use to select and move segments or groups; select segments or groups ready for copying, deleting, rotating, flipping, or resizing.

Pick tool

Shape tool

- **Shape tool** – use to edit lines or arcs; add new nodes; find the crossings across a segment; split the segment in half or thirds; partition the segment into even sections; stagger the segment into "half drop" sections.

Line tool

Arc tool

- **Line tool** – use to draw lines; click and hold as you drag to make a line, then release.

- **Arc tool** – use to draw arcs or curves; click and hold as you drag to make the arc, press the SPACEBAR on your keyboard if it is facing the wrong direction, then release.

Grid tool

- **Grid tool** – use to draw all the lines of a grid in one click; grids can be *even* (2 x 2 is a Four Patch, 3 x 3 is a Nine Patch, etc.) or *uneven* (2 x 10, 3 x 7, etc.); make columns or rows by setting one side to 1.

Block Width & Height

Graph Paper Cells

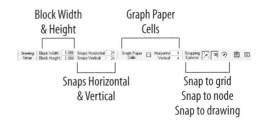

Snaps Horizontal & Vertical

Snap to grid
Snap to node
Snap to drawing

Notes
- There are shortcuts for block size, snap points, and graph paper in the Precision Bar. Click VIEW > Precision Bar to turn it on.

Line tool

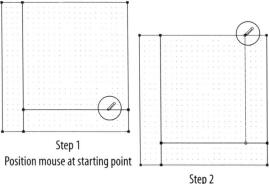

Step 1
Position mouse at starting point

Step 2
Click, hold, and drag to the end point of the line

Drawing with the Line and Arc Tools

When drawing with EasyDraw™, remember you are drawing the seam lines in your block. Therefore all lines must touch or cross other lines or the block edge. You cannot have any patches "floating" inside your block. You should also not draw lines on top of other lines. In EasyDraw™, lines *do* share lines with other patches, unlike with PatchDraw.

Drawing with the Line Tool

The line tool draws straight lines.

1   Position the mouse cursor where you want the line to start.

2   Click, hold and drag to where the line is to end, then release the mouse. The line draws as you drag. Make sure the line touches another line or arc, or the outside of the block, at a snap point, before you release the mouse.

Drawing with the Arc Tool

The Arc tool draws semi-circular arcs which may be edited to form deeper or shallower curves.

1   Position the mouse cursor where you want the line to start.

2   Click, hold and drag to draw the arc, pressing your keyboard SPACEBAR if the arc is facing the wrong direction, then release the mouse where you want the arc to end. Make sure the arc touches another line or arc, or the outside of the block, at a snap point, before you release the mouse.

Arc tool

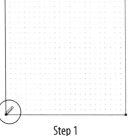

Step 1
Position mouse at starting point

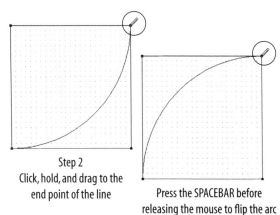

Step 2
Click, hold, and drag to the end point of the line

Press the SPACEBAR before releasing the mouse to flip the arc

Notes

• Advanced users: When drawing to snap points, be sure *Snap to grid* is turned on.

• When you release the mouse, the line may seem to move a bit. This is because lines drawn in EasyDraw™ will snap to points on a grid. The number of grid points can be adjusted using BLOCK > Drawing Board Setup > Snap Grid. Snapping to a grid helps ensure that your lines are connected. Any segments not connected to other lines or arcs will disappear or cause color to bleed through multiple patches.

Draw with Line and Arc Tools

Splitting Segments

You can split a line or arc with the Shape tool in EasyDraw™. Splitting a segment gives you more nodes to play "connect the dots" with.

Step 2
Shape

1 Start with an EasyDraw™ block on your screen. You can either draw it (see pages 223-225) or edit it from the Sketchbook (see page 121).

2 **Click the Shape tool > click on the line or arc in the block you want to split so it is selected.**

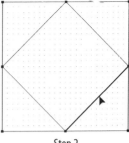

Step 2
Select the line

3 Choose one of the following ways to see the Edit Line or Edit Arc box:

• *on the button* – click the small red square in the bottom-corner of the Shape tool button.

• *right-click* – right-click in the middle of the worktable and click **Edit**.

• *from the menu* – click **BLOCK > Edit**.

Step 3
Edit Line box

4 **Click one of the buttons in the Edit Line or Edit Arc box to split the line or arc.** Once clicked, you will see one or more small black dots (nodes) along the old segment indicating it is split:

• **Half** – click this to split the segment into two equal pieces (in half)

• **Thirds** – click this to split the segment into three equal pieces (in thirds)

• **Partition** – choose the number first and then click the Partition button to split the line into that many equal pieces. You can either double-click the number and type over it or click the arrows to change it. (Allowable values are 3-15.)

• **Stagger** – choose the number first and then click the Stagger button to split the line into a "half-drop" version of that many equal pieces. You can either double-click the number and type over it or click the arrows to change it. (Allowable values are 3-15.)

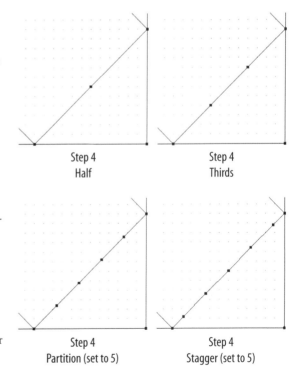

Step 4
Half

Step 4
Thirds

Step 4
Partition (set to 5)

Step 4
Stagger (set to 5)

Splitting Segments

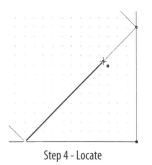

Step 4 - Locate

Line tool

Arc tool

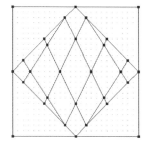

Step 5 - Draw lines or arcs using the new nodes

Step 6 - Color tab

Step 6
Paintbrush

The block has been colored

Step 7
Add to Sketchbook

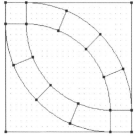

All four arcs - Partition, set to 4

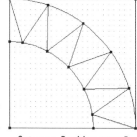

Outer arc - Partition, set to 5
Inner arc - Stagger, set to 5

- **Locate** – click this button, then click on the selected segment where you want to place the node.

- For information on **Xings**, see the Notes below.

5   If you don't like the placement of the nodes, click **EDIT > Undo** or press **CTRL+Z** on your keyboard.

   Otherwise, click the **Line** tool to draw lines or the **Arc** tool to draw arcs to the new nodes created.

6   **Click the Color tab when you are finished drawing > use the Paintbrush tool to color your block.**

7   Click the **Add to Sketchbook** button to make this block part of your project.

Notes

- The EasyDraw™ block outline cannot be split. However, lines drawn on top of the outline can be.

- Use Partition (set to the same number each time) on two segments to create a straight line effect.

- Use Partition on one segment and Stagger on another (both set to the same number) to create a zigzag effect.

- You will probably never need to use Xings unless you are drawing an extremely complex block. When you click the Add to Sketchbook button or switch back and forth from the EasyDraw and Color tabs, nodes appear at every intersection of every segment. If, however, you only wanted the nodes along one line, you would select it with the Shape tool and click Xings on the Edit box. The selected line would be split wherever another one crosses it. No other nodes would appear in the drawing where segments cross.

Splitting Segments

Drawing a Grid

1   Click **WORKTABLE > Work on Block,** or click the **Work on Block** button.

Step 1
Work on Block

2   Click **BLOCK > New Block > EasyDraw Block** to start a block with just a pieced layer, or **EasyDraw + PatchDraw** to start a block that can have appliqué motifs.

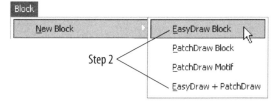

Step 2

3   Click the **Grid** tool.

4   Choose one of the following ways to verify the Grid Setup:

   • *on the button* – click the small red square in the bottom-corner of the Grid tool button.

   • *right-click* – right-click in the middle of the worktable and click **Grid Setup**.

   • *from the menu* – click **BLOCK > Grid Tool Setup.**

Step 3
Grid

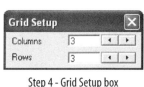

Step 4 - Grid Setup box

5   Double-click in the boxes for **Columns** or **Rows** and type a new number to change the grid. You can also click the right or left arrows to change the number.

6   The grid can fill the entire block or part of it. If you want the grid to fill the entire block, you should start at (or just outside) the top-left corner of the block and release at (or just outside) the bottom-right corner of the block. **Move your cursor to any part of the block, click and hold as you drag diagonally to make the grid, then release.**

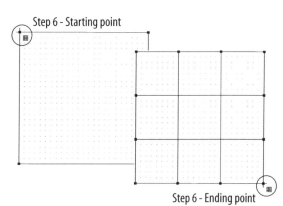

Step 6 - Starting point

Step 6 - Ending point

7   **Click the Color tab > use the Paintbrush tool to color your block.**

Step 7 - Color tab

Step 7 - Paintbrush

8   Click the **Add to Sketchbook** button to make this block part of your project.

Notes
• Make sure the grid works for the block size and snap points in that area. You will be able to draw the grid, but may get unexpected results when you try to draw other lines. Example: Don't drag out a 3x3 grid to fill a 7 inch block.

The block has been colored

Step 8
Add to Sketchbook

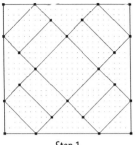

Step 1
Start with an EasyDraw™ block

Step 2

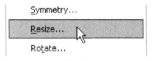

Step 3

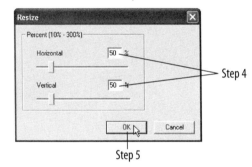

Step 4

Step 5

Shrinking a Block to a Quarter Patch

1 Start with an EasyDraw™ block on your screen. You can either draw it (see pages 223-225) or edit it from the Sketchbook (see page 121).

2 Click **EDIT > Select All.**

3 Click **BLOCK > Resize.**

4 Double-click the number for **Horizontal** and type **50**, then **Vertical** and type **50**. You can also drag the sliders to set the percentages.

5 Click **OK**.

6 While the pieces are still selected, click and hold in their center and drag the group to the top-left corner of the block so they snap into place.

7 While the pieces are still selected, make copies for the other three corners. Click **EDIT > Copy,** then **EDIT > Paste**. Move the pasted group to a different corner (as done in step 6), then repeat this step for the last two corners.

8 Be sure your new EasyDraw™ block is not breaking any EasyDraw™ rules (see page 222). You may need to draw a 2x2 grid in your block to complete it (see page 228).

9 **Click the Color tab > use the Paintbrush tool** to color your block.

10 Click the **Add to Sketchbook** button to make this block part of your project.

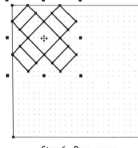

Step 6 - Drag group
to top-left corner

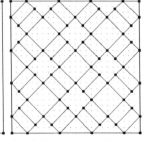

Step 7 - Paste the group 3 times
and drag to each corner

Step 9 - Color tab

Step 9 - Paintbrush

Step 10 - Add to Sketchbook

Notes

• Values for resizing by degree range from 10-300.

• When resizing an EasyDraw + PatchDraw block, you must resize the EasyDraw™ and appliqué layers separately.

• Resizing and moving blocks often leads to unconnected lines, because the block size and snap to grid settings of the original block do not work for the smaller version. Your colors may bleed into the next patch when you color. If this is the case, fix the Drawing Board Setup (see page 223) > convert the entire drawing to guides (see pages 252-253) > redraw the block from scratch with the Line and Arc tools.

Shrink Block to a Quarter Patch

Superimposing EasyDraw™ Blocks

As you've seen from the rest of this chapter, you can add or delete lines to existing EasyDraw™ blocks. Let's take this a little further and paste one on top of another.

1　Start with an EasyDraw™ block on your screen. You can either draw it (see pages 223-225) or edit it from the Sketchbook (see page 121).

2　Click **EDIT > Select All,** then **EDIT > Copy.** (Or, you can press CTRL+A, then CTRL+C on your keyboard.)

3　**Click the View Sketchbook button > Blocks section > find and select a different EasyDraw block > click the Edit button to put it on the worktable.**

4　Click **EDIT > Paste** (or press CTRL+V). The pasted block will be slightly off-center.

5　While the pasted block is still selected, click in its center and move it up and left so it snaps into the top-left corner of the block outline.

6　**Click the Color tab > click the EasyDraw tab.** This will make nodes where all the lines and arcs crossed.

7　You may want to clean up your drawing and delete unnecessary lines or arcs. See page 254.

8　**Click the Color tab > use the Paintbrush tool** to color your block.

9　Click the **Add to Sketchbook** button to make this block part of your project.

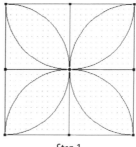

Step 1
Start with an EasyDraw™ block

Step 2
EDIT > Select All

Step 2
EDIT > Copy

Step 3
View Sketchbook

Step 4
EDIT > Paste

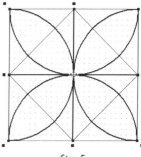

Step 5
Center the pasted block

Step 8
Color tab

Step 8
Paintbrush

Step 9
Add to Sketchbook

The block has been colored

PatchDraw Blocks

Quilt designed by Marla Whalen
Arlington, Tennessee

Section B

If you want to draw appliqué blocks, you must use PatchDraw. But this drawing style can also be used for drawing pieced blocks on special grids, or blocks combining piecing and appliqué. PatchDraw has its own requirements: if you intend to fill patches with color, each patch must be drawn as a complete, closed patch; and no patch can share a line with another patch. If you draw open patches, these lines will be considered threads (think redwork) and cannot be filled with fabric. PatchDraw's many drawing tools give you complete flexibility, but they need some study and practice to master. This chapter will help you understand exactly how these tools work.

Reference

Understanding PatchDraw

In PatchDraw, you draw blocks by creating patches. As long as your patches are closed, you can fill the patches with color. Any unclosed shapes, like cat whiskers, will be considered thread. To create a closed patch, be sure that whenever you start drawing a patch, you end back at its beginning, OR, that you use one of the automatic closed shape tools. **Patches cannot share lines and drawn segments should not cross one another as they would in a figure-eight.**

These patches are closed and can be colored.

These patches are open and will be treated as thread.

You can use PatchDraw to design pieced, appliqué, or combination blocks. Each new block you start can have a background square or not. There will be four typical uses for PatchDraw:

A *Appliqué Motifs with no background square*
(Block > New Block > PatchDraw Motif)

B *Appliqué Blocks with a plain background square*
(Block > New Block > PatchDraw Block >
Applique tab)

C *Pieced Blocks with no appliqué*
(Block > New Block > PatchDraw Block > Pieced
tab)

D *Pieced Blocks with appliqué motifs*
(Block > New Block > PatchDraw Block > use
both tabs)

If you are using any of the PatchDraw grids to design pieced blocks with the Polydraw tool, you'll need to start a PatchDraw block. Draw each line to close the shape and fit them together to form your pieced block. You cannot draw using the line method in EasyDraw.

If you plan to set the block on Layer 1 of a quilt, it needs to have the background square or be completely covered in patches (no holes), as with the Polydraw tool and PatchDraw grids. If you plan to set the block on Layers 2 or 3, you do not need the background square.

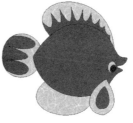 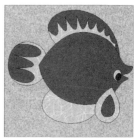

A A *motif* has no background square.

B A *block* has a background square.

C Draw pieced PatchDraw blocks (without any holes) on the Pieced tab.

D Draw patches on both tabs to make blocks combining piecing and appliqué.

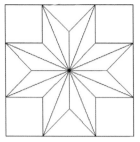

The patches in this finished block appear to share lines.

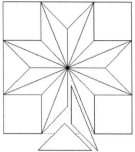

When pulled away, you can see each is its own closed shape.

Draw the basic elements of your design.

Reshape the patches to be perfect once they are drawn.

One of the biggest benefits of PatchDraw is the ability to create very realistic shapes. One way to achieve this is to use the special shape tools: heart, oval, diamond, teardrop and leaf, to name a few. The shape tools are nice because they create patches that are already closed. The other way to create realistic shapes is to use the Freehand tool and just draw as you like. No matter the tool used, you can reshape the patches after they are drawn. **Remember, "closed is better than perfect" and you can always edit later.**

To see examples of appliqué blocks and motifs drawn using PatchDraw, **go to LIBRARIES > Block Library > look at any of the blocks in 4 Classic Appliqué, 5 Contemporary Appliqué, or 6 Motifs.**

To see examples of pieced blocks drawn using PatchDraw, **go to LIBRARIES > Block Library > 1 Classic Pieced > and look at the last six blocks in Five- and Six-Pointed Stars.**

Understanding PatchDraw

Drawing a PatchDraw Block

Starting the Block

1   Click **WORKTABLE > Work on Block**, or click the **Work on Block** button.

2   Click **BLOCK > New Block > PatchDraw Block** to start a block with a background square, or **PatchDraw Motif** to start without the background square.

Verify Block Size, Special Grids, Snap Points & Graph Paper

Steps 3 – 7 are somewhat optional, but it is important to know how to change them if needed.

3   *Block Size* – Click **BLOCK > Drawing Board Setup > Block Size** (under General) to double-check the finished block size. **Width** and **Height** determine your rulers. Double-click in the box and type a new size to change it.

4   *Special Grids* – Click **Snap Grid** (under General). For more information on the different styles, see pages 238-239.

5   *Snap Points* – Click **Snap Grid** (under General), double-click in the box for Horizontal and Vertical grid points and type a new number for each. These should be a *multiple of your block size.* For example,

- **If you are working in inches and your block size is 6" x 6",** you should set both your horizontal and vertical snaps points to:
  6 (snap every inch, 6 x 1 = 6),
  12 (snap every 1/2 inch, 6 x 2 = 12),
  24 (snap every 1/4 inch, 6 x 4 = 24),
  48 (snap every 1/8 inch, 6 x 8 = 48), etc.

- **If you are working in centimeters and your block size is 15x15cm,** you should set both your horizontal and vertical snaps points to:
  15 (snap every cm, 15 x 1 = 15),
  30 (snap every 0.5cm, 15 x 2),
  75 (snap every 2mm, 15 x 5 = 75),
  150 (snap every mm, 15 x 10 = 150), etc.

Step 1
Work on Block

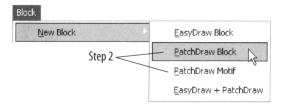

Step 2

Step 3
BLOCK > Drawing Board Setup

Change width and height

Step 3

Change snap points

Steps
4 & 5

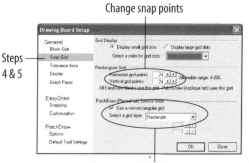

Change special grids (see pages 238-239)

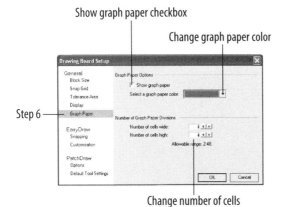

Show graph paper checkbox

Change graph paper color

Step 6

Change number of cells

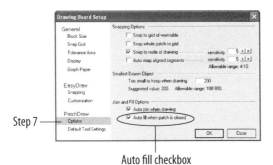

Step 7

Auto fill checkbox

> **Please note:**
> There are shortcuts for many Drawing Board Setup options and PatchDraw tool options in the Precision Bar. See HELP > Contents for more information.

Step 8

Pick tool

Shape tool

PolyLine

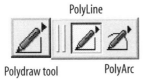

Polydraw tool   PolyArc

- **If your block is a rectangle at 6" x 10"**, you should set your snaps to be multiples of each number. Snaps would be 6 x 10, 12 x 20, etc.

6   *Graph Paper* – Click **Graph Paper** (under General)

- Click the checkbox next to **Show graph paper** to choose whether or not you want to see it.

- To change its color, click the down arrow next to **Graph paper color** and click a color in the list. (If you're using a Special Grid from step 4, be sure Graph Paper is set to a different color so you can tell them apart when drawing.)

- You can also set the number of cells that appear on the block. Double-click in the box and type a new number to change either **Number of cells wide** or **Number of cells high** (allowable values are from 2 to 48).

7   *Auto fill* – Choose whether or not patches fill when closed. Click **Options** (under PatchDraw) and check or uncheck **Auto fill when patch is closed**.

Using the PatchDraw Tools

8   If you are on the **Pieced** tab of a PatchDraw block, use any of these tools to draw or modify your design. All patches must be closed and the entire background must be filled with no overlapping patches:

- **Pick tool** – use to select and move one or more patches; pick any patches ready for deletion, rotation, flipping, or resizing.

- **Shape tool** – use to shape patches; add, delete, or move nodes to reshape the patch.

- **Polydraw tool** – choose the PolyLine or the PolyArc tool from the flyout menu; draw lines or arcs to form all sides of the patch; double-click the node where you started drawing to close the patch; double-click away from the drawing or press your keyboard **ESC key** to erase a patch in progress.

Drawing a PatchDraw Block

9 If you are on the **Applique** tab of a PatchDraw
block, PatchDraw motif, or EasyDraw +
PatchDraw block, use any of these tools to draw
or modify your design. **Any closed patches you
draw will be interpreted as appliqué and any
open patches or segments you draw will be
interpreted as thread.** It also helps if you draw
from the back to the front (ending with the
details of the block) so that you have the least
amount of re-layering to do:

- **Pick tool** – use to select and move one or
  more segments or patches; select segments or
  patches ready for deletion, rotation, flipping,
  or resizing; pick patches and send them to
  the front or back of the drawing.

- **Shape tool** – use to edit segments or patches;
  add or remove nodes from a segment or patch;
  move nodes to reshape a segment or patch.

- **Line tool** – draw lines; click and hold as you
  drag to make a line, then release.

- **Bezier Curve tool** – draw curves; click and
  hold as you drag to make the arc, then release.

- **Freehand tool** – draw freeform patches as
  you would on paper, see page 241.

- **Brush Stroke tool** – draw one segment in a
  freehand manner and it is the "invisible spine"
  of your future patch; this is great for vines and
  stems, see pages 242-243.

- **Rectangle tool** – drag out a rectangle or
  rounded rectangle, see pages 244-245.

- **Ellipse tool** – drag out an ellipse or circle;
  choose between a full circle, pie, or curve, see
  pages 244-245.

- **Oval tool** – drag out closed shapes; choose
  from hearts, leaves, teardrops, and more on
  the flyout menu, see page 246.

- **Polygon tool** – drag out closed shapes; choose
  from triangles, diamonds, and other polygons
  on the flyout menu, see page 246.

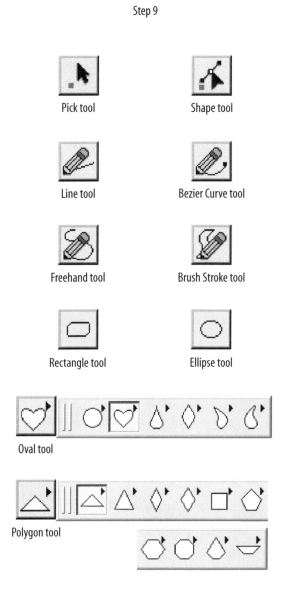

Step 9

Pick tool   Shape tool

Line tool   Bezier Curve tool

Freehand tool   Brush Stroke tool

Rectangle tool   Ellipse tool

Oval tool

Polygon tool

Drawing a PatchDraw Block

Step 1
View Sketchbook

Step 2

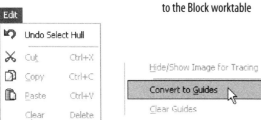

Edit the PatchDraw block
to the Block worktable

Step 3 - EDIT > Select All

Hide/Show Image for Tracing

Convert to Guides

Clear Guides

Step 4

Eliminating the PatchDraw Background

PatchDraw Blocks have a background. PatchDraw Motifs do not have a background. To eliminate the background, you need to copy and paste the appliqué into a new PatchDraw Motif.

1 **Click the View Sketchbook button > click the Blocks section > find and click on your PatchDraw Block > click the Edit button.**

2 Click the **Applique** tab.

3 Click **EDIT > Select All**, then **EDIT > Copy**. (You can also use keyboard shortcuts: CTRL+A, CTRL+C.)

4 *(Optional)* Click **BLOCK > Convert to Guides**.

5 Click **BLOCK > New Block > PatchDraw Motif**.

6 Click **EDIT > Paste**.

7 *(Optional)* Reposition the pasted motifs.

• *If you would like the design centered,* be sure you have the Precision Bar turned on. Click **VIEW > Precision Bar** if it is off. Then, click the **Move selected segments to center of block** button.

• *If you would like the design to be in its original location,* click and hold in the center of the pasted motif while they are still selected and drag them to cover the guides you made in step 4.

8 **Click the Color tab > use the Paintbrush tool** to color your block.

9 Click the **Add to Sketchbook** button to make this block part of your project.

Step 5

Step 6

The patches are
pasted in the motif

Step 7
Move selected segments
to center of block

The new motif does not
have a background

Notes
• To reverse these directions and add a plain block to the background of a motif, choose BLOCK > New Block > PatchDraw Block in step 5.

Using PatchDraw Grids and the Polydraw Tools

When drawing pieced blocks in PatchDraw, you can use other grids than just square or rectangular.

Step 1
Work on Block

Choose Your Grid

1   Click **WORKTABLE > Work on Block**, or click the **Work on Block** button.

2   Click **BLOCK > New Block > PatchDraw Block**.

Step 2

3   *Block Size* – Click **BLOCK > Drawing Board Setup > Block Size** (under General) to double-check the finished block size. **Width** and **Height** determine your rulers. Double-click in the box and type a new size to change it.

Step 3
BLOCK > Drawing Board Setup

4   *Special Grids* – Click **Snap Grid (under General) > click to put a check next to *Use a non-rectangular grid* > click the down arrow next to *Select a grid style* > click *your choice* > click OK**. Choose from the following:

  • *Rectangle (select this to turn off the grid)*
  • Circle
  • Arc
  • Eight Point Star
  • Kaleidoscope
  • Octagon

Change width and height

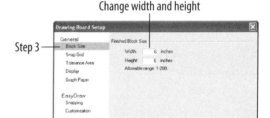

Step 3

Draw the Block

5   **Click and hold on the Polydraw tool > click the PolyLine tool to draw lines** (Rectangle, Eight Point Star, Kaleidoscope, and Octagon grids) or the **PolyArc tool to draw arcs and straight lines** (Circle and Arc grids).

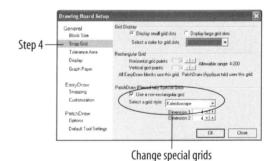

Step 4

Change special grids

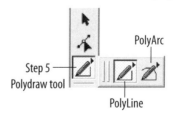

PolyArc

Step 5
Polydraw tool

PolyLine

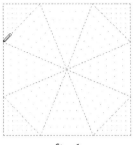

Step 6
Click a grid point

Step 7
Click grid points to place nodes

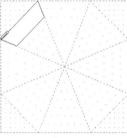
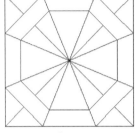

Step 8
Double-click on the starting point to close the patch

Step 9
Fill the entire block with patches

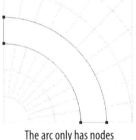

Notice the gaps between the arcs

The arc only has nodes in the corners

To avoid gaps click each spoke on the grid

6   Once you begin drawing, you must complete the patch by returning to the initial point. To start over at anytime, press the ESC key. **Click on a grid point to start.** (Nodes automatically snap to the nearest grid point.)

7   **Click another grid point to place a node.** Continue clicking to place the nodes that form your patch. If you are using the PolyArc tool on a Circle or Arcs grid, it will draw arcs when you are drawing along the same ring and draw straight lines otherwise. Do not cross your lines in one patch (as with a figure-eight).

8   **Double-click to end the patch at the beginning point.** If auto fill is turned on, you'll see the patch fill.

9   Continue drawing complete patches until the entire block is filled. Don't leave any holes or overlap patches.

Notes
- If you click accidentally and begin the drawing process and didn't want to, either press the keyboard ESC key or double-click to release the mouse and delete the line.

- If you click accidentally in the middle of drawing at a place you did not want to click, hold the keyboard SHIFT key and click to release the last node that was placed.

- Holding the SHIFT key and clicking multiple times will release each node, one at a time, back until the initial node.

- You must complete an entire patch when drawing with these tools. You cannot draw part of a patch, start a different patch then come back to the first patch to finish it. You must complete an entire patch to be able to see it and edit it.

- Don't draw lines on top of existing lines within the same patch.

- If you notice gaps between patches, delete one patch and redraw it, clicking on each node along the way (even if it is a straight line or simple arc).

Drawing with the Line and Bezier Curve Tools

The Line and Bezier Curve tools are available on the Applique tab.

1   Click **WORKTABLE > Work on Block**, or click the **Work on Block** button.

2   Click **BLOCK > New Block > PatchDraw Block, PatchDraw Motif, or EasyDraw + PatchDraw.**

3   Click the **Applique** tab.

4   Click the **Line** tool to draw lines or **Bezier Curve** tool to draw curves.

5   **Position your cursor inside the block outline > click and hold to start the segment > drag your cursor across the screen to change its length > release to stop that segment, but do not move your mouse cursor.**

6   **Continue from the stopping point of the last segment > click and hold to start the next segment > drag to the desired ending point > release, but do not move your mouse to stop that segment.**

7   Repeat step 6 until you stop where you started in step 5. This will close the patch. If auto fill is turned on, you'll see the patch fill.

Notes
- If you turned off *Snap to Node* in the Precision Bar, your segments will not connect.

- The Bezier Curve tool is not like the Freehand tool. A single arc drawn with this tool can never be more complicated than an "S" curve. To draw a complex shape with this tool you must "build it up" by joining together several arcs.

- If you want to draw a patch combining lines and curves, use the Bezier Curve tool and CTRL key. When you draw with the CTRL key held down – it will draw lines; with it released – it will draw curves.

Step 1
Work on Block

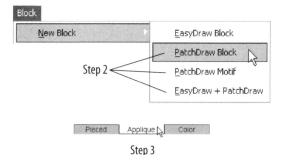

Step 2

Step 3

Step 4
Line

Step 4
Bezier Curve

 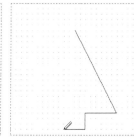

Step 5 - Drag out the first segment

Step 6 - Drag out each segment from the ending point of the segment before

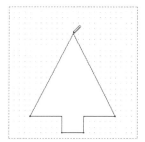

Step 7 - End at the starting point to close your appliqué patch

Step 1
Work on Block

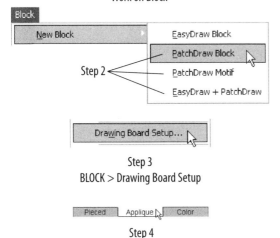

Step 2

Step 3
BLOCK > Drawing Board Setup

Step 4

Drawing with the Freehand Tool

The Freehand tool is available on the Applique tab (on all blocks other than EasyDraw™ Blocks).

1 Click **WORKTABLE > Work on Block**, or click the **Work on Block** button.

2 Click **BLOCK > New Block > PatchDraw Block** to start a new block with a PatchDraw background, **PatchDraw Motif** to start a new block without a background, or **EasyDraw + PatchDraw** to start a new block with an EasyDraw™ background.

3 Click **BLOCK > Drawing Board Setup**. Double-check your block size and snap points to be sure they are set as you'd like. Click **OK**.

4 Click the **Applique** tab.

5 **Click the Freehand tool > position your cursor inside the block outline > click and hold > move your cursor around freely > end the patch at the beginning point > release the mouse.** The patch will smooth out. If auto fill is turned on, the patch will fill.

6 If you do not like your patch, click **EDIT > Undo** and start over from step 5.

7 *If you ended the patch accurately at the beginning, it will close.*

If you missed the beginning point, **click the Shape tool > click and hold on the ending node with the Shape tool to pick it up > drag it over and drop it on top of the beginning node.** The patch should close and will fill if auto fill is turned on.

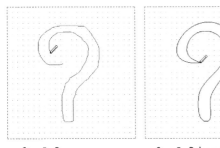

Step 5 - Drag your mouse around freely to form the patch

Step 5 - Release the mouse at the starting point

Step 6

Step 7
Shape

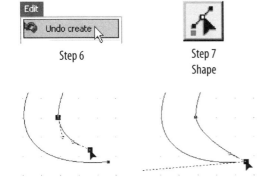

Step 8 - Drag the ending node on top of the beginning node

Notes

- Do not draw lines in a shape that cross (as with a figure 8). Do not draw patches extending past the block outline.

- Any unclosed shapes will be interpreted as thread.

- Use the Freehand tool to trace pictures, see pages 262-264.

- You can adjust the freehand smoothness of the patch through the Drawing Board Setup, see HELP > Contents.

Drawing with the Freehand Tool

Drawing with the Brush Stroke Tool

The Brush Stroke tool is available only on the Applique tab. The Brush Stroke tool is great for drawing stems, vines, buds, and basket handles.

1   Click **WORKTABLE > Work on Block**, or click the **Work on Block** button.

2   Click **BLOCK > New Block > PatchDraw Block** to start a new block with a PatchDraw background, **PatchDraw Motif** to start a new block without a background, or **EasyDraw + PatchDraw** to start a new block with an EasyDraw background.

3   Click **BLOCK > Drawing Board Setup**. Double-check your block size and snap points to be sure they are set as you want them. Click **OK** when you are done.

4   Click the **Applique** tab.

5   Click the **Brush Stroke** tool. If the Brush Stroke tool is not on your toolbar, see page 304.

6   *To draw the spine,* **click the Brush Stroke tool > position your cursor inside the block outline > click and hold > move your cursor around freely to draw the "spine" of your patch > release the mouse.** This is a drawing-in-progress, so it will not fill automatically if you have auto fill turned on. The "spine" can still be edited. You will see two equidistant lines on either side of the spine. These sides are the edges of the real patch and are controlled by Minimum Width and Boldness.

7   *To reshape the spine,* **click the Shape tool > click the spine to select it > click and hold on any node > drag it to a new position.** You can also click a node to see its handles. **Click and hold on the handle > drag it to a new position.**

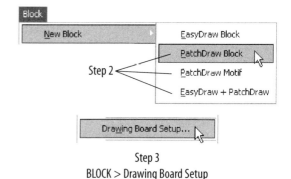

Step 2

Step 3
BLOCK > Drawing Board Setup

Step 4

Step 5
Brush Stroke

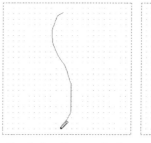 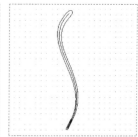

Step 6 - Drag the cursor freely   Step 6 - Release the mouse
to draw the patch spine   to see the in-progress patch

Step 7
Shape

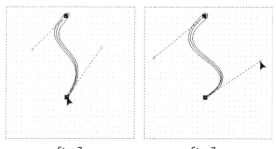

Step 7   Step 7
Drag a node to a new position   Drag a handle to a new position

Step 9
Pick

Step 9
Stroke Style

Step 9
Stroke End

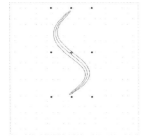

Step 9 - Stroke Style and Stroke End choices applied

Minimum Width: 1.500
Boldness: 5.000

Step 10

Step 10 - Minimum Width and Boldness choices applied

Step 11
Convert to Patch

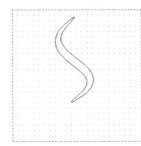

The Brush Stroke has been
converted to a patch

8 If you do not see the Precision Bar below the Project toolbar, click **VIEW > Precision Bar** to turn it on.

9 *To change the style of the stroke's body or ends,* **click the Pick tool > click the brush stroke to select it > click the down arrow next to Stroke Style and click a different style in the list > click the down arrow next to Stroke End and click a different style in the list.** Your brush stroke will update to reflect your changes.

10 *To change the thickness of the stroke,* you can change the minimum width or boldness.

- **Minimum Width** – All of the stroke styles, with the exception of the first one, have a place at the beginning, end, or middle where the stroke tapers in. This is "the location" in the stroke where the width is at its minimum. Set the minimum width to zero and this "location" will be basically flat (no width). As the minimum width number increases, this "location" will grow wider.

- **Boldness** – Boldness or "fatness" refers to the size of the stroke around the spine. If you set it to 1, you have a very narrow stroke surrounding the spine. As you increase this number, the stroke gets fatter and fatter, or bolder and bolder, surrounding the spine. The overall style of the stroke does not change so it still has a "location" where it's tapered and that area does not get fatter unless you change the Minimum Width for it.

11 When you are finished editing the spine and changing the settings, click the **Convert to Patch** button on the Precision Bar or click the **Color** tab.

Notes
- Before clicking *Convert to Patch* or the Color tab, you can reselect and change the settings for a brush stroke by selecting it with the Pick tool.

Drawing with Brush Stroke Tool

Drawing with the Rectangle and Ellipse Tools

The Rectangle and Ellipse tools are available on the Applique tab and may not be on your toolbar by default, see page 304.

1   Click **WORKTABLE > Work on Block**, or click the **Work on Block** button.

2   Click **BLOCK > New Block > PatchDraw Block, PatchDraw Motif, or EasyDraw + PatchDraw.**

3   Click the **Applique** tab.

4   *To add the Rectangle and Ellipse tools to your toolbar,* **right-click on the Drawing toolbar > click Add/Remove Buttons > click the Rectangle tool > click the Ellipse tool > click away from the Add/Remove list to turn the list off.**

5   Click the **Rectangle** tool to make squares, rectangles, or rounded rectangles OR the **Ellipse** tool to make circles, ellipses (ovals), pies, or wedges.

6   **Position your cursor inside the block outline > click and hold to start the shape > optional: hold down your keyboard CTRL key to make a perfect square or circle > drag your cursor across the screen to change the size > release to stop the shape.** This is a drawing-in-progress, so it will not fill automatically if you have auto fill turned on.

Notes
• These shapes are not filled when you first draw them so that you can edit them as geometric objects. For example, using the Shape tool or the Precision Bar, you can change the angles of a pie shape, or the amount of rounding at the corners of a rectangle. Once you apply *Convert to Patch* to fill the object it can no longer be edited in this way.

Step 1
Work on Block

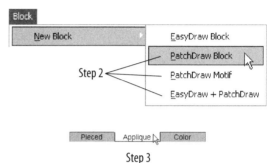

Step 2

Step 3

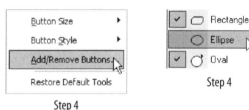

Step 4

Step 5
Rectangle

Step 5
Ellipse

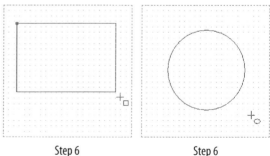

Step 6
Using the Rectangle tool

Step 6
Using the Ellipse tool and holding down the CTRL key to create a perfect circle

Drawing with Rectangle / Ellipse

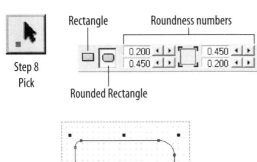

Step 8
Pick

Rectangle

Roundness numbers

Rounded Rectangle

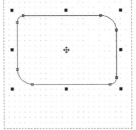

Step 8 - Rounded rectangle choices applied

Ellipse   Arc   Starting angle

Partition evenly
into sections

Pie   Ending angle   Stagger initial/
final sections

Change the
number of
sections

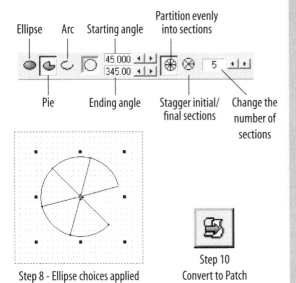

Step 8 - Ellipse choices applied

Step 10
Convert to Patch

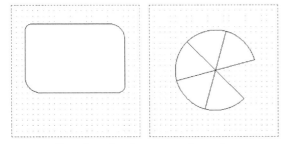

These shapes have been converted to patches

Steps 7-9 are a group of optional steps. If you are happy with your drawing skip to step 10. Otherwise, do all the steps in the shaded box.

7   *(Optional)* If you do not see the Precision Bar below the Project toolbar, click **VIEW > Precision Bar** to turn it on.

8   *(Optional)* **Click the Pick tool > click on the line of the shape you just drew to select it > change the settings on the Precision Bar to modify the shape:**

- **Rectangle button** – click this to make the corners sharp (90 degrees).

- **Rounded Rectangle button** – click this to make rounded corners; click the arrow buttons next to the roundness numbers to make the corners more or less round.

- **Ellipse button** – click this to make your ellipse or circle have no gaps

- **Pie button** – click this to turn your ellipse into a pie; click the arrow buttons for starting and ending angles to increase any gap in the pie.

- **Arc button** – click this to turn your ellipse into an arc; click the arrow buttons for starting and ending angles to increase any gap in the arc.

9   *(Optional)* If you are making an ellipse, pie or arc, you can section it into pieces. Click either the *Partition evenly into sections* button or *Stagger initial/final sections* button. Then, click the arrows beside *Change the number of sections* box to divide the ellipse, pie or arc.

10   When you are finished, click the **Convert to Patch** button on the Precision Bar or click the **Color** tab. If auto fill is turned on, you'll see the patch or patches fill.

Notes
- If you accidentally deselect the patch and haven't converted it to a patch yet, click it with the Pick tool to continue editing.

Drawing with the Oval and Polygon Tools

The Oval and Polygon tools are available on the Applique tab. They draw closed shapes automatically.

1 Click **WORKTABLE > Work on Block**, or click the **Work on Block** button.

2 Click **BLOCK > New Block > PatchDraw Block, PatchDraw Motif, or EasyDraw + PatchDraw.**

3 Click the **Applique** tab.

4 These tools have flyout menus for all the different shapes. To see all the styles, click either the Oval or Polygon tools and *hold down* the mouse button until the flyout menu appears, displaying the styles. **Click to select the style you like.**

5 **Position your cursor inside the block outline > click and hold to start the shape >** *optional: hold down your keyboard CTRL key to make a perfect shape or draw at a perfect angle* **> drag your cursor in any direction across the screen to change the size or orientation > release to stop the shape.** The drawing is complete and will fill automatically if you have auto fill turned on.

Step 1
Work on Block

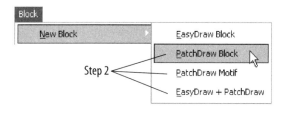

Step 2

Step 3

Oval tool   Polygon tool

Step 4
Click and hold to see the flyout menus

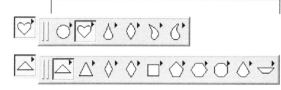

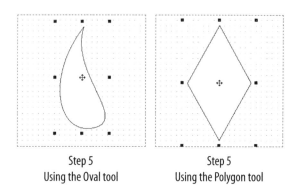

Step 5
Using the Oval tool

Step 5
Using the Polygon tool

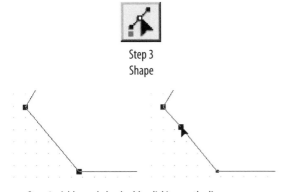

Step 3
Shape

Step 4 - Add a node by double-clicking on the line or curve

Step 4 - Delete a node by double-clicking on it

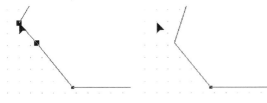

Step 4 - Move a node by clicking and dragging it to a new location

Step 5 - Shape a curve or node by clicking
to select it and moving the handles

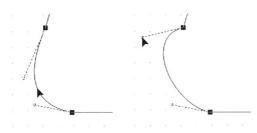

Edit Node box –
The buttons available
depend on what is
selected

Shaping Patches

Nodes and handles are the key to shaping patches. Nodes are the black dots between segments. Handles are attached to nodes only near curves (not lines).

1   Click the **View Sketchbook** button. Click the **Blocks** section and double-click your block.

2   Click the **Applique** tab.

3   **Click the Shape tool > click a line or curve in the patch you want to shape.**

4   *To add nodes,* double-click on the line or curve at the point where you want a node.

   To delete nodes, double-click on the node to delete it. (Every patch needs at least two nodes.)

   To move nodes, click and hold on the node in the patch, then drag it to a new location.

5   *To shape a curve,* click the curve to see the handles, then click, hold, and drag the handles to new positions.

   To shape a node, click to select the node to see its handles, then click, hold, and drag the handles to new positions.

6   *To change a line to a curve or vice versa,* click to select the line or curve. Right-click on the line or curve, click **Edit**, and then click the **to Curve** or **to Line** button on the Edit box that appears.

7   *To change the smoothness of a node's handles,* click to select the node. Right-click on the node, click **Edit**, then click any of the following options:

   • **Corner** – makes the handles independent.
   • **Smooth** – straightens the handles out to be 180 degrees from one another.
   • **Cusp** – lincs the handles up on top of one another.
   • **Symm**(etrical) – smoothes the node as much as possible, by making the handles the same length and 180 degrees apart from one another.

Making a Wreath

WreathMaker is available on the Applique tab and is used to make original wreath designs. This feature can be used on patches you draw or on patches from existing Library blocks. WreathMaker repeats and rotates any selected patches for you.

1   Click **WORKTABLE > Work on Block** or click the **Work on Block** button.

2   Click **BLOCK > New Block >** *Your Choice* (anything except EasyDraw Block).

3   Use any of the PatchDraw tools to draw the shape you want to repeat. Remember that orientation matters. You will make different wreaths with horizontal patches than vertical. To learn how the PatchDraw drawing tools work, see pages 240-247.

4   **Click the Pick tool > click the shape you drew.** To select more than one patch, click the first, hold down your keyboard **SHIFT key** and click the others. Or, press CTRL+A to select all.

5   Click **BLOCK > WreathMaker** (or right-click on the selected patches and click WreathMaker).

6   *Number of clusters* – drag the slider bar to any position or double-click the current number and type a new number to change the number of patch groups. (Range: 3-20)

7   *Cluster spacing* – drag the slider bar to any position or double-click the current number and type a new number to change the amount of space between patch groups. (Range: 0-100%)

8   *Resize cluster* – drag the slider bar to any position or double-click the current number and type a new number to change how much the patch groups are resized. (Range varies, 100% = no change in size)

9   Click **OK** and the wreath will appear.

10 If you do not like the way it looks, click **EDIT > Undo** and start over at step 5.

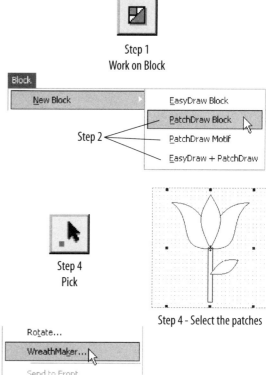

Step 1
Work on Block

Step 2

Step 4
Pick

Step 4 - Select the patches

Step 5

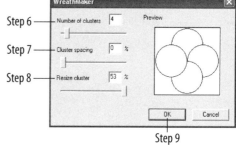

Step 6

Step 7

Step 8

Step 9

The finished wreath

Wreath Recipes

Original   Result

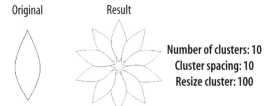

Number of clusters: 10
Cluster spacing: 10
Resize cluster: 100

A small number for Cluster spacing will keep your
clusters close together or even overlap them.

Original   Result

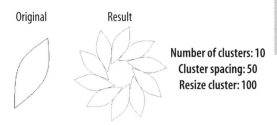

Number of clusters: 10
Cluster spacing: 50
Resize cluster: 100

If your original is not vertical, you can make more "twisted" designs.

Original   Result

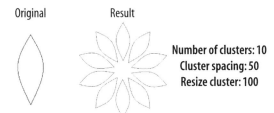

Number of clusters: 10
Cluster spacing: 50
Resize cluster: 100

A larger number for Cluster spacing
will place your clusters farther apart.

Original   Result

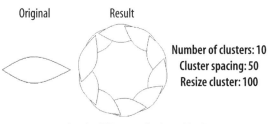

Number of clusters: 10
Cluster spacing: 50
Resize cluster: 100

See the difference a horizontal leaf
makes compared to a vertical leaf?

Notes

- You may want to relayer your wreath's patches, see page 250. Keep in mind, one patch will always have to be on top.

- You can WreathMaker a wreath to see interesting effects. WreathMaker is also great for creating quilting stencils.

- Wreaths are automatically centered in the block.

- If you set *Cluster spacing* to 0% the wreath will be touching in the center. If you set it to 100%, WreathMaker may automatically change the value for Resize cluster to ensure that the wreath fits inside the block.

- If you set *Resize cluster* to 100% the patches will not change size. If you set it to anything higher than 100%, the patches will increase in size.

Original   Result

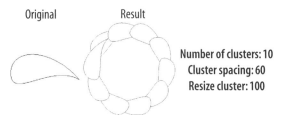

Number of clusters: 10
Cluster spacing: 60
Resize cluster: 100

Look at the effect drawing a shape differently can have on a
wreath. Compare this wreath to the one below.

Original   Result

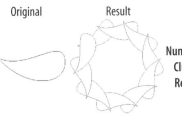

Number of clusters: 10
Cluster spacing: 60
Resize cluster: 100

Making a Wreath

Layering Patches in PatchDraw

When patches overlap, you'll sometimes want to move a patch in front of or behind another. You can layer patches on the Applique tab (patches on the Pieced tab should never overlap).

Step 1
Work on Block

1   Click **WORKTABLE > Work on Block**, or click the **Work on Block** button.

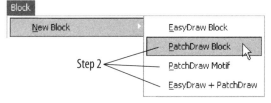

Step 2

2   Click **BLOCK > New Block > PatchDraw Block, PatchDraw Motif, or EasyDraw + PatchDraw.**

3   Click the **Applique** tab.

4   **Draw your block.** Once your block is drawn, you can move patches in front of or behind other patches.

Step 3

Step 4

5   Click the **Color** tab at the bottom of the screen. You will be looking at your block as a black and white line drawing.

Step 5

6   **Click the Pick tool > click a patch you want to re-layer.** Use SHIFT+click to select more than one patch. The outline of selected patches will be bold.

Step 6
Pick

8   Click **BLOCK > Send to Front** and the patches will be the top layer or **BLOCK > Send to Back** so the patches will be the bottom layer. (You can also right-click anywhere on the drawing and choose Send to Front or Send to Back.)

Notes

- Patches are automatically layered in the order they are drawn: first patch drawn = bottom; last patch drawn = top. Save time and draw them in the correct order.

- You can change the layering before or after you've colored patches.

- If you change a layer and you don't like the new look, you can choose EDIT > Undo to take back your most recent change.

- You can also relayer patches on the Applique tab while drawing. Use the shortcuts on the Precision Bar.

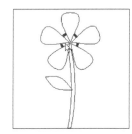

Step 6 - Click the patch to re-layer

Step 7

The flower center is now
on top of the petals

Precision Bar shortcuts

Send to front

Send to back

Quilt designed by Emily Haigh
Peoria, Arizona

All Blocks

Section C

This section helps with both EasyDraw™ and PatchDraw. It gives block drawing steps that work the same way no matter which drawing style you're using. And it contains helpful information for everyone. Even beginners will be interested in how Serendipity lets you make new blocks without drawing so much as a line! More advanced designers will want to see the importing and tracing information. So be sure to at least page through this section no matter your drawing experience.

Reference

Using Graph Paper and Guides

Guides and Graph Paper are not part of your finished design, but they can help you to draw blocks. You can use one or both when drawing.

1   Click **WORKTABLE > Work on Block**, or click the **Work on Block** button.

2   Click **BLOCK > New Block >** *Your Choice.* You can use graph paper and guides with any block style.

Using Graph Paper

3   Click **BLOCK > Drawing Board Setup > Graph Paper** (under General).

4   Click to put a check in **Show graph paper** so you can see it.

5   Click the down arrow next to **Graph paper color** and click on a color in the list to change its color. (You want this color to be lighter and different than the black lines you will be drawing.)

6   Double-click in the box and type a new number to change either **Number of cells wide** or **Number of cells high** (allowable values are from 2 to 48). Examples: Set it to 2 x 2 and you will know where the center of your block is, or set it to 3 x 3 and you will have a 9-patch graph behind your block.

7   Click **OK**. You will see the graph paper in the selected color and number of cells you chose.

Step 1
Work on Block

Step 2
BLOCK > *Your Choice*

Step 3
BLOCK > Drawing Board Setup

Step 4   Step 5

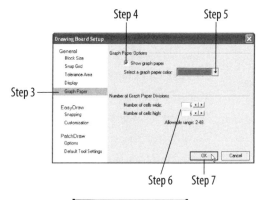

Step 3

Step 6   Step 7

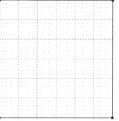

The block now has graph paper

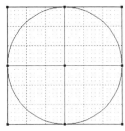

Step 8 - Draw guides

Step 9 - EDIT > Select All

Step 9
Pick

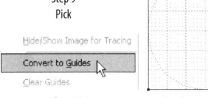

Step 10

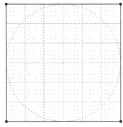

The drawing has been
converted to guides

Step 11

Step 12

Step 13

Step 14

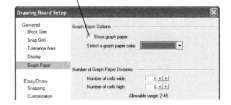

Using Guides

8 Use any of the tools to draw your guides.

9 Convert all or part of the drawing to guides:

- *All of the drawing* – Click **EDIT > Select All**.

- *Part of the drawing* – Click the **Pick** tool and click on the part of your drawing you want to be guides. To select more than one line, arc, or patch, select the first one, then **SHIFT+click** the others.

10 Click **BLOCK > Convert to Guides.** You will see the guides in the color they are set in Drawing Board Setup.

11 If you do not like this color, click **BLOCK > Drawing Board Setup > Display** (under General). Click the down arrow next to **Select a color for guides** and click on a color in the list. (You want this color to be lighter and different than your black lines you will be drawing.)

12 Click **OK**.

Clearing Guides or Turning off Graph Paper

13 To clear the guides from the worktable, click **BLOCK > Clear Guides.**

14 To turn off the graph paper, click **BLOCK > Drawing Board Setup > Graph Paper (under General) > click to uncheck Show graph paper > click OK.**

Notes

- **You can right-click on the worktable and convert selected segments to guides.**

- **If you are trying to get two different blocks to match at the sides, convert the first block to guides, start a new block and draw where the guides meet the edge of the block outline.**

- **If you turn on the Precision Bar, you will have shortcuts for these tasks. Click VIEW > Precision Bar to turn it on. See page 224 for illustration.**

- **To convert a rectangle, ellipse, or stroke to guides you must first use *Convert to Patch*.**

Using Graph Paper and Guides

Copying & Pasting or Deleting Lines or Patches

You can copy and paste or delete any part of your drawing, whether you are in EasyDraw™ or PatchDraw.

1   Click the **Pick** tool.

2   **Click the segment or patch you want to copy or delete.** To select multiple segments or patches, click the first one and **SHIFT+click** the others.

3   *To copy and paste the selection,* click **EDIT > Copy,** then **EDIT > Paste.** (Or press CTRL+C, then CTRL+V on your keyboard.) The pasted version will now be selected and you can move it into place. Position your cursor over the move icon in the center of the pasted segments. Click and hold, then drag the segments to the new location.

   To delete the selection, click **EDIT > Clear.** (Or press the DELETE key on your keyboard.)

4   If you pasted or deleted the wrong thing, click **EDIT > Undo** (or press CTRL+Z on your keyboard). Then go back to step 2 to verify what indeed was selected.

Notes

*   **You can add Copy, Paste and Cut buttons to the top toolbar to use as shortcuts, see page 301.**

*   **To delete a line or patch immediately after drawing it, click EDIT > Undo.**

*   **When you delete segments in an EasyDraw™ block, verify that the new drawing does not break the rules of EasyDraw™ now, see page 222.**

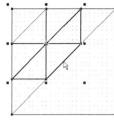
Step 2
Click segment(s) to copy

Step 3
EDIT > Copy

Step 3
EDIT > Paste

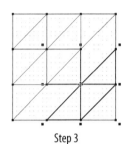
Step 3
The selected segments have been pasted and moved to the lower-right corner

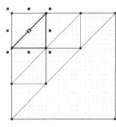
Step 2
Click segment(s) to delete

Step 3
EDIT > Clear

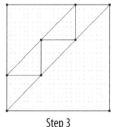
Step 3
The selected segments have been deleted

Step 2
Pick

Original block rotation

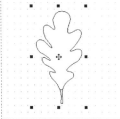

Step 2 - Select the segments
or patches to rotate

Rotating or Flipping a Drawing

1   Start with any block on your screen. You can either draw it (see pages 223-224 or 234-235) or edit it from the Sketchbook (see page 121).

2   **Click the Pick tool > click on the segment or patch in the block.** If you want to rotate or flip multiple segments or patches, click the first one, then SHIFT+click the others.

Rotating

3   *To rotate by specific degrees* – Click **BLOCK > Rotate > type in a specific degree or drag the slider bar (1 to 359 degrees) > click OK.**

4   *To rotate by common degrees* – Click **BLOCK > Symmetry > then click Rot 90, Rot 180, or Rot 270.**

Step 3

Step 4

Notes
There are three ways to bring up the Symmetry box:
- *on the button* – click the small red square in the bottom-corner of the Pick tool button.

- *right-click* – right-click in the middle of the worktable and click Symmetry.

- *from the menu* – click BLOCK > Symmetry.

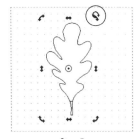

Step 5
CTRL+click to rotate

The selection has been
rotated using the mouse

5   *To rotate using the mouse* – **CTRL+click in the center of the segment(s) on the crosshair icon > position your cursor over a corner handle > spin handle around the center of the segment(s).**

Flipping

6   *To flip the segment(s)* – Click **BLOCK > Symmetry > then click Flip H, Flip V, Flip D, or Flip O.**

Step 6

Step 7

Step 8
Add to Sketchbook

The selection has
been flipped vertically
from the original

7   **Click the Color tab > use the Paintbrush tool to color your block.**

8   Click the **Add to Sketchbook** button to make this block part of your project.

Rotating or Flipping a Drawing

Resizing Lines or Patches

At any point while you're drawing, you can resize one or many lines or patches.

1   With your block on the Block worktable, click the **Pick** tool.

2   **Click the line or patch you want to resize.** If you want to resize multiple lines or patches together, hold down your keyboard **SHIFT key** and click the other lines or patches. The selected items will appear highlighted and be surrounded by little black squares, called handles.

3   Resize the selection by percentage or by the way they look on the screen:

- *To resize by percentage,* click **BLOCK > Resize. Type a new number for the horizontal percentage > press the TAB key twice on your keyboard > type a new number for the vertical percentage.** Resizing values can be from 10-300%.

- *To resize by the way things look on the screen,* **Position your cursor over one of the handles. Click, hold and move the handle to a new position.** The selected items will resize as you move the handle.

Notes
- To resize the entire drawing (not the block outline), choose EDIT > Select All in step 2.

Step 1
Pick

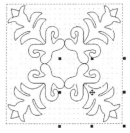

Step 2
Select the patch to resize

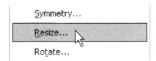

Step 3
BLOCK > Resize

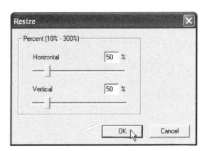

Step 3
Resize by percentage

The selected patch has
been resized by 50%

Step 3
Resize by the way things
look on the screen

Resizing Lines or Patches

Step 2
Work on Block

Step 3

Step 4
Select a frame

Step 5
Select a Sketchbook block

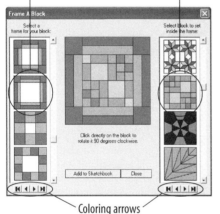

Coloring arrows

Step 6
Click to rotate

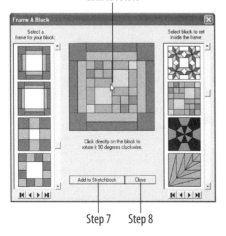

Step 7   Step 8

Framing Blocks with Serendipity

You can make new blocks without drawing a single thing by using Serendipity from the BLOCK menu. Use Frame Block to add any of our pre-designed frames around the outside of your block.

1 Start with blocks in your Sketchbook (see pages 128-129, 223-224, or 234-235).

2 Click **WORKTABLE > Work on Block**, or click the **Work on Block** button. It does not matter what block is on your screen.

3 Click **BLOCK > Serendipity > Frame Block.** The Frame A Block box will appear. It has three sections: the frame, the result, and the block.

4 In the left column, use the vertical scrollbar to see all the frame choices. **Click the frame you want to use.** (*Optional:* Use the coloring arrows below the column to choose the frame color-uncolored or grayscale.)

5 In the right column, use the vertical scrollbar to see your Sketchbook blocks. **Click the block you want to frame.** (*Optional:* Use the coloring arrows below the column to choose from the block colorings as they appear in the Sketchbook.)

6 In the center, you will see the resulting block. This picture is interactive. If your block is asymmetrical (not the same on all sides), **click on the block in the picture to rotate it 90 degrees with each click.**

7 If you like the new framed block, click **Add to Sketchbook**. If you don't like it, start over at step 4.

8 Repeat steps 4-7 to try framing other blocks or click **Close** to return to the worktable.

Notes
• **These frames are all pre-drawn for you. If you'd like to draw your own frames, try Merge Blocks instead (see page 259).**

Tilting Blocks with Serendipity

You can make new blocks without drawing a single thing by using Serendipity from the BLOCK menu. Use Tilt Block to rotate or tilt the block inside a square (like Diamond in the Square at varying angles).

1 Start with blocks in your Sketchbook (see pages 128-129, 223-224, or 234-235).

2 Click **WORKTABLE > Work on Block**, or click the **Work on Block** button. It does not matter what block is on your screen.

3 Click **BLOCK > Serendipity > Tilt Block.** The Tilt A Block box will appear. It has three sections: the block, the result, and a slider to control the tilt.

4 In the left column, use the vertical scrollbar to see your Sketchbook blocks. **Click the block you want to tilt.** (*Optional:* Use the coloring arrows below the column to choose from the block colorings as they appear in the Sketchbook.)

5 At the bottom, **drag the slider rectangle to the desired tilt.**

6 At the top, you will see the resulting block. This picture is interactive. If your block is asymmetrical (not the same on all sides), **click on the block in the picture to rotate it 90 degrees with each click.**

7 If you like the new tilted block, click **Add to Sketchbook**. If you don't like it, start over at step 4.

8 Repeat steps 4-7 to try tilting other blocks or click **Close** to return to the worktable.

Notes
• Put blocks on-point by setting the tilt to 45 degrees in step 5.

Step 2
Work on Block

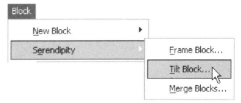

Step 3

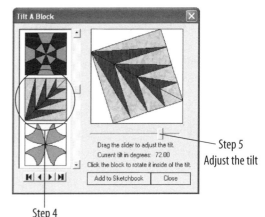

Step 5
Adjust the tilt

Step 4
Select a Sketchbook block

Step 6
Click to rotate

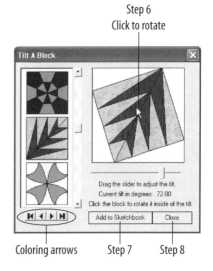

Coloring arrows   Step 7   Step 8

Tilting Blocks with Serendipity

Step 2
Work on Block

Step 3

Step 4   Step 5

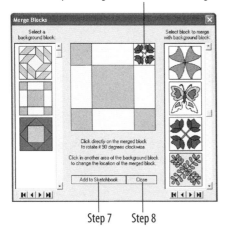

Coloring arrows

Step 6 - Change the location of the merged block

Step 7   Step 8

Merging Blocks with Serendipity

Use Merge Blocks to put any block inside an EasyDraw™ block that has a square, rectangle, or other 4-sided spot as part of its drawing.

1   Start with blocks in your Sketchbook (see pages 128-129, 223-224, or 234-235).

2   Click **WORKTABLE > Work on Block**, or click the **Work on Block** button. It does not matter what block is on your screen.

3   Click **BLOCK > Serendipity > Merge Blocks.** A box will appear with three sections: the background block, the result, and the inner block.

4   In the left column, use the vertical scrollbar to see your Sketchbook EasyDraw™ blocks that have 4-sided spots as part of their drawing. (Not all blocks will show because they do not fit the criteria.) **Click the block you want as the background.** (*Optional:* Choose the block coloring with the coloring arrows.)

5   In the right column, use the vertical scrollbar to see all your Sketchbook blocks. **Click the block you want to merge into the background.** (*Optional:* Choose the block coloring with the coloring arrows.)

6   In the middle, you will see the resulting block. This picture is interactive in two ways:

   • If there is more than one square, rectangle, or 4-sided spot in the background block, **click a different spot of the background block to change the location of the merged block.**

   • If your block is asymmetrical (not the same on all sides), **click on the block in the picture to rotate it 90 degrees with each click.**

7   If you like the new merged block, click **Add to Sketchbook**. If you don't like it, start over at step 4.

8   Repeat steps 4-7 to try merging other blocks or click **Close** to return to the worktable.

Merging Blocks with Serendipity

Drawing Sash or Border Blocks

These directions are for drawing non-square blocks.

Step 1
Work on Block

1   Click **WORKTABLE > Work on Block**, or click the **Work on Block** button.

2   **Click BLOCK > New Block > EasyDraw Block, PatchDraw Block, or EasyDraw + PatchDraw.**

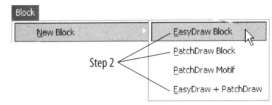

Step 2

3   *Block Size* – Click **BLOCK > Drawing Board Setup > Block Size** (under General) **> double-click the number for Width, then Height and type a new number for each.** These should be proportional or equal to your sash or border dimensions. Example: If your sash is 15x3, type in 15x3. If your border is 110x8, you may need to type in 55x4.

Step 3

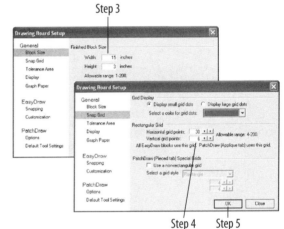

4   *Snap Points* – In **Snap Grid** (under General), verify the numbers for horizontal and vertical snap points. **Double-click in the box and type a new number to change them.** These should be a multiple of your block size. For example, if your sash is a rectangle at 15x3, set your snaps to be multiples of each number. Snaps would be 15x3, 30x6, 60x12, etc.

Step 4   Step 5

5   Click **OK**.

6   Draw your block (see page 224 for EasyDraw or pages 235-236 for PatchDraw tools).

Step 6
Draw the block

7   Click the **Add to Sketchbook** button.

Step 7
Add to Sketchbook

8   Click **WORKTABLE > Work on Quilt**.

9   Click the **Set Block** tool.

Step 8

Step 9
Set Block

10   Find and click on the last block in the palette, click in the sash or border space in your quilt.

Notes

- Blocks cannot be set into mitered borders.

- If you need help determining the size of the sash or border, go to the Quilt worktable and either measure on the quilt with the Tape Measure tool (approximate) or click the Layout or Borders tabs to see the settings (exact).

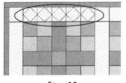

Step 10
Set the block in a sash space

Note:
All blocks look square in the Sketchbook and in the Blocks palette. It is up to you to set them in the rectangular spaces for which they were designed.

Drawing Sash or Border Blocks

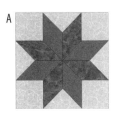

A

Click the Applique tab and draw motifs

Initial design:
Pieced PatchDraw block

B

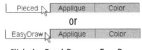

Click the PatchDraw or EasyDraw
tab and draw the background

Initial design:
PatchDraw motif

C

Draw the pieced part of your
block on the PatchDraw tab

Initial design:
PatchDraw block

D

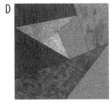

Click the Applique tab and draw motifs

Initial design:
EasyDraw™ block

Combining Piecing and Appliqué

1   Have the block to be copied in your Sketchbook and **click the View Sketchbook button > click the Blocks section**.

2   **Double-click the block you want to use.**

3   Follow these instructions according to which tabs you see and the type of block you're using:

A *EasyDraw or Pieced tab, Applique tab, pieced block with no motifs* – **Click the Applique tab > draw your appliqué motifs > *(optional)* click the Color tab and color > click Add to Sketchbook.**

B *Applique tab, motifs only with no background square* – Follow the directions for *Eliminating the PatchDraw Background* (see page 237). But, in step 5, choose **BLOCK > New Block > PatchDraw Block or EasyDraw + PatchDraw** instead, depending on the tools you want for your pieced block. **Click the Pieced or EasyDraw tab > draw according to the rules of the style you chose > *(optional)* click the Color tab and color > click Add to Sketchbook.**

C *Pieced tab, Applique tab, motifs with a plain background square* – **Click the Pick tool > click to select the block outline > press your keyboard DELETE key > draw the pieced part of your block filling the entire block with patches > *(optional)* click the Color tab and color > click Add to Sketchbook.**

D *EasyDraw tab, pieced block with no motifs* – **Choose EDIT > Select All. EDIT > Copy. BLOCK > Convert to Guides. Then choose BLOCK > New Block > EasyDraw + PatchDraw. Click the EasyDraw tab, choose EDIT > Paste**, reposition the design to cover the guides you made. **Click the Applique tab > draw your appliqué motifs > *(optional)* click the Color tab and color > click Add to Sketchbook.**

Importing Images to Trace

If you have a picture which you would like to trace to make a block, you can import it into EQ6. The picture must be saved on your computer in one of these file formats: BMP, GIF, JPEG, PNG or TIFF.

If you are tracing a finished quilt block image in EasyDraw, it may be difficult to match the line positions in the image to the EasyDraw snap to grid points. It may be easier to not import an image, but just look at the block, determine its basic grid structure, and draw from scratch.

1   Click **WORKTABLE > Work on Block.**

2   Click **BLOCK > New Block >** *choose a drawing style best-suited for drawing your image.*

3   Click **BLOCK > Import Image for Tracing.** A standard Windows file box will appear.

4   **Click the down arrow beside the Look in: box.** Go to the drive where the image is located. Double-click through the folders until you open the folder containing your image files.

5   **Click the image file you want to import.**

6   **Click Open.** (If you are replacing an old tracing image with a new one, click Yes at the prompt.) The Import Image box appears.

7   *To make the image fit the block size on the worktable,* click **Fit image to block size**.

   To crop out part of the image and resize it to fit your block, click **Crop and resize**.

If you import a rectangular image, it must "stretch" to fit into a square block. To avoid this, either crop now to make your image square, or change your block size later to be a rectangle of the same proportions as your image (BLOCK > Drawing Board Setup).

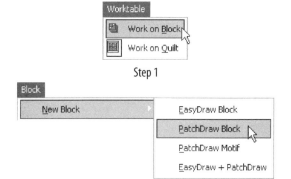

Step 1

Step 2
BLOCK > New Block > *Your Choice*

Step 3

Step 4

Step 5

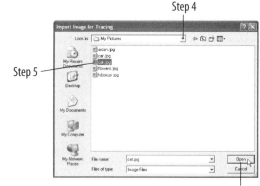

Step 6

Step 7

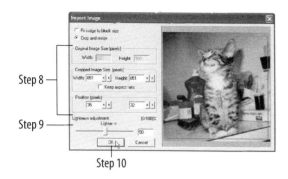

Step 8

Step 9

Step 10

Step 11

Please note:
Don't worry if your picture looks a little funny, this is because of lightness adjustment and high-resolution images trying to condense lots of information into a small space. This image is for tracing only, and the image will be clearer when you zoom in.

8 Around the outside of the image is a dotted box that is the same size as your image. **If you chose Crop and resize, crop your image:**

- *To crop and resize manually* – put your cursor over any corner of the dotted box around your image, watch until the cursor changes to a double-arrow. Click, hold and drag in toward the image center. The dotted box gets smaller and this is now your cropped selection.

- *To reposition the dotted crop box manually* – click and hold in the center of the dotted crop box and drag it to a new a new location.

- *To crop and resize by pixels* – under Cropped Image Size, click the Width and Height arrows to resize the crop box. Click Keep aspect ratio to keep your cropped image the same proportion as your block size (as it is set in Drawing Board Setup).

- *To reposition the dotted crop box by pixels* – under Position, click the arrows to reposition the box by pixels. (You are positioning the top-left corner of the dotted crop box.)

9 Lightness Adjustment controls how transparent your image is when drawing. *Recommended:* **leave the setting at 50 to begin, then re-import if you are not satisfied (start at step 3).**

10 Click **OK.** (If the imported image file size is large, you may experience a slight delay before seeing your image.) The image will appear on the Image tab of the worktable. It will always appear as dark as the original on this tab.

11 **Click the EasyDraw, Pieced, or Applique tab.** (The tabs you see depends on the block style chosen in step 2.) If you find the image too light to see well, or so dark that it might make your drawing lines hard to see, import again (step 3) and change the Lightness Adjustment (step 8).

Notes
• Now you may want to see Tracing Images on page 264.

Importing Images to Trace

Tracing Images

1   We recommend using PatchDraw to trace images. Before drawing, study your imported image, considering how you will divide your image into patches which can be sewn.

2   Understand that each drawn patch must be a complete, closed patch. No patch can share a line with another patch.

3   Understand that any unclosed shapes will be considered quilting lines, not patches. Lines can be colored using the Set Thread tools, but they cannot be printed as Template patterns or filled with fabric, as patches can.

4   Be aware that the drawing order of patches determines the layering order. You can change the patch layering order at any time, but it is easier to draw them in the order you'd like them layered: first drawn = bottom; last drawn = top.

5   Click the Hide/show image for tracing button on the Precision Bar, when you want to hide the image and see only your drawing. If you want to delete the image, click the Image tab > right-click the image > click Delete.

6   If your image is relatively simple and geometric, use the Oval and Polygon tools. If your image is more complex, use the Freehand tool.

7   Imported images are not saved in the project file or with the block. An imported image will only remain in the project during that working session. If you partially draw a block and need to exit, add your partial drawing to the Sketchbook and make a new image to import if you cropped the original. (Click the Image tab > click FILE > Export Marquee Selection, drag to form a box along the block outline lines > release and save the file somewhere you can find it again.) To finish drawing the block at a later time, open the project, find the block in the Sketchbook, double-click it to put back on the worktable, then import the new image and continue drawing.

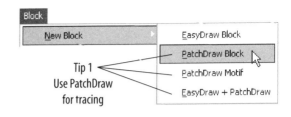

Tip 1
Use PatchDraw
for tracing

Tip 3
The cat's body is made up of closed patches, but its whiskers are only lines and therefore are considered quilting stitches

Tip 5
Use the *Hide/show image for tracing* button to see your drawing without the image behind it

Hide/show image for tracing button

Tip 7
Save your tracing image if you have to close EQ6 before completing the drawing

Click the Image tab

Click FILE > Export Marquee Selection

Printing and Exporting

Quilt designed by Linda Erickson
Albuquerque, New Mexico

Chapter 9

EQ6 gives you twelve different possibilities for printing patterns, colored block and quilt pictures, yardage estimates, photographs, and even quilting stencils. This chapter describes them all. And it also shows you how to export blocks and quilts out of the program to use in other software.

Reference

Printing Patterns Overview

There are many ways of printing block patterns in EQ6, but the basic steps are the same. Usually, the best way to print is to select the block, check *Use size from quilt*, and preview the pattern. The full directions are described below.

1   *To print from the Quilt worktable,* **click the Select tool > click the layer on which you set the block, motif, or stencil > click the block, motif, or stencil to select it.**

    To print from the Block worktable, **click the Color tab** to verify there are no drawing or coloring errors.

2   Click **FILE > Print >** *Your Choice.*

3   Finished block size is on the first tab or screen of all printout styles, but on the Options tab of Foundation Patterns. Under **Finished Block Size**, you have two options:

    • **Use size from quilt (recommended)** – If you are working on a quilt on the Quilt worktable, click *Use size from quilt*. The finished block size will show in gray because EQ6 is reading the sizes you set on the Layout tab of this quilt. (If you question the size, be sure to see information on how blocks are measured by looking up the layout style you are using, see pages 149-155 and 159.)

    • **Custom Block Size** – To type in a size, click *Custom block size,* then double-click inside the **Width** box and type a size; double-click inside the **Height** box and type a size.

4   Under **Copies**, double-click in the box and type the number of printouts you want (1 to 99).

Step 1
Select

Step 2

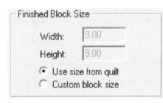

Step 3
Use size from quilt recommended on Quilt worktable

Step 4

Step 5

Print button   Close button

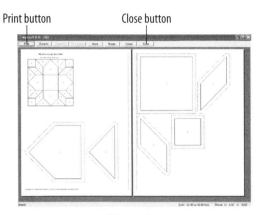

Print preview

5 Click any of the buttons across the bottom of the box for more options:

- **Page Setup** – click to change margins, paper size, orientation, or the printer (see page 286).

- **Fonts** – click to change fonts or font size (see page 285).

- **Preview (recommended)** – click to preview your printout. From the preview, click Print to print or Close to return to this window.

- **Print** – click to print your block, motif, or stencil without previewing.

- **Close** – click to return to the worktable without printing.

Notes
- EQ6 will print blocks that are clipped in half or a quarter, such as blocks along the edges in on-point quilts or border strips, if the quilt is designed in EQ6. EQ6 cannot print clipped blocks for quilts or borders made in previous EQ versions that are opened or *imported* through EQ6.

- If multiple-page printouts are missing the right-edge guideline, click Page Setup and increase your Right page margin.

- Previewing a template or foundation pattern printout can save you paper. You can delete or move templates or foundation sections. You can also rotate templates 90 degrees to fit better on a page.

Printing Patterns Overview

Printing a Block, Motif, or Stencil

Step 1
Select

1   *To print from the Quilt worktable,* **click the Select tool > click the Layer tab on which you set the block, motif, or stencil > click the block, motif, or stencil to select it.**

To print from the Block worktable, **click the Color tab** to verify there are no drawing or coloring errors.

2   Click **FILE > Print > Block**.

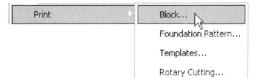

Step 2

3   *Choose your finished block size. (Use size from quilt* is recommended if printing from the quilt, see page 266.)

4   Under **Printing Style**, choose from the following:

• **Outline drawing** – black and white solid lines showing how patches overlap.

• **Quilting stencil** – black and white dotted lines. If you are printing stencils colored using the Thread tool, choose *Showing fabrics* instead.

• **As applique pattern** – black and white solid lines with white-filled patches showing how patches are layered.

• **Showing fabrics** – prints the block in color as displayed in the Print Block box. This option also prints a stencil in the thread color, style and weight you have chosen.

5   If you chose Showing fabrics, click the **coloring arrows** beneath the block picture to select the coloring you want to print. The displayed coloring will print, regardless of which coloring is showing on the worktable.

6   *Choose desired number of copies* (see page 266).

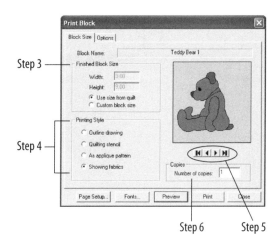

Step 3

Step 4

Step 6   Step 5

Outline drawing

Quilting stencil

As applique pattern

Showing fabrics

Printing Block, Motif, or Stencil

Step 7
Options tab

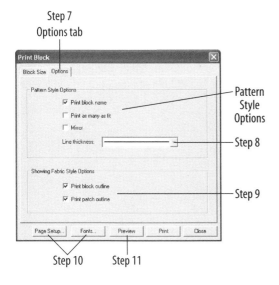

Pattern
Style
Options

Step 8

Step 9

Step 10   Step 11

Sample printout of *Showing fabrics*

7   **Click the Options tab > under Pattern Style Options, click to check the options you want:**

- **Print block name** – prints the name at the top of your printout from the block's Sketchbook notecard. If you did not name your block, it will say "Unnamed." (Naming a block is different than naming a project. See page 123.)

- **Print as many as fit** – prints as many full blocks on one page as possible, when you are printing smaller blocks

- **Mirror** – prints the block flipped horizontally

8   For **Line thickness**, click the down arrow to show the styles, then click directly on the thickness you want.

9   If you chose Showing fabrics, the outline choices under **Showing Fabric Style Options** will be enabled. (Other styles listed in step 4 automatically print outlines.) Put a check next to the options you want.

- **Print block outline** – prints a black outline around the block

- **Print patch outline** – prints black outlines around the patches

10 *Change the Page Setup or Fonts* (see pages 285-286).

11 *Click Preview, then Print.*

Notes
- EQ6 will print blocks that are clipped in half or quarter, such as blocks along the edges in on-point quilts or border strips, if the quilt is designed in EQ6. EQ6 cannot print clipped blocks for quilts or borders made in previous EQ versions that are opened or *imported* through EQ6.

Printing Block, Motif, or Stencil

Printing a Foundation Pattern

Foundation patterns are also known as paper piecing patterns. If you've used PatchDraw to draw your block or if your EasyDraw™ block has curves, you will need to section and number the block yourself. See Sections and Numbering on the next page.

Step 1
Select

1   *To print from the Quilt worktable,* **click the Select tool > click the Layer tab on which you set the block > click the block to select it.**

To print from the Block worktable, **click the Color tab** to verify there are no drawing or coloring errors.

2   Click **FILE > Print > Foundation Pattern**. The Print Foundation Pattern box appears. (This box is resizable to help you section or number complicated patterns. Position your cursor over the box edge or corner, then click and drag to enlarge the entire box.)

Step 2

Options

3   **Click the Options tab**.

4   *Choose your finished block size.* (*Use size from quilt* is recommended if printing from the quilt, see page 266.)

5   **Seam Allowance** – check *Print seam allowance* if you want seam allowance added around each section. Double-click the number and type a new number, if you need to change it.

6   **Line Thickness** – click the down arrow to show the styles, then click directly on the thickness you want.

7   *Choose desired number of copies* (see page 266).

8   *Options* – click to check the options you want, see the Options list to the right.

9   **Click Preview to see the pattern.** If you don't like how the block is sectioned or numbered, click **Close**, then change it (follow steps 10-15). Otherwise, click **Print**. If your pattern says *Unnamed*, see page 123.

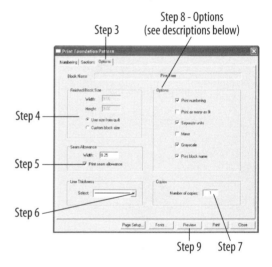

Step 3

Step 8 - Options
(see descriptions below)

Step 4

Step 5

Step 6

Step 9   Step 7

Options:
- **Print numbering** – prints letters and numbers on the pattern.
- **Print as many as fit** – prints as many full blocks on one page as possible, when printing smaller blocks. (Separate units must *not* be checked.)
- **Separate units** – separates pattern according to sections defined on Sections tab.
- **Mirror** – flips pattern horizontally. (Depending on your technique, use this so your block doesn't end up backwards.)
- **Grayscale** – prints the pattern with gray shading. Works with library blocks or drawn blocks with first coloring only containing white, black, dark gray (RGB 128) and light gray (RGB 192).
- **Print block name** – prints the name at the top of your printout from the block's Sketchbook notecard. If you did not name your block, it will say "Unnamed." (Naming a block is different than naming a project. See page 123.)

Printing a Foundation Pattern

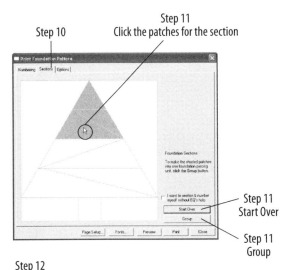

Step 10

Step 11
Click the patches for the section

Step 11
Start Over

Step 11
Group

Step 12

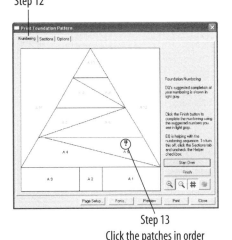

Step 13
Click the patches in order

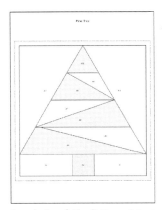

Sample Foundation Pattern printout

Sections

10   Click the Sections tab. Blue lines surround the areas denoted as sections (units).

11   To resection the block, **click Start Over > click the patches you want in a section > click the Group button > continue grouping sections until your are satisfied.** To undo your last click, SHIFT+click the same patch before you group it, otherwise click Start Over.

Numbering

12   Click the Numbering tab. You'll see numbers and letters in the sections of your block.

13   To renumber the block, **click Change Numbers > click the patches in the order you want them numbered.** (EQ6 will help, ensuring your block is still foundation pieceable. But if you do not want help, click the Sections tab and click the *I want to section & number myself without EQ's help* box, then click the Numbering tab again.)

Here you can also take your most recent click back if you SHIFT+click the same patch again, otherwise click Start Over.

14   *Change the Page Setup or Fonts (see pages 285-286).*

15   *Click Preview, then Print.*

Notes

- To undo your changes, click the Sections tab > click Start Over > click Preview.

- To make your sectioning and numbering permanent for this Sketchbook block, edit the block > follow steps 2-14 > click Preview > Close > Close > Save button. You may want to save this block in your My Library to make it accessible from other projects, see pages 143-144.

- EQ6 will print blocks that are clipped in half or a quarter, such as blocks along the edges in on-point quilts or border strips, if the quilt is designed in EQ6. EQ6 cannot print clipped blocks for quilts or borders made in previous EQ versions that are opened or *imported* through EQ6.

Printing a Foundation Pattern

Printing Templates

You can print templates for any block, no matter if it is pieced or appliqué. Templates are block patterns. Each patch is printed as a separate piece (surrounded by seam allowance if you so choose).

Step 1
Select

1   *To print from the Quilt worktable,* **click the Select tool > click the Layer tab on which you set the block or motif > click on the block or motif to select it.**

   To print from the Block worktable, **click the Color tab** to verify there are no drawing or coloring errors.

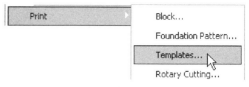

Step 2

2   Click **FILE > Print > Templates.** The Print Template box appears.

3   *Choose your finished block size.* (*Use size from quilt* is recommended if printing from the quilt, see page 266.)

4   **Seam Allowance** – check *Print seam allowance* if you want seam allowance added around each template. Double-click the number and type a new number, if you need to change it. *(See Notes at the end of this topic for seam allowance tips.)*

5   **Print Key Block** – the *key block* is a small drawing of your block, with each patch identified by a letter. This "key" helps you know how to fit your template patches back together. Click to choose one:

   • **None** – choose when you don't need a key block, and want more room for templates.

   • **Small** – choose when your block does not have many small patches.

   • **Large** – choose when your block has so many tiny patches that the patch letters would not fit or read well on a small key block.

6   **Line Thickness** – click the down arrow to show the styles, then click directly on the thickness you want.

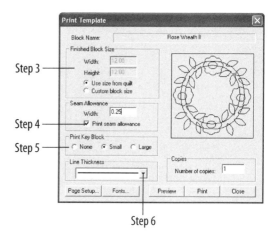

Step 3

Step 4

Step 5

Step 6

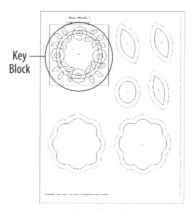

Key Block

Template printout

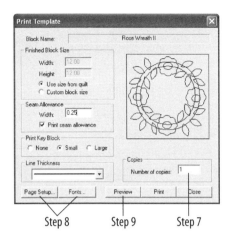

Step 8   Step 9   Step 7

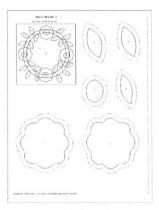

Sample Template printout

7 *Choose desired number of copies* (see page 266).

8 *Change the Page Setup or Fonts* (see pages 285-286).

9 *Click Preview, then Print.*

Notes
- The block name is set through the Sketchbook notecard. See page 123 to change it.

- EQ6 will print blocks that are clipped in half or a quarter, such as blocks along the edges in on-point quilts or border strips, if the quilt is designed in EQ6. EQ6 cannot print clipped blocks for quilts or borders made in previous EQ versions that are opened or *imported* through EQ6.

- If your printer prints the seam allowance faintly, you can darken it by clicking FILE > Preferences > General. Under "Printing Options" change the "Minimum line size in pixels" from 1 (default) to 2, 3 or 4. See which thickness you prefer with your printer.

- If you are printing directly onto freezer paper or EQ's Self-Adhesive Template Sheets and plan to hand-cut seam allowance around the patches, uncheck Seam Allowance. Then see pages 274-275 for how to move or delete unnecessary patches from your printout, so you can fit as much on one page as possible.

Printing Templates

Changing Foundation and Templates Printouts

Sometimes you may want to delete repeated templates or foundations, or move them so they don't extend across more pages than necessary. You can tailor your printout before printing by using the available buttons on your print preview.

1   *To print from the Quilt worktable,* **click the Select tool > click the Layer tab on which you set the block or motif > click on the block or motif to select it.**

   To print from the Block worktable, **click the Color tab** to verify there are no drawing or coloring errors.

2   Click **FILE > Print > Templates (or Foundation Pattern)**. The Print box appears. Choose your settings and sizes (see pages 270-271 and 272-273).

3   Click the **Preview** button. The preview shows what your printout currently looks like.

Notes
- Templates have a key block option that appears at the top-left of the printout. You can choose not to print it, or to print it small or large. But you should make this choice before moving or deleting templates. If you close the print preview your printout will reset, then you'll have to start deleting, moving, and rotating all over again.

Deleting

When you delete pattern pieces, the remaining pieces reorganize. So, delete pieces before moving them.

If you are printing appliqué blocks, you may want to delete the large background square and cut that later.

4   Click the **Delete** button. You are now in "delete-mode."

5   **Click a section or patch to select it > press your keyboard DELETE key to delete it.** It will disappear and the other pieces will move up to take the deleted one's place.

Step 1
Select

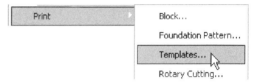

Step 2

Key block   Step 4

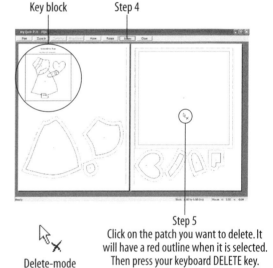

Step 5
Click on the patch you want to delete. It will have a red outline when it is selected. Then press your keyboard DELETE key.

Delete-mode cursor

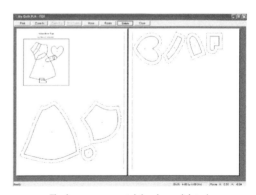

The large square patch has been deleted.

Step 7

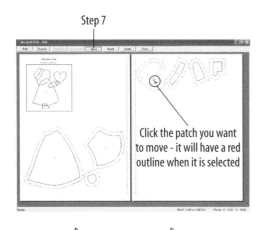

Click the patch you want to move - it will have a red outline when it is selected

Move-mode cursor

Rotate-mode cursor

Step 10

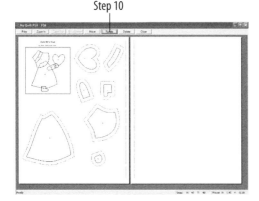

Step 12   Clicking Close will undo all changes

Blank pages will not print

Patch has been rotated 90 degrees

6 You are still in "delete-mode," so repeat step 5 to delete other pieces as desired. If you delete enough pattern pieces to clear a page, that blank page will not print.

Moving

7 Click the **Move** button. You are now in "move-mode."

8 **Click in the center of a section or patch to select it > click, hold, and drag it to another position > release the mouse when the pattern piece is where you want.**

9 You are still in "move-mode," so repeat step 8 to move other pieces as desired.

Rotating (Templates Only)

10 Click the **Rotate** button. You are now in "rotate-mode."

11 **Click on a template to rotate it 90 degrees with each click.** You may need to repeat steps 7-9 to move it again.

12 Click **Print** when the pattern looks the way you want it. If you click Close the pattern will reset and you'll have to start over.

Notes
• **If you accidentally delete a template or foundation you still need, click Close and click Preview again to start over.**

Changing Foundation/Templates

Printing a Rotary Cutting Chart

This type of printout is not available for all blocks, because some blocks are not ideal for rotary cutting. Blocks made up of squares, triangles, rectangles, parallelograms or diamonds, however, work best. If you notice patches missing from the printout, it's because they are not able to be rotary-cut. Print the block again as Templates to get these "missing" patches.

Be sure to read the next topic on how to avoid rounding and also the "best practices" to use when rotary cutting. See pages 278-279.

1   *To print from the Quilt worktable,* **click the Select tool > click the Layer tab on which you set the block > click on the block to select it.**

To print from the Block worktable, **click the Color tab** to verify there are no drawing or coloring errors.

2   Click **FILE > Print > Rotary Cutting**. The Print Rotary Cutting Chart box appears.

3   *Choose your finished block size. (Use size from quilt* is recommended if printing from the quilt, see page 266.)

4   **Seam Allowance** – choose the seam allowance width you want added around each piece. Double-click the number and type a new number, if you need to change it.

5   **Print Key Block** – the *key block* is a small drawing of your complete block, with each patch identified by a letter. This "key" helps you know how to fit your patches back together. Click to choose one:

   • **Small** – click if your block does not have many small patches.

   • **Large** – click if your block has so many tiny patches that the patch letters would not fit or read well on a small key block.

Step 1
Select

Step 2

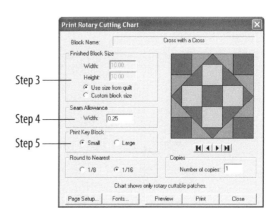

Step 3
Step 4
Step 5

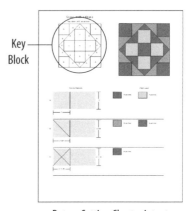

Key Block

Rotary Cutting Chart printout

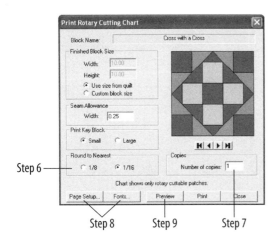

Step 6

Step 8   Step 9   Step 7

6   Round to Nearest *(available when working in inches; metric automatically rounds to nearest millimeter)* – click to select whether you want EQ6 to round to the nearest 1/8 or 1/16 inch when calculating. Rounding to the nearest 1/16 gives you the most accurate rotary cutting instructions (see pages 278-279).

7   *Choose desired number of copies (see pages 266).*

8   *Change the Page Setup or Fonts (see pages 285-286).*

9   *Click Preview, then Print.*

Notes

• The block name is set through the Sketchbook notecard, see page 123 to change it.

• EQ6 will print blocks that are clipped in half or a quarter, such as blocks along the edges in on-point quilts or border strips, if the quilt is designed in EQ6. EQ6 cannot print clipped blocks for quilts or borders made in previous EQ versions that are opened or *imported* through EQ6.

Understanding the Cutting Diagrams

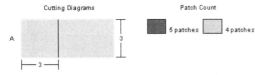

Means cut 5 squares of one fabric and 4 squares of another.

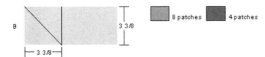

Means cut 4 squares of one fabric, then cut diagonally, to make 8 patches. Then cut 2 squares of another fabric, cut diagonally, to make 4 patches.

Means cut 1 square, then cut diagonally both ways, to make 4 patches.

Printing a Rotary Cutting Chart

How to Avoid Rounding in Rotary Cutting

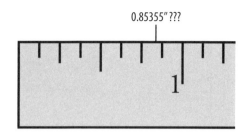

Rotary cutting dimensions are nearly always approximations. For example, the 7/8 inch that quilters conventionally add for half-square triangles is really 0.85355 inches, rounded off to the nearest 1/8 inch so it can be read on a ruler. (Experienced quilters in fact cut a little "shy" in this case, since 0.85355 is a little less than 7/8 or 0.875.)

This applies to the dimensions given in EQ6 rotary cutting printouts as well as to dimensions in books. Because of this, the rotary cutting instructions may not always be the best way to cut your block. Here are some things that you should know when deciding on the best type of pattern to use for a given block.

EQ6 Gives Conventional Results

With simple cases (rectangles and triangles at even sizes), EQ6 gives the same results as conventional quilter's wisdom. It adds 1+1/4 inches to the finished size of quarter-square triangles, just like the books.

But, EQ6 gives rotary cutting dimensions *even in cases where the conventional rules of thumb do not apply.* Here you need to be aware that rounding off to the nearest 1/8 or 1/16 inch may produce inaccuracies. The example illustrates this point very well.

A block 7 across by 5 down, should be printed at **7" x 5"** or **14" x 10"** or **21" x 15"**, etc. If the size is not a multiple of the grid, print templates instead.

The inaccuracies produced by "rounding off" can become significant if the finished sizes of patches are not easily measured on common rulers. The illustrated block has 7 patches across by five patches down. If you wanted a 10 inch square block, this would mean that each rectangle has a finished size 1.428571" by 2". The measurement 1.43 is not to be found on your ruler.

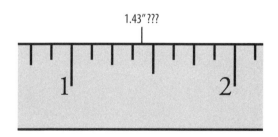

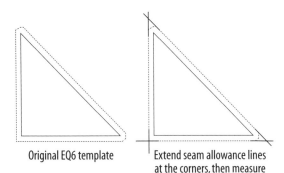

| Original EQ6 template | Extend seam allowance lines at the corners, then measure |

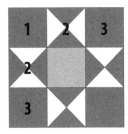

Best Practices 1
Make note of a block's grid or structure.
The Ohio Star shown is on a 3x3 grid.

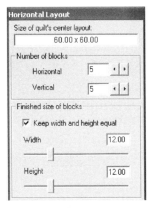

Best Practices 2
Make finished block size a multiple of the block grid

Best Practices 3
Click *Use size from quilt* when printing

EQ6 would add the 1/4 inch seam allowance, round off (say, to the nearest 1/8 inch), and tell you to cut rectangles 1-7/8" by 2-1/2". If you then pieced together these patches (assuming you use accurate quarter-inch seams), the finished size of the actual block would come out to be 9-5/8" by 10", a full 3/8 inch too narrow! If you round off to the nearest 1/16 inch, the block will be 10-1/16" x 10", and still 1/16 inch too wide.

Use Templates to Verify Sizes

EQ6 templates are always 100% accurate. If you are uncertain about rotary cutting dimensions in some cases, print the templates as a check. The actual, un-rounded dimensions for rotary cutting may be measured by the dotted seam allowance lines on the templates. First, extend the seam allowance lines at the corners until they cross. Then, measure the resulting total length and height.

Best Practices

1   **Make note of a block's grid or structure.** (For example, a Nine Patch and all its variations and stars are on a 3x3 grid.)

2   When setting up a quilt on the **Layout** tab, **set the finished block size to be a multiple of that grid**. (Nine Patches would be best at 3, 6, 9, 12, 15, 18, etc.)

3   When printing rotary cutting, **print the block at a multiple of that grid and round to 1/16 of an inch**. (Click the *Use size from quilt* option to print the block the same size as specified on the Layout tab.)

4   **Print templates to cross-check the sizes** (especially if the block is complex and the grid is not apparent). Tape these to the underside of your acrylic ruler to verify the actual width of the patches to be cut and to keep the templates from sliding away.

Avoid Rounding in Rotary Cutting

Printing Border or Sash Blocks

Printing border or sash blocks is like printing other blocks: you select the block, choose your pattern type, then print. What's confusing is that the whole border won't print as one pattern. Most borders require multiple print jobs, because they are made up of multiple blocks or sections. (See notes below about using the Auto Borders for printing convenience.)

Printing a Block in your Border or Sash

1 **Click the Select tool > click the Layer 1 tab > click the border, sash or corner block you want to print.** The whole block will select, whether it is a long strip, a whole block, or a clipped block.

2 Click **FILE > Print > *Your Choice*.** (Use Templates, Foundation Pattern, or Rotary Cutting to get a pattern.)

3 Under **Finished Block Size**, click *Use size from quilt*. The finished block size will show in gray.

4 *Choose desired number of copies* (see page 266).

5 *Change the Page Setup or Fonts* (see pages 285-286).

6 *Click Preview, then Print.*

Notes
- **If you want the convenience of having your whole border print in one print job, use a border from the Single Block Patterns Auto Border category. See page 192.**

- **If you notice patches are missing on rotary cutting charts for border, sash or sash corner blocks, it's because those patches are not able to be rotary-cut. Print the block again as Templates to get these "missing" patches.**

- **EQ6 will print blocks that are clipped in half or a quarter, such as blocks along the edges in on-point quilts or border strips, if the quilt is designed in EQ6. EQ6 cannot print clipped blocks for quilts or borders made in previous EQ versions that are opened or *imported* through EQ6.**

Printing Border or Sash Blocks

Step 1
Select

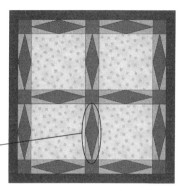

Step 1
Click the sash
to print

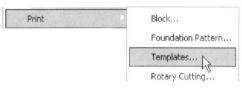

Step 2

Check *Use size from quilt* to ensure your printouts are correct

If you forget to check *Use size from quilt* your printout will be wrong

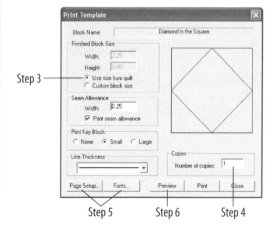

Step 3

Step 5   Step 6   Step 4

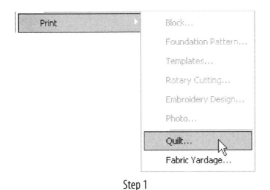

Step 1

Step 2

Step 3

Step 4

Step 5   Step 6

Options:
- **Print name** – prints the name at the top of your printout from the quilt's Sketchbook notecard. If you did not add your quilt to the Sketchbook and name it, the printout will say "Unnamed." (Naming a quilt is different than naming a project. See page 123.)
- **Print overall size** – prints the dimensions of your quilt at the top of your printout
- **Print block outline** – prints a black outline around each block
- **Print patch outline** – prints black outlines around each patch

Printing a Quilt

To print a quilt, you must be on the Quilt worktable with the quilt you wish to print on your screen.

1   Click **FILE > Print > Quilt.** The Print Quilt box will appear.

2   Under **Printing Style**, choose either:

- **Outline drawing** – to print your quilt as a line drawing with no color

- **Showing fabrics** – to print your quilt filled with the current fabrics and colors

3   *Options* – click to check the options you want. See a description of these options on the left.

4   *Choose desired number of copies (see page 266).*

5   *Change the Page Setup or Fonts (see pages 285-286).*

6   *Click Preview, then Print.*

Notes
- **If the line drawing printout of your quilt has overlapping shapes, especially with appliqué, try coloring the entire quilt white. Then print the white quilt *Showing fabrics*.**

- **To print out a smaller picture of your quilt, try making your margins smaller (see page 286) or exporting your quilt and printing from another program (see pages 288-289).**

- **If you would like to select part of a quilt to print, click FILE > Export Selected Area > drag the mouse on the quilt to select the area you want to print > click Print.**

Printing a Quilt

Printing Photos or Embroidery

To print a photograph or embroidery design from your quilt, you must be on the layer on which you set the photo or embroidery design. Photos can be set on Layers 1, 2 or 3. Embroidery can only be set on Layer 3.

Step 1
Select

1   **Click the Select tool > click the Layer tab on which you set the photo or embroidery > click the photo or embroidery in your quilt to select it.**

2   Click **FILE > Print > Photo** or **Embroidery Design**. The appropriate Print box will appear.

3   *Choose your desired size (Use size from quilt recommended; see page 266).*

4   *Choose desired number of copies (see page 266).*

5   *Change the Page Setup or Fonts (see pages 285-286).*

6   *Click Preview, then Print.*

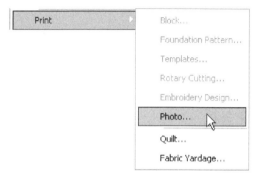

Step 2

Notes
*   If you are printing photos on fabric, for sewing into a quilt, you may want to print them slightly larger than the size you will sew (have the color extend into the seam allowance). Then, when you sew, you won't see any white lines from unprinted fabric along your seam line.

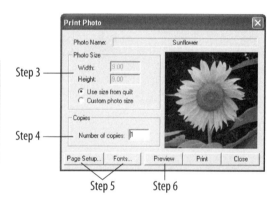

Step 3

Step 4

Step 5   Step 6

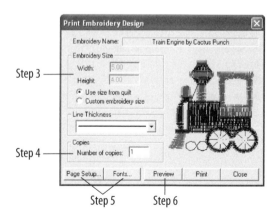

Step 3

Step 4

Step 5   Step 6

Printing Photos or Embroidery

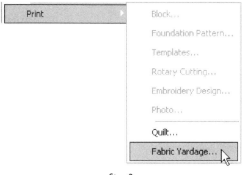

Step 2

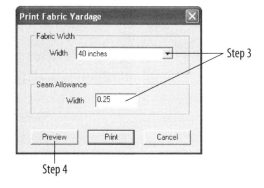

Step 3

Step 4

Step 4

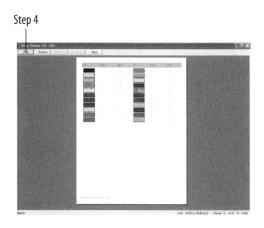

Printing Fabric Yardage Estimates

EQ6 will estimate yardage for your quilt. Remember that these are estimates. You may find you need less fabric depending on your quilt style.

1 **Click the View Sketchbook button > click the Quilts section > find your quilt > double-click on it.** This will send the quilt to the worktable.

2 Click **FILE > Print > Fabric Yardage**. The Print Fabric Yardage box will appear.

3 Select the *Fabric Width* and *Seam Allowance* settings you want.

4 Click **Preview**, then **Print**.

Notes

Here is how EQ6 figures yardage:

- It adds the seam allowance you select to each patch.

- It places an imaginary rectangle around each patch at the seam allowance.

- It places these rectangles on fabric of the selected Fabric Width.

- Each time a "row" is filled, it begins a new row, counting the entire strip as required yardage.

- The result is usually an over estimate. Shapes like on-point sashes tend to give exceptionally large yardage figures.

- The estimate for the border generally requires a length of fabric as long as the longest border strip. If you want a border pieced in strips, use the Blocks border style.

- Backing and binding are not estimated.

Print Fabric Yardage Estimates

Special Notes on Fabric Yardage Estimates

1 **EQ6 gives you yardage for your borders as you have them designed on the screen.** If you are going to sew long, *unpieced* borders around your quilt, then set the borders to be long and unpieced in EQ6. If you plan to *piece* the borders, then piece them in EQ6 by choosing a different border style (such as Blocks).

2 **Color your center and borders differently to see where yardage is going.** If your quilt center and borders use the same fabric swatch (let's say a light blue check), the yardage will show as one number for both in the estimate. Leave your quilt center colored in the light blue check fabric, but change your border to be a light blue solid color. If you re-print fabric yardage, they'll show up as separate numbers in the estimate.

3 **For quilts with many blocks colored exactly the same each time, you can use the yardage estimate to count the number of blocks you need to sew.** Click the Paintbrush tool > click the Colors tab within the palette > click a solid color (not used anywhere in your quilt and not close in color to any of the fabrics you have used) > CTRL+click one patch in one block on the quilt. This should make all matching blocks color in the same position. If you preview the yardage now, the number of patches needed for the solid color chosen will equal the number of blocks colored that way on the quilt.

4 **Fabric yardage may not figure backing, but if you design a second quilt that *is the back* you can print yardage for that as well.** Start a new Custom Set quilt (the same size as your quilt front) and set a plain square which covers the entire center rectangle. Or, design a pieced back in any layout style (the same size as your quilt front) and color it with fabric. To see how large your quilt front is, look in the bottom-right corner of your screen and find Quilt. This is the finished size of the quilt (including borders).

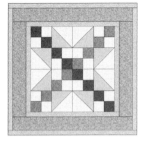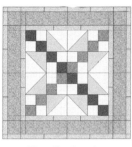

Unpieced borders give you unpieced estimates

Pieced borders give you smaller estimates

Initial design - borders and center colored in same fabrics

Modified design to see yardage needed for center versus border

CTRL+click a patch in one block and preview the yardage to get a block count

Fabric key	Number of patches	Yardage estimate
	16	1/2

Quilt front - 66" x 98"

Quilt back - 66" x 98"

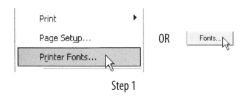

Step 1

Changing Fonts

Use this to make your printouts easier to read by changing the style or point size of your font.

1 Click **FILE > Printer Fonts.** OR, if you have the Print box on your screen, click the **Fonts** button. The Printer Font box appears.

2 Click the down arrow next to the **Choose font for:** box, and click the item you want to change.

- **Symbol (default is Arial, 8)** – On templates and rotary cutting charts, it labels the key block. It also labels each template.

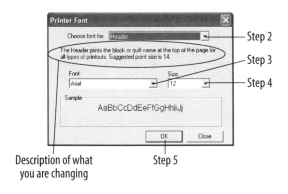

Step 2
Step 3
Step 4
Step 5

Description of what you are changing

- **Number (default is Arial, 8)** – On quilts, it is the overall size of the quilt (below the Header). On foundation patterns, it labels the individual patches in a section. On templates and rotary cutting instructions, it labels the key block size. On fabric yardage estimates, it is the main font used.

- **Header (default is Arial, 12)** – The header prints the block or quilt name (as it appears on the notecard) at the top of the page.

- **Footer (default is Arial, 7)** – The footer prints in the lower-left corner of all printouts.

- **Data (default is Arial 8)** – The data font prints on rotary cutting instructions only. This is used for the legend for cutting diagrams, patch counts, and patch labels.

3 Click the down arrow next to the **Font:** box, and click the font style you want.

4 Notice the suggested point size for the part of the printout you are changing. Click the down arrow next to the **Size:** box, and click the point size you want.

5 Click **OK** to keep your changes, or click **Close** to cancel them.

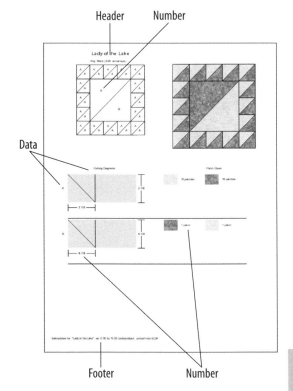

Header   Number

Data

Footer   Number

Notes
- **To change fonts for Fabric Yardage estimates, choose Printer Fonts from the FILE menu before printing.**

Changing Fonts

Changing Page Setup or Printers

Use this to change the page orientation, margins, paper size, printer or paper source.

1 Click **FILE > Page Setup.** OR, if you have the Print box on your screen, click the **Page Setup** button. The Page Setup box appears.

2 *(Optional)* If you are changing printers, **click the Printer button > click the down arrow next to the Name box > click the printer you wish to use > click OK.**

3 Under Paper, click the down arrow next to the **Size** box to choose your paper size.

4 Under Paper, click the down arrow next to the **Source** box to choose where the paper is fed from (which paper tray, or manual feed, for example).

5 Under Orientation, click **Portrait** if you want your printout to be tall (normal) or **Landscape** if you want your printout to be wide (sideways).

6 Under **Margins**, double-click in each box and type the size you want to set the left, right, top and bottom margins. Margins are the spaces around the edges of your printout. If you make them too large it will take more pages to print the information. Your printer determines how small they can be.

7 Click **OK** to keep your changes, or click Close to cancel them.

Notes
• When changing printers, you may also want to view the printer's other settings by clicking the Properties button.

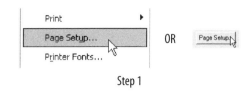

Step 1

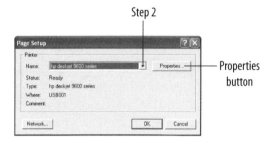

Step 2

Properties button

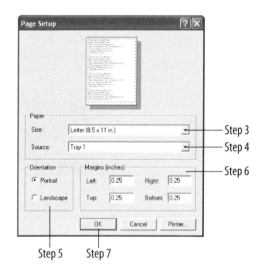

Step 3
Step 4
Step 6

Step 5   Step 7

Changing Page Setup or Printers

Step 1

Step 2

Step 3

Save a File

Step 4

Step 5

Step 6

Copy to Windows clipboard

Step 5

Exporting Selected Areas

1 Have the quilt or block on the worktable. Click **FILE > Export Marquee Selection.** Your cursor will change to a magnifying glass with a crosshair.

2 **Position the crosshair's center at the top-left of the area to be exported > click and hold > drag diagonally down and right to form a box > release when the box encloses the image you want to export.** A box will appear with three choices:

Save a File

3 Click the **Save a file** button.

4 **Click the down arrow next to *Save in:* to see the list of drive choices > click the appropriate drive.** Browse through folders until you reach the folder where you want to save the image. (Or click My Documents > My Pictures, to save there.)

5 Click inside the *File name:* box. **Type a name for your file.**

6 Click **Save**. Your file will be saved as a bitmap (.bmp).

Copy to Windows Clipboard

3 Click the **Copy to Windows clipboard** button.

4 Click **START > All Programs**, and open a drawing, imaging or word-processing program.

5 Create a new image, file, or document. Click **EDIT > Paste** (or press CTRL+V). Your image will appear in the document.

Print

3 Click the **Print** button. Your image will print.

Notes

• To print the entire screen, press the PRINT SCREEN key > open a new document in a program such as Word > press CTRL+V to paste the screen image. This is handy for writing EQ6 teaching materials.

Exporting Selected Areas

Exporting Images

EQ6 lets you export images, perfect for everything from Web pages to books – in techno-speak, images of low to high resolution.

1 Have the quilt or block on the worktable. Click **FILE > Export Image.** An Export Image box appears.

2 **Click the down arrow next to *Save in:* to see the list of drive choices > click the appropriate drive.** Browse through any folders if necessary until you reach the folder where you want to save the image. (Or click My Documents > My Pictures, if you want to save there.)

3 **Click the down arrow next to *Save as type:*** and choose the desired file type:

   • **TIFF** is the most widely used file format in desktop publishing today on both Macs and PCs. Use this, for instance, for images to be sent to publishers.

   • **JPEG**, **GIF** and **PNG** files can be used on the Web. (Some older browsers may not support PNG files.)

4 Click inside the *File name:* box. **Type a name for your image.** If you are using this image for the Web, do not type any spaces.

5 Click **Save**. An Export Image File box appears. You will want to export the image at the size and resolution you need for your document.

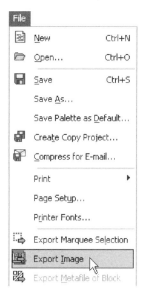

Step 1

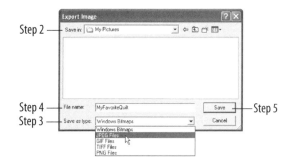

Step 2 — Step 3 — Step 4 — Step 5

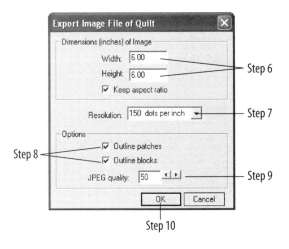

Step 6

Step 7

Step 8

Step 9

Step 10

6   **Under *Dimensions of Image*, enter the size you need by double-clicking inside each box and typing a new size.** If you are exporting a quilt image, leave *Keep aspect ratio* checked to keep your quilt correctly proportioned when changing height or width.

7   **Click the down arrow next to *Resolution* and click the resolution you need.** Resolution depends on how you'll use the image:

- *75 dpi (low resolution)* – for images to be emailed or used in Web pages.

- *150-300 dpi* – for images to print from your home printer.

- *300-600 dpi* (high resolution) – for images to be used in books or magazines.

8   **Under *Options*, you can uncheck the *Outline patches* and *Outline blocks* boxes if you do not want a black line around blocks and patches.**

9   **If you chose to export a JPEG or TIFF file, set the other options:**

- **JPEG files** – JPEG quality (set to 50 by default; available choices 0 – 100; 100 is the highest quality/largest file size; 0 is the lowest quality/smallest file size)

- **TIFF files** – Compression (LZW or none) and Depth (24 bit or 32 bit).

10 Click **OK**.

Notes
- When in doubt, try several settings and choose the one that works best for your use.

- In general, you want to export the image at the size you plan to use it in the document. The number of pixels in an image is fixed. Increasing or decreasing image size after the image has been created can lead to resolution and printing issues in your document.

Exporting Images

Exporting Metafiles

You can export metafiles of blocks (not quilts) and import them into another software application, such as Word, to make piecing diagrams.

1   Begin on the Block worktable, on any tab, with the block you want to export. (If your block is colored with fabrics, those fabrics will change to solids in the exported block.)

2   Click **FILE > Export Metafile of Block**. The Export Metafile box will appear.

3   Under *Quality*, choose **Draft quality**, **Medium** or **High**.

4   Under *Options*, choose one:

   • Choose **Outline and Fill** to get a colored block with outlines.

   • Choose **Outline only** to get a line drawing.

   • Choose **Fill only (recommended)** to get a colored block without outlines.

Notes
• If you choose *Outline and Fill* or *Fill only*, the fill colors can only be solid colors. If your block is filled with fabrics, they will be changed to their average solid colors in the metafile.

5   You can save the metafile as a file or copy it to the clipboard:

   • If you choose **Save as Windows metafile**, a standard Windows Save box will appear. In the *Save in:* box, click the down arrow and navigate to the folder in which you want to save your metafile. Click inside the *File name:* box, and type a name for your metafile. Click Save. EQ6 automatically adds the three-letter file extension of .emf.

   • If you choose **Copy to Windows clipboard**, the metafile is copied to the Windows clipboard. After exporting, open the document you want to paste into, and choose **EDIT > Paste** (or CTRL+V) to paste the metafile.

Step 2

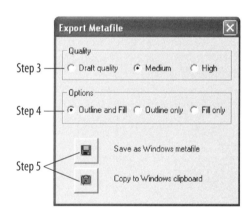

Exporting Metafiles

Step 1
Resize metafile

Step 2
Edit Picture

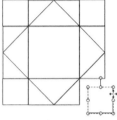

Step 2
Drag patch

Step 3
Color a patch or add an outline

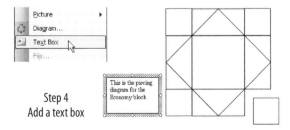

Step 4
Add a text box

Exploding Metafiles to Make a Piecing Diagram

These instructions work with Microsoft® Word documents (not WordPerfect® or Microsoft® Publisher). Each Word version varies; so these instructions are simplified and basic. You may have to experiment a little to make it work with your software. Start by having a metafile pasted in your new Word document (see page 290).

1 *To resize it –* **double-click the center of the metafile > click the Size tab > uncheck Lock aspect ratio > type in the Height and Width for the image > click OK.** The image will resize.

2 *To explode the block –* **right-click the center of the metafile > choose Edit Picture. Click and hold on any piece > drag it away from the rest.** To select multiple patches to move together, hold down your keyboard **SHIFT key** as you click on them.

Notes
- If you chose *Outline and Fill* as your option, be aware that Word treats the outline and fill as two separate items. Select them both by first carefully clicking the patch outline, then holding down your keyboard SHIFT key, and clicking the center of the fill. Both should then be selected and will move together.

3 *To color a patch or add an outline –* **double-click the center of a selected patch or patches > click the Colors and Lines tab > under Fill Color or Line Color, click a new color > click OK.**

4 *To add text or a label –* **click Insert > Text box. Click and hold > drag to form a text box. Type what you want > format it if necessary (bold, italics, a different font, etc.), then click outside the box to deselect.** The text box has a black outline and white fill color that can cover your patches. The next step will change that.

Metafiles / Piecing Diagrams

5   *To format the text box* – **Double-click on the border of the text box > click the Colors and Lines tab > under Fill Color, choose No Fill > under Line Color, choose No Line > click OK.**

6   *To move a text box* – **click and hold on the text box border > drag it to a new location.**

7   *To add an arrow* – click **VIEW > Toolbars, and put a check next to Drawing. Click the thin black arrow (not the white cursor arrow) on the Drawing toolbar. On top of the piece you want to mark, click and drag to form an arrow.** Arrows also have a line color. For dark patches, consider double-clicking the arrow once it's drawn, clicking the Colors and Lines tab, and changing the Line color from black to white.

Step 5
Format the text box

Notes
- Sometimes a metafile has an outer box around it, called a Drawing Canvas. Keep your metafile pieces, labels and arrows all together either inside or outside the canvas (not part in - part out). To keep all inside, enlarge the canvas by clicking on its outline. When your cursor looks like an "L" (corner), drag the corner bigger. To keep all outside, drag all the items outside the canvas edge, select the canvas outline, then press your keyboard DELETE key.

Step 6
Drag text box to
new location

Step 7
Turn on the Drawing toolbar

Step 7
Click the black arrow button on the toolbar

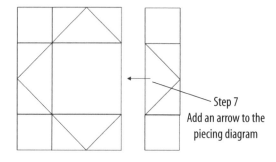

Step 7
Add an arrow to the
piecing diagram

Index

Index

The Toolbars

Project Tools

 New

 Open

 Save

 Create Copy Project*

 Compress for E-mail*

 Print

 Export Selection*

 Export Image*

Export Metafile of Block*

 Undo*

 Cut*

 Copy*

 Paste*

 Add to Sketchbook

 View Sketchbook

 Zoom In

 Zoom Out

 Refresh

 Fit to Worktable

 Watch a Video

 Display Dynamic Help

 Work on Block

 Work on Quilt

 Customize Toolbars

* These tools are not on the toolbar by default. To add them to the toolbar, click the Customize Toolbars button > click Add/Remove Buttons > click to put a check next to the tools you want to add. Click away from the list to close it. (To restore the default tools at any time, click Customize Toolbars > Restore Default Tools.)

The Toolbars

Quilt Tools

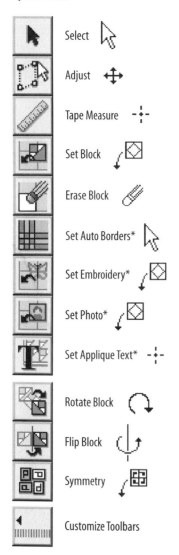

Select

Adjust

Tape Measure

Set Block

Erase Block

Set Auto Borders*

Set Embroidery*

Set Photo*

Set Applique Text*

Rotate Block

Flip Block

Symmetry

Customize Toolbars

* These tools are not on the toolbar by default. To add them to the toolbar, click the Customize Toolbars button > click Add/Remove Buttons > click to put a check next to the tools you want to add. Click away from the list to close it. (To restore the default tools at any time, click Customize Toolbars > Restore Default Tools.)

Color Tools (Quilt worktable)

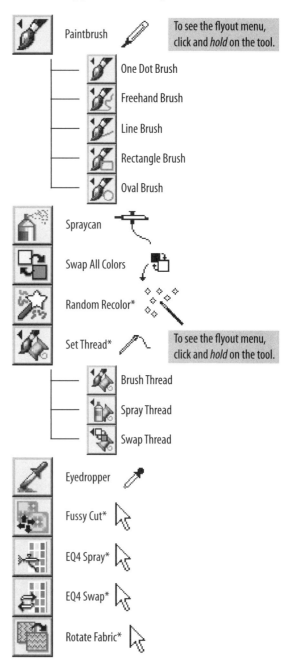

Paintbrush

To see the flyout menu, click and *hold* on the tool.

One Dot Brush

Freehand Brush

Line Brush

Rectangle Brush

Oval Brush

Spraycan

Swap All Colors

Random Recolor*

Set Thread*

To see the flyout menu, click and *hold* on the tool.

Brush Thread

Spray Thread

Swap Thread

Eyedropper

Fussy Cut*

EQ4 Spray*

EQ4 Swap*

Rotate Fabric*

The Toolbars

EasyDraw™ Tools

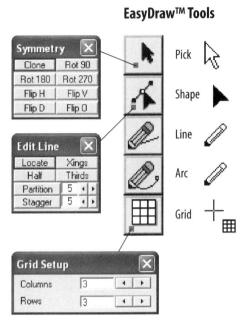

Pick	
Shape	
Line	
Arc	
Grid	

Tracing Tools

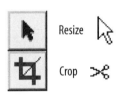

Resize	
Crop	

Color Tools (Block worktable)

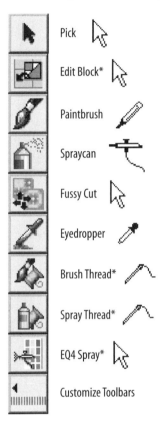

Pick	
Edit Block*	
Paintbrush	
Spraycan	
Fussy Cut	
Eyedropper	
Brush Thread*	
Spray Thread*	
EQ4 Spray*	
Customize Toolbars	

* These tools are not on the toolbar by default. To add them to the toolbar, click the Customize Toolbars button > click Add/Remove Buttons > click to put a check next to the tools you want to add. Click away from the list to close it. (To restore the default tools at any time, click Customize Toolbars > Restore Default Tools.)

The Toolbars

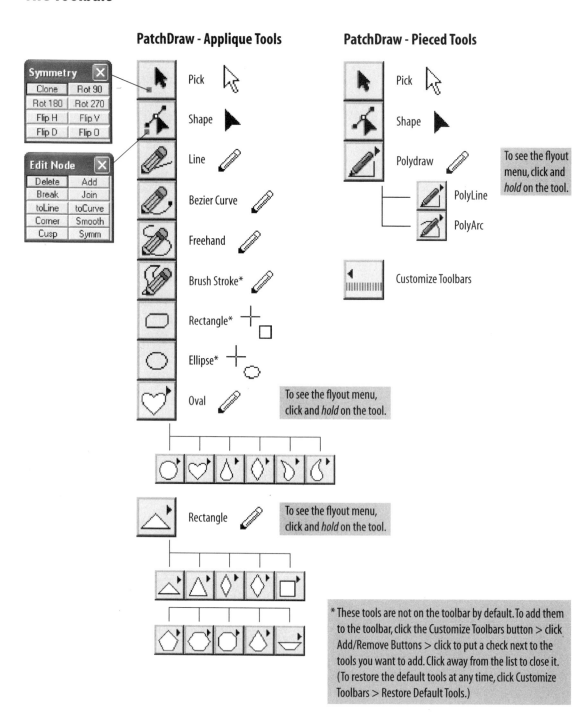

PatchDraw - Applique Tools

Symmetry

Clone	Rot 90
Rot 180	Rot 270
Flip H	Flip V
Flip D	Flip 0

Edit Node

Delete	Add
Break	Join
toLine	toCurve
Corner	Smooth
Cusp	Symm

Pick

Shape

Line

Bezier Curve

Freehand

Brush Stroke*

Rectangle*

Ellipse*

Oval

To see the flyout menu, click and *hold* on the tool.

Rectangle

To see the flyout menu, click and *hold* on the tool.

PatchDraw - Pieced Tools

Pick

Shape

Polydraw

PolyLine

PolyArc

Customize Toolbars

To see the flyout menu, click and *hold* on the tool.

* These tools are not on the toolbar by default. To add them to the toolbar, click the Customize Toolbars button > click Add/Remove Buttons > click to put a check next to the tools you want to add. Click away from the list to close it. (To restore the default tools at any time, click Customize Toolbars > Restore Default Tools.)